John

July 1776 111

Y REALLY SO AWFUL?

ARE THEY REALLY SO AWFUL?

A CAMERAMAN'S CHRONICLE

CHRISTOPHER CHALLIS

JANUS PUBLISHING COMPANY
London, England

First published in Great Britain 1995
by Janus Publishing Company
Edinburgh House, 19 Nassau Street
London W1N 7RE

Reprinted 1995

British Library Cataloguing-in-Publication Data.
A catalogue record for this book is available
from the British Library.

ISBN 1 85756 193 7

Printed & bound in England by
Antony Rowe Ltd, Chippenham, Wiltshire.

Contents

	Foreword by Stanley Donen	vii
	Preface	xi
1.	The beginning	1
2.	A foothold in features	9
3.	Footsteps to India	13
4.	Ice cold in Delhi	20
5.	World windows	27
6.	Prelude to the war	33
7.	RAF film production unit	41
8.	A Matter of Life and Death	48
9.	A 'DP' at last	54
10.	The End of the River	60
11.	The Red Shoes	72
12.	Korda	77
13.	The Tales of Hoffman	81
14.	Gone to Earth	87
15.	Genevieve	94
16.	Saadia	98
17.	MGM	115
18.	ABPC	125
19.	HMS Defiant	131
20.	The Victors	137
21.	The Vikings	144
22.	The Vanquished	152
23.	Yugoslavia revisited	158
24.	Stanley Donen	166
25.	Pasta and Chianti	176

26. Back in Paris 185
27. The Little Prince 190
28. Cutting the crap 199
29. The corset 207
30. Under contract 218
31. Under water 223
32. A matter of seconds 233
33. Under no illusions 241
34. The riddle of profits and losses 248
Detailed list of the author's film credits 256

Foreword by Stanley Donen

To INTRODUCE Chris Challis to you I want to describe his nature and that wasn't easy for me to discover. Chris is loath to expose his deep feelings. You might think, even after getting to know him, that he is a person without convictions, but you would be wrong. He's a strong-willed bugger and you wouldn't want to cross him. He's great as a friend but you wouldn't want him as an enemy. He listens to expert opinions, but he questions authority and he can spot a phoney a mile away. On the other hand, if he questions a person on his or her field of expertise and the specialist replies, 'I don't know', then Chris is his champion. He can't abide lies to cover lack of knowledge but honesty will get to him every time. There is no one with whom I have worked who fights harder to do a good job. He loves his work and enjoys the difficulty and adventure of finding a better way to show how we feel and behave.

As an example, in *Staircase*, Rex Harrison was to play a barber who had a glorious head of hair. I wanted him to look like Beethoven and we had seven wigs made, in different styles, to see which was best on Rex. I explained to Rex, before shooting a test of him wearing each of them, that we were testing only the wigs, as I wanted to get a hard look at them at their worst. With that understanding we shot the test. Chris, Rex and I were in a projection room looking at the film when Rex started to mumble: 'I look terrible'. Then more muttering: 'this is awful – this is the worst photography I have ever seen' . . . then shouting: 'I will not be photographed like this! Do you understand, Chris, I will not let you photograph me like this', Chris responded to Rex's assault without hysteria or shouting: just a quiet and firm rebuttal, in his most calm and elegant way: 'Rex, you will be photographed any way that Stanley wants you to be'. Rex was speechless. He had tried his usual routine of intimidation in order to get the upper hand but he couldn't frighten Chris. Chris won the round!

Over the years, I found him to be a strong and loyal friend. By the time we were making *Two for the Road* we had been friends for seven years. I was having difficulty in my personal life and we were far from home, shooting in St Tropez, while my wife and family stayed back in London. I received a very distressing phone call from my wife's doctor in London telling me that she was extremely depressed, that I must hurry back to London as she needed my support and he feared that she wouldn't live through the crisis. Chris was with me when I received the call, saw my distress and asked what was the trouble. When I explained, he said I should go back to London for as long as needed; he would assume responsibility for the company in St Tropez and see that no member of the crew or cast was upset about my leaving. He also said he wouldn't take any money, if there was a delay in filming, as a result of my absence. Because of his help I was able to leave and support my wife, while Chris held the fort for me.

While shooting *Arabesque,* we had an extremely complicated shot which I only wanted to shoot once because it involved Sophia Loren's clothes getting dirty, her hair being messed up and, if we had to do it twice, it would take a considerable amount of time for the second take. We got it on the first take. I was very happy and breathed a sigh of relief. Chris came to me after we moved the company to the next location and said we had to go back and reshoot the last shot. I said angrily, 'Why didn't you tell me before we broke everything up?' It was going to be time-consuming and costly and I wanted to know why we had to go back. He said he was sorry but he had misread the light meter; it was his fault but we must reshoot immediately as the shot was unusable. Naturally I was furious and was very vocal about it. I said I had made it quite plain that I only wanted to do the shot once, why hadn't he been more careful? He took it without flinching, again saying he was sorry but he had made a mistake and we must reshoot. Chris asked me please not to print the take as it would embarrass him, but I insisted. Then he told me that the clapper/loader, the lowest member of the camera crew, had neglected to put film in the camera. Chris hadn't misread the light meter at all but he was trying to take the blame himself, rather than let the poor clapper boy be humiliated.

Another of Chris's attributes is that he likes to laugh, has a sharp wit and he is always ready to deflate a rising ego. I often had difficulties keeping my concentration while working with him because we laughed so much

Also during *Arabesque,* I found myself outside, on a rooftop, huddled with Chris and Austin Dempster, the camera operator, shooting down on a scene where Gregory Peck and Sophia try to steal horses from a stable. Greg was supposed to have a fight with a stable boy, knock him out, grab the horses, put Sophia on one, get on another and ride away. In every take, during the scuffle, the horses would run away so that Greg couldn't get them. After each take Chris suggested another way of keeping the horses there. I tried his suggestions but none of them worked. I began to worry that we weren't going to get the shot before it was too dark to shoot. Austin suggested that the stable boy should hold the reins and when he fell, the horses couldn't bolt because their reins were in his hand. We tried it and, to my great relief, it worked. Chris looked at me and said, 'That's what I meant'. The tension was broken and Chris jokingly taking the credit for Austin's idea was terribly funny; we nearly fell off the roof laughing.

Finally, let me say only this, he is a wonderful cameraman, a man of excellent character and a person I treasure as a friend. I have only now discovered that he is also a good writer and you have a treat in store as you turn to the first page.

Preface

I HAVE OFTEN wondered what drives people, usually in their declining years, to write about themselves. The very word autobiography implies, to me, a certain sense of self-satisfaction, a job well done during an upright and honourable life. Politicians and generals seem to feature largely in the list, rushing into print on retirement in order to set to rights public misconceptions about the seamier and less successful episodes of their careers. The time of publication is well chosen, with those who might answer back safely dead or already discredited.

Then of course there are those who have a scandal to uncover, a life of dissipation to lay bare, either their own or someone else's. These publications, less erudite than the former category, nevertheless enjoy great success and usually make better reading.

Finally, we have those who have made a great contribution to learning and society throughout the world, and who have a duty to leave a record of their accumulated wisdom for others to benefit from. These, I feel, are fully justified in thinking that others want to know about them.

So where does this meditation leave me – nearing the end of an unimportant life, with little to show but a few cans of coloured celluloid and an accumulation of anecdotes about movies and the people who make them, which could well be dismissed as trivial?

As I sit before the first blank sheet of paper, the weight of authorship heavy on my shoulders, the thought occurs that it might well be better if I left the paper in its pristine whiteness and retired into the garden to cut the lawn.

So, why am I attempting it anyway? For years, no doubt to the point of boredom, I have recounted my anecdotes to friends and family alike, and it is they who are responsible for me sitting here, pen in hand.

Perhaps, after all, it is for the best. The memories will finally be laid to rest, perhaps to be read at a later date by my grandchildren with a chuckle here and there.

I have already been warned by acquaintances in the publishing world that a chap like me cannot hope to write the sort of light-hearted book I have in mind. 'You have to be a David Niven or a Peter Ustinov', they tell me, 'a widely-known and acclaimed figure on the world's stage. If you must write a book, make it technical, stick to the things you know about.'

And if I do, who will want to read it? Perhaps a few starry-eyed graduates from film school. Of one thing I am certain; if I write anything at all it must be what I want, and not what someone else thinks it should be. This may well be a recipe for disaster, in which case I have the comforting knowledge that there are always the grandchildren, making up an eager public of seven.

I have always believed that we are all endowed by nature with a gift of some kind, an inborn ability for which we ourselves deserve no credit, apart perhaps from the credit for recognising it and putting it to good use. Upon careful reflection, I am not convinced that my bent lies in the field of authorship or even cinematography, but I do have a sense of the ridiculous, a commodity which abounds in the world of films. This sense is absolutely essential if one is to survive and remain sane. The same, I feel certain, could be said of politics and the law, and the fact that it is lacking in so many who enter these professions no doubt accounts for much that occurs in public life.

Just as Oscar Wilde's plays have sometimes been considered only a vehicle for his epigrams, so this book is just an excuse for stringing together anecdotes spanning 50 years of films. I hasten to point out that this comparison has no literary connotations.

My memories are not aided by studiously kept diaries or notes but just drawn at random from the past, not necessarily in chronological order, and certainly not in order of merit. Being the person I am, the things that remain are mostly the absurdities, which seem to abound. My intention is not to imply that insanity is total but, rather, that it is widespread.

My thanks, which are due to so many people who have helped me on my way, I will confine to just a very few. This does not imply ingratitude to the many others, but is merely an attempt to be less boring and to avoid the accusation of being a 'name dropper'.

The late Michael Powell and Emeric Pressburger thought fit to give me my first chance as a lighting cameraman, and, much later in my career, Stanley Donen prolonged it. All three had the outstanding courage to entrust the photography of their many projects to my often shaky hands. At times hard taskmasters, for me they shared the ability to engender great personal loyalty, together with an unswerving belief in the subject in hand. Not always universally acclaimed or successful financially, their films were always original and exciting to work on. Apart from being creatively and technically challenging, you always had fun.

Actors, directors, producers, even cameramen, tend to live in a world largely made up of fantasy and imagination, the border line between the real and the unreal at times somewhat confused. With crisis a constant bedfellow, they 'strut and fret their weary hour (often in overtime) upon the stage, and then are heard no more.' This may well explain what may be regarded as the curious choice of incidents which I have drawn from the subconscious. Maybe the memory has a built-in form of censorship which automatically rejects the things that are not worth remembering.

1

The beginning

'NOW, YOUNG MAN, you must be one of these film people. Come and sit next to me, and tell me, are they really so awful?' The question is posed by a large, somewhat formidable lady and the setting is the drawing room of the Governor's Residence in Malta, in 1956. We are on location for *The Battle of the River Plate*. Our production manager is John (Lord) Brabourne, son-in-law of Earl Mountbatten, and this fortunate relationship has resulted in the closest co-operation from the Royal Navy. Presumably this same relationship has elicited invitations for a chosen few of the film crew to a formal dinner and reception at Government House. I am among the few. Very young and dressed in a very cheap dinner suit which, I notice, is unimproved by six weeks at sea with the Mediterranean Fleet. I am dragged down forcibly onto a sofa and covered with a sense of confusion and social disadvantage. To the strains of a military band playing discreetly in the background, I nervously compose some sort of fatuous answer, the drift of which, thankfully, slips my memory.

* * *

For me it all started during my last year at school. Then, as distinct from now, cinema-going was a twice-weekly habit and, in common with many others of my age, I was hooked on the movies. This fascination was coupled with a keen interest in photography, and by a stroke of good fortune I was given a 16mm cine-camera by a friend of my father. I conceived the idea of making a school newsreel of the year's events and, having talked the headmaster into supplying the filmstock out of school funds, I set about my first production. The result enjoyed considerable success when it was shown to school and parents on Speech Day and I became firmly convinced that this business of film making was a 'piece of cake'.

At the age of 18 the world lay before me, but the moment of truth arrived when I had to decide what to do for a living. The decision was simple. Much against firmly-expressed parental wishes it had to be the film industry. But how? Once again fortune smiled upon me, completely convincing me of my destiny. My father, in the course of business, happened to meet a gentleman by the name of Castleton-Knight, at that time managing director of Gaumont British News. After much persuasion on my part, and with subtle contrivance on my father's, my name and plight were introduced into a totally unrelated conversation. An extremely weary Castleton-Knight suggested that I make an appointment to come up and see him together with my much vaunted 'first production'.

At least half an hour early, on the fateful day I presented myself at Film House in Wardour Street and was taken down to a large, gaudily decorated theatre in the basement. I had been instructed to bring my projector with me as they had no facilities for screening 'home movies'. What confidence I had arrived with rapidly evaporated as I set up my equipment among the seats of the third row, balancing the projector precariously on a plank of wood and piles of old *Film Weekly*.

Castleton-Knight arrived and seated himself in the back row with the idea, I felt, of distancing himself as far as possible from what was about to take place. As he settled himself down without speaking a word, the lights dimmed and the curtains glided silently back to reveal a vast and empty screen. Its very blankness seemed to mock my effrontery and as I pressed the projector switch, there in the bottom left hand corner of the screen appeared the flickering, jumpy images which were my sole claim to fame and prosperity. Naturally, as is the habit of all home movies, the film broke several times and continually jumped off the sprockets, causing the images to leap wildly.

Only the darkness of the theatre remained to bring comfort to my acute embarrassment. After 20 minutes of agony even this refuge was removed as the lights came up again and the curtains closed over the scene of my undoing. Out walked Castleton-Knight, again without a word, and with shaking hands I packed up my miserable belongings. Clutching the projector and the can of film which contained, as I had once thought, the key to my future, I slunk unheeded through a side entrance and into the gathering gloom which by now had begun to enshroud Soho.

The dusk was indicative of my feelings and the cheerless realisation that mine was the shortest film career in history. I struggled with the knowledge that I must at once cast from my mind all thoughts of a job in films and turn my endeavours towards more mundane things. In total despair I returned home, quite unable to discuss my utter humiliation with anyone.

Two days later came a letter from Gaumont British offering me a job as assistant cameraman, salary to be one pound per week and expenses, to commence in two weeks' time when I was to report to Film House.

The two weeks of waiting were spent roughly divided between moments of wild excitement and growing doubt and fear. As time passed, the latter seemed to gain ascendancy. I really knew nothing about photography or indeed of what would be expected of me. To repair these manifest shortcomings I combed the local libraries and second-hand bookshops for anything and everything to do with films and especially camerawork, only to discover that little or nothing existed. It became clear that my heroes from behind the cameras were not men of letters. I switched my inquiries to works on pictorial composition and the science of optics, which only resulted in my confusion and feeling of inadequacy increasing unchecked as days of feverish study passed without apparent reward.

At last the crucial Monday arrived. I reported promptly at 8.30 to the newsreel's general manager, Mr Bishop. A man of genial appearance and friendly manner, he explained to me that I was to become an entirely new animal in the newsreel world, a trainee assistant cameraman. Hitherto the need for such a creature had not been felt to be necessary, the cameras used being light and portable. The cameramen worked alone, more akin to newspaper reporters, using their own discretion as to how a story should be covered. With the advent of live sound and extreme long-focus lenses, the equipment had grown in size and complexity and help became essential. My spirits rose immediately at the prospect of so quickly coming to grips with the intricacies of professional cinematography, and my ambitions soared as I accompanied Mr Bishop downstairs to meet the cameramen. We descended to the basement and he kicked open a battered door next to the theatre which had been the scene of my earlier humiliation. A smoke-filled room was revealed, furnished with a number of largely broken chairs, a dilapidated sofa or two, and an assortment of tables. The denizens of this underground vault closely resembled a scene from a Hogarth painting. Several animated poker games were in progress and conversation, or rather what one could decipher of it through the general noise level, did not seem to indicate an atmosphere of rare artistic and creative concern. My introduction over, Mr Bishop departed, leaving me to my fate. Hardly an eye had been raised and I got the distinct feeling that my appointment did not arouse great enthusiasm. No doubt I was looked upon as a friend of the management, maybe even a front office plant. There they all were: Peter Cannon, Sydney Bonnett, Hal Morely, 'Sludge' Pryke and Eddie Edmonds, the father figure of them all.

I reported daily to this 'den of iniquity' sharp at 8.30, remaining until 6 or 7 each evening, and my contribution to British films consisted of making countless cups of tea, running errands, and collecting vast quantities of bacon sandwiches from the café next door. My intellectual contact with the creative world of films was, to say the least, severely limited. As I listened to the conversation going on around me, the picture of what it would be like, which I had built up in my no doubt fertile imagination, was gradually destroyed, to be replaced by another of rather more stark reality. Nobody requested my willing services apart from the domestic chores already mentioned and I remained among them all largely an outcast.

Sometime during the second week, Bishop allocated me forcibly to Eddie Edmonds, who was to go out next day on a sound interview. Facing up to the inevitable, Eddie took me aside for a heart-to-heart talk. Firstly, to set at rest any fancy ideas I might have, he explained that my function was to hump the gear, get the inevitable tea, and generally make myself useful. On no account was I to touch the camera or lenses. He then went on to explain at great length the significance of the word 'expenses' in my letter of engagement. It quickly became apparent that this somewhat innocent word had far-reaching connotations. In fact it represented a valuable source of supplementary income, and the more obscure methods of its application were a closely guarded secret, one to which I had now to be admitted. It appeared that there existed a sort of unwritten agreement, which could hardly be described as gentlemanly, between the 'office' and cameramen, and a going rate for almost every contingency had been established. As an example, if you were fortunate enough to be allocated a position in the Royal Enclosure at Ascot you could book the price of a tip-top lunch when in fact you, of course, took sandwiches and a bottle of beer. You could also claim for the hire of a morning suit and this concession was turned to profit since they owned collectively several of these attires which were, over the years, passed around to great advantage. The same rules applied to Wimbledon, Henley and a host of other events.

I soon discovered that my main source of income was to be the good old London taxi. At that time film was on a nitrate base and consequently highly inflammable. There existed, so I was told, a law prohibiting its carriage on any form of public transport. The newsreel laboratories were situated at Shepherd's Bush, and after shooting it was my job to get the negative there with the utmost dispatch. Now it so happened that by far the quickest way from a London location was the underground railway, and by travelling that way I was serving the company well and, by a strange coincidence, enhancing my own meagre earnings. I quickly learned to carry with me at all times a supply of brown packing paper and string and soon became adept at turning a pile of film cans into an innocent parcel. In the inner sanctum of that underground lair at Film House, hidden from prying eyes there existed a complete scale of taxi fares from pretty well anywhere in London to Shepherd's Bush which were accepted as fair and equitable by both management and crews. From time to time new avenues were explored in the realm of what could be claimed or not and, once accepted, became part of the lore.

Each man had an expense book which was submitted twice weekly for approval and, if passed, the cash could be drawn from a mean-faced and highly suspicious accountant, fondly know as 'padlock pockets'.

I was duly given a book of my own by Eddie, with strict instructions never to submit it for signature before he or someone else of comparable experience had vetted its contents in order to ensure that I had adhered strictly to the unwritten code. The days passed accompanied by much humping of gear, hundreds of cups of tea, bacon rolls and sandwiches, and the running of countless personal errands. Slowly suspicions were allayed and I was becoming acceptable. No doubt my eager interest in 'expenses' had much to do with this fact and the worst fears that I might be a management 'spy' receded into the background. I became fully integrated into the 'underworld' life of Film House, and the demand for my services increased by the day. I learned to load and unload film magazines and even practised threading cameras, but that was as near as I got to expressing my artistic talents.

In 1935, before the advent of television, newsreels were big business in the cinema. Every theatre included one in its programme and in the West End of London and other major cities there were cinemas which showed nothing else. The reels were changed and brought up to date several times a week and, in the case of major sporting events and other big stories, even daily. Great competition existed between the 'big four', Gaumont, Movietone, Pathé and Universal, and the rush to be out first with a story often assumed hectic proportions. Motor cycle dispatch riders and even light aircraft were kept at the ready to gain valuable minutes and be first on screen. The companies vied with each other for the exclusive rights to big events like the Cup Final, a Test Match, or Wimbledon and paid large amounts of money to get them. Immediately, the unlucky bidders laid plans to 'steal' the events. Cameras were smuggled into the stadium sewn in cushions, hidden under coats and concealed in sandwich boxes. Ingenuity knew no bounds in the attempts to get past the opposition's security.

Gaumont succeeded in obtaining the rights of the Grand National and had the bright idea of engaging a band of thugs, who were instructed to roam the course and confiscate any unauthorised camera. The day ended with hundreds of 'home movie' enthusiasts being forcibly relieved of their cameras. The argument and litigation which followed went on for many months.

This newsreel war reached its climax with a Test Match at The Oval. The opposition companies had found themselves vantage points on roof tops, in windows, and even up trees. With the use of long-focus lenses they were able to get excellent results. This was immediately countered by shining mirrors in their lenses and putting up a screen of large balloons with streamers hanging from them to obscure the view. An enterprising cameraman availed himself of a pair of long-handled shears and, standing on top of a van, was driven round the ground cutting the balloons adrift. All this activity no doubt produced a not unpleasant alternative to a dull day's cricket, but consternation manifested itself at the MCC and it was agreed from henceforth that permissions would be granted on a rota basis, and the film would be available to all companies.

Gaumont had the bright idea of carrying their two sound units in a couple of Rolls Royce limousines, even going to the length of dressing the sound man, who also did the driving, in chauffeur's livery to complete the illusion. By this subterfuge they were often able to bluff their way, uninvited, into some exclusive gathering, gaining a distinct advantage over Universal, who turned up in a battered old van with 'Universal News' emblazoned on the side.

Naturally enough this all created an exciting atmosphere for one of my tender years, and during my time at Film House I went just about everywhere, becoming as the months passed ever more accomplished with the expense book and picking up a point or two about the art of cinematography.

My great moment came when I was finally allowed to take a battered old DeVry camera home with me. It was the custom for the cameramen to do this in case a story broke locally overnight. The very next morning, driving up Piccadilly with my father on the way to work, we saw a crowd gathered round a tree in Green Park. In a flash I was out of the car and, with my camera, embarked on my first story. An eagle had escaped from the Zoo and, adopting an aggressive stance amid the branches of a tree, was successfully resisting all attempts at its capture by two keepers armed with nets on long poles. Cheered on by a derisory crowd, the eagle flew up and down from the tree, attacking the two men and eluding the wildly sweeping nets. The whole affair had a distinct air of comedy about it and only reached a successful conclusion when another expert arrived from the Zoo armed with a more sophisticated type of net. I had it all 'in the can' and it made the News Theatres that afternoon. I was called into the office and congratulated by Mr Bishop, who announced a rise in salary of five shillings per week!

I look back with great fondness on those early days. I managed to pack a lot of experience into a very short time and met with kindness on all sides. The cameramen were in general a pretty tough bunch, and composition and lighting were certainly not their forte, but they showed great tolerance towards me. If my knowledge of the finer points of cinematography was not greatly advanced, I certainly learned a great deal about life. Among them all I count it a great privilege to have known and worked with Sydney Bonnett, who made history by flying over, and filming, Everest with the Houston Expedition; and Herbert Ponting, then an old man, who had been the official photographer on Scott's expedition to the South Pole. He managed to take some wonderful cine-film and stills as well as producing a series of beautiful water colours. The film, both still and cine, was all processed by him in a tiny dark-room on board *Discovery,* and, as anyone who has dabbled in dark-room work will realise, this was a major feat in itself.

Much as I had enjoyed it all, I began to realise that newsreel photography was not what I really wanted as a career. My interest was in the creative side of cinematography and the only way to gain experience in that field was somehow to gain a foothold in feature films. Once again the question was how!

2

A foothold in features

Colour was rapidly becoming popular and Technicolor had already made several full length pictures in Hollywood. Pressure was on among the producers to get in on this new market. In 1937 I read in a trade paper that Technicolor were coming to England to film the first colour picture to be made here, which was to be called *Wings of the Morning* and was to be shot at Denham Studios and in Ireland.

Full of confidence, I decided to go down and offer them my valuable services. I was duly interviewed by George Cave, the head of the camera department. A quiet, white-haired American, he asked me a number of searching questions about my experience and aspirations which made me realise very quickly that I was not the great gift to Technicolor that I had so recently imagined. Perhaps impressed by my obvious enthusiasm, if not my knowledge, in his compassion he offered to take me on as a trainee loader, salary three pounds and ten shillings per week, but no expenses!

I emerged from his office walking on air. At last I was into features and into the money, too. Technicolor was a highly complicated process involving a special camera which exposed three black and white films simultaneously through tri-colour filters and a beam splitter and, because of the complexity of all the equipment, they supplied all the staff necessary to operate it. They were all highly trained, mostly having degrees in engineering and cinema from the University of California. This was an enormous change from the rough and ready world I had just left. It was all highly organised and professional and I was much in awe of them all. I realised only later that in a creative world one can be too academic. Although the early Technicolor pictures were excellent, it was only when established cameramen and art directors broke this stranglehold, and with it the strict set of rules which had been laid down regarding lighting and the use of colour, that really creative work started to appear.

In those early days Technicolor retained a contractual power of veto on the way things were done, and this was administered by what was called the colour control department. This was ruled over by Natalie Kalmus, wife of the managing director. A lady of advanced years, which she attempted to disguise by the injudicious use of make-up, and with a bizarre taste in clothes more or less matched by her artistic ability to stand in judgement over protesting art directors, she succeeded in engendering massive ill-will during her reign, and her passing was marked with relief and discreet rejoicing.

I spent five months on *Wings of the Morning*, almost entirely closeted in the dark-room and not encouraged to venture onto the studio floor. The occasional glimpse of artists on their way from make-up to their dressing rooms or the restaurant reassured me that I was in fact a very small cog in the very big wheel of a feature film.

During the making of *Wings of the Morning* the black and white negative was processed nightly by Technicolor staff in a conventional laboratory taken over for the purpose, and a black and white print made for 'rushes' next day. The negative was then shipped to Hollywood for colour printing and a gap of several weeks ensued before the colour pilots were returned. This must have proved a harassing experience for director, cameraman and art director alike, particularly since it was such a new medium. The results were outstanding, largely due to the more diffused light in England and Ireland as compared to California, and as a result of the interest aroused and the prospect of future pictures, it was decided to build a laboratory in England to cater for the needs of European production.

Technicolor were very reluctant to show anyone colour prints until they were completely happy with the result, and since the permutations available during printing were myriad, this often caused long delays and altercations between producer and laboratory. A delay usually signified trouble of some sort, typified by an occasion on *Wings of the Morning* when no amount of pressure from the producers could achieve the return of a scene shot in Ireland. It finally transpired that the 'plant' were finding it next to impossible to get the post boxes red: in Ireland they happen to be green!

The new laboratory was to be at Harmondsworth and I was

offered a job as trainee technician, salary five pounds per week. There seemed to be no end to my good fortune and the prospect of riches. I spent the next nine months working in all departments as the imported machinery was set up and tested. This was a marvellous opportunity to really understand how the process worked and proved a great help in later years. We had only three cameras, which were sent over from the States. The lenses and beam-splitters were supplied by Taylor Hobson and had to be mounted and tested in the newly equipped engineering shop, and once again I was lucky to be involved. There was no comparable training available elsewhere in England and I became the first English technician to be fully employed by them. I owe Technicolor a very great debt for what amounted to a degree course in cinematography.

At last Technicolor England was declared operational, and the first production was to be a documentary film about England and the English, to be released with a colour film of the forthcoming Coronation of King George VI. Apart from myself, the camera crew was entirely American. Bill Skall, a small irascible man, much given to various stomach ailments, both real and imaginary, was the 'Director of Photography'. Due no doubt to internal weaknesses, he appeared to live almost entirely on a diet of bicarbonate of soda and Vichy water. Now, in England in the year 1937, Vichy water was not readily available outside Soho and a few major hotels. Since our film was to be shot in the depths of the English countryside, not to mention the Highlands of Scotland, where the commodity was entirely unknown, Vichy water began to rapidly assume enormous proportions in my life, particularly as it was made abundantly clear that its provision was to be my sole responsibility. The problem was further aggravated by the fact that he liked it iced!

I soon abandoned all pretence of being an embryo artist and devoted my life, somewhat unwillingly, to the procurement of Vichy water (iced) 24 hours a day for two months. The culmination of this film was the Coronation procession, and I was allocated to a position on the roof of the lodge-house at Hyde Park Corner. Owing to the amount of equipment, we were instructed to be in position on the evening before and we spent a miserable night wrapped in blankets and fortified by a bottle of whisky. Even Bill Skall sampled this in the early hours, at which time I felt that Vichy water was losing its attraction!

During the previous month Technicolor had contracted to film *The Drum* for London Films. An A. E. W. Mason story set in India, it was to have the first big location ever undertaken in colour. To my intense delight I had been asked by George Cave if I would like to go to India on the second unit as trainee technician. By today's standards the crew was unbelievably small – Geoff Boothby, the director; Osmond Borradaile ('Bordy'), the lighting cameraman; Henry Imus, Technicolor technician; and myself.

3

Footsteps to India

A COMMON SHORTCOMING with all productions is that after months of prevarication and pre-production argument, once the die is cast, the unreasoning desire to start shooting, unprepared, and usually at the wrong time of the year for weather, transcends all common sense which may possibly have existed at an earlier date.

The Drum was no exception to this rule. Great consternation was caused at London Films because all the colour cameras were needed on the Coronation. Our departure for India had to be delayed until after the great procession through the streets of London and it was decided that Boothby and Borradaile should go on ahead, leaving me to follow as soon as possible by air with the camera, lenses and film stock.

Long distance air travel at that time was something of an adventure and this was certainly the first occasion that a location unit had travelled this way. Technicolor had never tackled a foreign location of this nature before and, in consultation with Hollywood, every aspect of the conditions that might be encountered was gone into in the smallest detail. The heat and dust would obviously be a great problem, particularly with regard to the film stock. Because of lack of communications it would not be possible to send back the exposed film for processing during our expected stay of several months, so a method of packing it had to be devised. Since the camera used three films simultaneously, 1000 feet of print footage meant 3000 feet of negative. Apart from the obvious bulk, fire risks and insurance, the question of air freight was crucial. Cargo space was limited and we were told that the film and equipment would have to travel in the passenger compartment, which entailed buying half the available seats.

It was decided to make special metal drums, each to take six rolls of film and a packet of special drying agent to control humidity. The lids were soldered on and the joint taped over and coated with shellac. Several weeks were spent checking over every detail and separating what was to go by sea. I was given a not over-generous allowance to equip myself with personal requirements and dispatched to a firm in Shaftesbury Avenue who were reputed to be experts in such matters. It became apparent later that, judged from their West End emporium, their idea of what we were to encounter was as far removed from reality as that of the Technicolor experts in their air-conditioned Hollywood offices. I was fitted out with a tropical dinner suit, shorts, shirts and other garments deemed necessary for the East. The final item was a topee, rather on the large side, but necessary still as the hallmark of a Sahib in those dying days of the Raj. The outfitters claimed considerable experience in air travel and had available a special cabin trunk made of some sort of fibre, light in weight and looked upon with favour, so they said, by Imperial Airways. It was impressed upon me that, owing to shortage of space, I would have to pack all my possessions in this one bag.

The Coronation film completed, I had one clear day for a final check, the others having departed some weeks before, and a final interview with George Cave, who gravely impressed on me the extent of my responsibilities to Technicolor and to the producer, Alexander Korda, a demi-god who dwelt, as yet unseen by me, in a world which according to popular belief was one of elegance and extreme luxury, peopled mostly by creatures of great physical beauty. In return for my undivided allegiance I was to receive seven pounds and ten shillings per week but once again there was no mention of expenses, that magic element of a contract to which I had so early become accustomed. After a final handshake he handed to me a sheaf of papers, neatly bound in Technicolor blue, which were, as he explained, the result of several weeks' research into the behaviour of negative stock under conditions of extreme heat and humidity, together with advice as to what action to take should conditions become adverse.

Apparently the report had been specially commissioned from Hollywood for our impending trip and no doubt compiled in yet another air-conditioned refuge far removed from the heat-stricken, dusty plains of India.

The flight started from Southampton in the Imperial Airways flying boat *Canopus*, and next morning I was safely aboard complete with camera, lenses, fifty drums of film and my fibre cabin trunk. First stop was Marseilles for lunch, then on to Rome, where we landed on Lake Bracciano, and where we were scheduled to spend the first night. It is hard to realise now how very comfortable those flying boats were, with masses of room to move around on two decks, and even including a smoking room in the nose beneath the cockpit, furnished with club chairs and a small bar. There was a constant supply of drinks and snacks, and since the aircraft was not pressurised we flew within easy sight of the ground, with plenty to look at as the ever-changing countryside of France and Italy passed below. I was considerably reassured when told by a crew member that in the event of trouble it was far easier to land a flying boat in a ploughed field than a conventional aircraft in the sea!

After dinner and a sightseeing trip around Rome, we were off again in the morning for Brindisi, and then Athens for the second night. Take-off proved a problem as the day was quite windless and the surface of the lake like glass. It was explained to us that the suction of the hull made it impossible to get airborne under these conditions. After a number of abortive and rather disturbing attempts, the services of a number of motor launches were called upon to zigzag across our path and break up the surface. At last we were away, and the second night in Athens was largely a repetition of the first, with a comfortable hotel and a trip to the Acropolis. The third night stop was Alexandria, and the even tenor of our ways started to fall apart. The hotel and the food were awful, and the heat, noise and flies an abrupt shock to my Northern constitution. No sooner had I entered my room than an uninvited gentleman forced his way in, no doubt by the use of a duplicate key, and without more ado attempted to shave me and cut my hair. Only by a show of physical violence was I able to eject him and escape his unwelcome services. I discovered soon afterwards that my loose change and a fountain pen had departed with him.

The next day we transferred to the *Hadrian*, one of those early four-engined aircraft that gave the appearance of being built of corrugated iron. Most of the route was over featureless desert to Rutbah Wells for lunch, following the clearly visible oil pipeline and, with a number of refuelling stops, on to Baghdad for the night. The fuel stops appeared to be nothing more than fairly level stretches of desert in the middle of nowhere. The job was carried out by Arabs straight from *The Seven Pillars of Wisdom*, the petrol being pumped by hand from large battered drums which lay about in some confusion. The only sign of life in this forlorn landscape was usually a small hut, where we were given very hot and very sweet coffee. We were always glad to climb back on the aircraft for, although the temperature inside was well over a hundred, it contained a supply of ice and the prospect of a drink.

As I mentioned earlier, Baghdad was the night stop-over. Set between the Tigris and the Euphrates, in the very cradle of civilisation, it was to be my first real contact with the magic of the East. Lulled into a delightful stupor by the drone of the engines and a number of gin and tonics. I conjured up visions of a city watched over by spires and minarets, its streets peopled by dusky maidens hurrying back to the harems, soft eyes behind the slits in their yashmaks averted from the foreigners' bold gaze. The smell of scent and spices wafted on the balmy night air, and all this beneath the canopy of a velvet, star-studded sky. The grim reality was the Maude Hotel, its name forever an enigma to me. The heat was appalling and the flies and mosquitoes abounded. My luggage was mislaid and the only aroma carried by the night air was from a long row of lavatories on the second floor, none of which appeared to be connected to any conventional form of plumbing.

After a cold wash with rather dirty water from a jug in my room, I repaired, tired and rumpled, having no change of clothes, to the extremely dingy bar on the ground floor. Its only other occupant was a middle-aged fellow countryman who, having accepted the offer of a drink with unseemly alacrity, went on to explain that he had spent the last seven years out here, all of them in the Maude Hotel, a fact which probably accounted for any eccentricities in his behaviour. He assured me that the local population were the most accomplished thieves in the world, far more adept than the Egyptians and even the Greeks. They had discovered, he insisted, a method of melting a small hole in the bottom of a bottle of whisky, extracting part of the contents and topping it up with cold tea. They would then skilfully seal the hole, leaving the top of the bottle untouched. 'You must always examine the bottom of the bottle and run your fingers over it, laddie,' he intimated. At around midnight I left him in the bar alone facing, with admirable stoicism, the prospect of several more years at the Maude and countless more bottle bottoms to be examined.

My slowly disintegrating cabin trunk, the subject of much abuse by disapproving porters along the way, had now turned up in my room. I was already suffering acutely from a largely unexplained phenomenon which afflicts all travellers. A carefully packed case with adequate room for everything, can, once opened, never be again induced to accept its original contents. After four nights *en route,* at least a third of my possessions were tied to the outside with string. How I grew to envy my fellow passengers, who, lacking the advice of the outfitter in Shaftesbury Avenue, were equipped with conventional luggage and even overnight bags.

Our next objective was Sharjah, an RAF station on the shores of the Persian Gulf. We landed at Bahrain for lunch and fuel, and took off with half a dozen new passengers, well dressed and obviously wealthy Arabs, who passed the flight examining pearls which they all seemed to carry in leather pouches secreted beneath their robes. We landed at Sharjah as dusk was falling and were greeted by a heavily armed guard of honour, provided by the local Sheikh on the occasion of each flight as a token of his desire for our safety and well-being. Their general appearance did not inspire great confidence, and these feelings were justified later when I discovered that the *Hadrian* had been surrounded by a portable barbed wire fence and an armed RAF guard. The next, and final, day was across the Gulf of Oman to Karachi. Spare seats were removed, together with anything else considered superfluous, in order to save weight and be able to carry the maximum amount of fuel for the long 'hop' across the sea.

I found myself almost the only passenger, with so much of the space taken up with the film drums and gear. Once over the sea I thought I would occupy the time by studying the report handed to me by George Cave, and as yet unopened. It consisted of several closely-typed sheets, accompanied by various graphs and charts, the purpose of which was to establish the expected usable life of the film at differing temperatures. A quick glance showed that in excess of 100°F the expectancy was reduced to days. In view of the last three days over the desert, I began to wonder whether in fact it was worth going on. I hastily put away the unpleasant piece of paper and placed my trust in Higher places and the fond hope that the Hollywood boffins were a bunch of pessimists.

After what seemed an eternity, we started our approach to Karachi, over the vast airship hangar built for the ill-fated R101.

'Bordy' was there to meet me and our first priority was to find a suitable place to leave the film. This was finally deposited with a cold storage company and at last I could sit back and take a look at India. That night, in the privacy of my hotel room, I developed a hand test on a sample of film taken from two of the drums. I had previously made up my mind that, in the event of disaster, I would steal from the hotel under cover of darkness in search of the first boat home – and if that proved difficult, there was always suicide! Fortunately, neither course was necessary as the test showed all was well so far.

As I sat in my room recovering from this period of intense anguish, my eye alighted upon the remnants of my cabin trunk, carefully deposited on a collapsible trestle by a disdainful member of the hotel staff. There on the side of it was affixed a large and very ugly mauve and orange label advertising the fact that I had spent the night at the Maude, Baghdad. This piece of effrontery proved almost impossible to remove, thereby proving beyond all doubt that their glue was more reliable than their sanitation.

Bordy, who already had a great deal of experience of India derived from the shooting of *Elephant Boy,* ordered a tailor to the hotel after breakfast the next day and I was measured for a suit, shorts, shirts and several pairs of army-type sandals. I had a fitting that evening and the goods were delivered the following afternoon, handmade and perfect in every detail. He also purchased a bedroll and blankets for me, an essential when travelling by train. Next came a 'bearer' or personal servant. Most hotels only provided service in the public rooms, your bedroom and personal needs being taken care of by your own servant, who travelled everywhere with you, on trains or anywhere else you ventured to go.

Next day we were to leave by train for Delhi, where we would meet up with Geoff Boothby. A journey of some 900 miles, crossing the Sind desert *en route,* it promised to be extremely hot. 'What about the film stock,' I inquired of the agent, 'are the coaches air conditioned?' My query seemed to cause considerable amusement. I soon learned that the European section of the train consisted of large, individual compartments containing a leather-covered settee which became a bed by night, a lavatory and shower, the windows covered with mosquito nets and louvred shutters, and suspended from the ceiling a number of lazily revolving fans or 'punkahs'. The luckless travellers attempted to mitigate the overpowering heat by having large galvanised baths containing huge blocks of ice, some 80 pounds in weight, and known as maunds, placed on the floor. These were replenished wherever possible along the route. It was arranged that I should have three in my compartment, and the plan was to pile the film drums round them, covering the lot with a hastily acquired tarpaulin. I purchased several thermometers to place at various strategic points under the cover and made up my mind to keep an hourly log.

At midday we were at the station, the temperature 103°F in the shade if you were fortunate enough to find any. I had the largest compartment available and was finally settled with my travelling companions, the film drums and the baths of ice. Inside, the compartment assumed the appearance of an elongated igloo with just room enough for me to move about. The temperature in the carriage steadily increased as the departure time came and went, with no sign of action apart from the ice, which was melting as I watched. After what seemed an eternity we moved off on our painful way, stopping for fresh ice and an evening meal. By now totally exhausted, I climbed across the tarpaulin to my bunk, already made up by Abdul. The shutters were closed and the fans whirred slowly overhead. The tarpaulin, whose origins were unknown, emitted a strange dank smell strongly reminiscent of cats, which grew steadily stronger as the time passed. The night rapidly assumed the proportions of a nightmare. I was up and down each hour, clambering over the mound of film and ice to read my thermometers, and taking on more ice as the opportunity presented itself. By morning the compartment and all that it contained was under a heavy layer of dust. The water in the baths had overflowed and the floor was coated with half an inch of brown mud. And so it continued, all 1000 miles of it at what seemed a snail's pace, until at last we arrived at Delhi.

4

Ice cold in Delhi

WITH THE FILM once again in cold storage, and further hand tests removing the necessity for immediate suicide, I could relax. Geoff Boothby had been busy with permissions, an audience with the Viceroy to gain his approval, and discussions with the Army, who were to provide our 'extras'. We were short of only one thing, the script, without which we were in a cinematic limbo. Of course we knew the broad outline of our assignment, which was to film the battle scenes, get general background shots of the countryside, and, with the aid of doubles for the principal actors, shoot a series of linking scenes which would marry in to what was being done in the studios. Without detailed knowledge it was impossible to arrange any of this work. Great problems had arisen with the script just prior to our departure, a not uncommon eleventh hour predicament, and it was agreed that the revised work would be sent out to us the moment it was completed. Two more weeks elapsed before it arrived by surface mail, a no doubt prudent economy on the part of the postal clerk responsible for its dispatch.

The Cecil Hotel consisted of a series of small bungalows set in a large garden, each one being a private apartment. The dining and public rooms and the bar were in a central block some distance away. After dinner on the first night I walked back to my room in the darkness, the night full of the sound of strange unfamiliar insects, and my thoughts turned to the subject of snakes, scorpions, and even tigers. Before retiring I searched my room thoroughly, looking under the bed and furniture for the presence of any unwelcome visitors and, reassured, flopped down on the bed in the welcome draught from the large fan hung from the ceiling and turned out the light. Just as the first waves of sleep began to sweep over me, something dropped on my chest and wriggled down my body.

With a tremendous shout I rose vertically from the bed, wildly searching for the light. Abdul came running from his place on the verandah and smilingly assured me, 'Only lizard, Sahib, lizards good in house, they eat insects.'

Geoff Boothby had recruited the services of six retired Indian Army Subadah Majors, who were to act as assistant directors, and they set about the task of finding doubles for Sabu, Valerie Hobson, and the other actors, and finding costumes to dress some of the troops as tribesmen.

Peshawar, at the foot of the Khyber Pass, was our first location, which involved another long and traumatic train journey. More tin baths and many mounds of ice later, we arrived in the midst of a terrific dust storm with visibility down to yards. Immediately Henry Imus and I set out, followed by a straggling line of coolies and rickshaws bearing the equipment and film stock in search of the cold store. Later, back at our hotel, more hand tests were undertaken to reassure ourselves that our efforts were still worthwhile.

During the weeks that followed we shot scenes in and around the old, mud-walled city, choosing the cooler part of the day and endeavouring to avoid the dust storm which arrived with surprising regularity each evening. Every night we had to dress for dinner, for without formal attire entry to any hotel dining room was barred. The Europeans lived in the cantonment area outside this Pathan city. Set in a flat, dusty landscape, with a backdrop of the distant mountains, it was a green oasis of neatly laid out roads lined with large bungalows, carefully segregated into the civil and military lines. The central points of this carefully tended piece of England were the club and the church. I still have with me the memory of the evening drink by the club pool, the air heavy with the scent of exotic flowers and shrubs, and the smell of hot, wet earth as it was watered by a seemingly endless chain of gardeners with goatskins of water on their backs.

Our next and more important location was Landi Kotal at the head of the Khyber Pass, where the Army maintained a large camp. The Pathan villages and houses were built of mud and each resembled a small fort. Tribal and family feuds were the local equivalent of football and sudden death by ambush was a daily hazard happily accepted as part of the fun. Whilst up there, we were taken to a primitive factory situated in tribal territory where they produced copies of Lee Enfield rifles made out of stolen railway lines, correct in every detail, even to the V.R. engraved on the butt. Historically they were a little behind the times, but no less lethal. They also made a sort of shotgun, with muzzle loading and fired by a flint. These were charged with powder and small stones and gave a good sport at short range when waylaying someone from behind a boulder on a narrow mountain track.

The main part of our work was to be in Chitral, a tribal state set in the Hindu Kush mountains on the borders of Afghanistan. In its very centre stood Tirich Mir, a 25,000 foot peak of spectacular beauty, its summit crowned in perpetual snow. Our journey was to be by truck to Malakand, then on foot or pack pony through the territories of Dir and Swat by a winding mountain trail, the final obstacle being the Lowarai pass at a height of 11,000 feet. Having reached Malakand, all our gear was laid out and divided into loads for the mules and ponies. The drums of film were put in large leather boxes and packed around with straw and ice brought down from the nearby glaciers. These boxes were slung one on either side of a pony, each box containing two drums. We were each allocated a pack pony equipped with a primitive form of saddle designed for acute discomfort or even injury. The track soon became very narrow, with a sheer drop of many hundreds of feet on one side and a more or less vertical rock wall on the other. The ponies were accustomed to carrying bulky loads and had the hair-raising habit of walking on the extreme outside edge of the path to avoid the load bumping on the inner wall. Having spent the first day with half my person suspended over the frightening void below, and the pony stumbling on the loose stones along the outer edge of the track, I decided that the equestrian arts were not among my ambitions and from then on I walked, with increasingly protesting feet, for the next two weeks.

The overnight stops were under canvas or in ancient forts which lined the route at intervals of a day's march, and had been built to give shelter and protection to traders on their way to India. We soon discovered by bitter experience that they were to be avoided at all costs, since they were infested with every known type of bug. Bathing was achieved in inadequately small tin baths carried as part of our equipment, in cold water taken from the river.

Henry Imus, the American technician, was a tall, lanky Californian much given to personal hygiene, and he viewed the murky river water with grave suspicion and distaste since it was shared by local sheep and goats. He had come well prepared for just this situation, with a personal store of various disinfectants. He set great store by potassium permanganate crystals which he used liberally in his bath. The sight of him sitting in his tin bath, the water bright red, surrounded by admiring local inhabitants, was a daily occurrence not to be missed With only his feet and backside immersed, these portions of his anatomy became dyed a deep red as the journey progressed. This startling appearance, more fitting to the monkey house in a zoo, remained with him long after our return home.

At last we reached Chitral and the first view of Tirich Mir. The warmth of the afternoon sun sent avalanches rumbling down its upper slopes, shrouding the summit in a glistening white cloud against the brilliant blue sky. It was here that the main battle sequences were to be filmed. The local ruler, known as the Mehtar, had a fairly substantial private army, trained by officers seconded from India who did a tour of duty extending to about two years. There were five of them in all, ranging from a Lieutenant-Colonel to two subalterns, all living under canvas. Our camp was set up on a barren rocky hillside overlooking theirs, and an invitation was extended to us by the Colonel to mess with them during our stay. It was made politely clear that we should be required to dress for dinner. Abdul retrieved my dinner jacket from the bedroll, where it had been rolled up for the past few weeks, together with a rather dirty, creased, white shirt, and I set about preparing myself for dinner. The bedroll was lined with a very cheap and hairy brown blanket, a large part of which had adhered itself to my suit, and which resisted all attempts at removal. Lacking a clothes brush, we finally gave up the struggle and I set out for the mess tent, picking my way among the rocks, looking like some strange sort of yeti in the gathering darkness.

The mess tent was aglow with candlelight and the table impeccably set. We were invited to be seated and there followed a very formal dinner, such as one might find in a London club, accompanied by equally formal conversation. I was completely fascinated by the total incongruity of the situation, the nine of us sitting there, separated from our nearest fellows by 300 miles of wild mountains yet preserving all the trappings of society. This ritual was repeated throughout our stay without any relaxation of the strict formality.

The days were hot and once again the problem of the film stock reared its ugly head. We chose a position near the base of a small glacier, where we dug a large pit in the stony ground, and into which went the drums of film, which were then covered with straw and ice from the glacier, fetched daily by the porters. The only drawback was that our 'ice house' was situated some four miles from the main location, which meant that at the end of filming each day I had to make the journey back to the film store with the exposed magazines slung on poles and carried by porters, with myself mounted on an even mangier and less sure-footed pony than before. This animal had the same disconcerting habit of walking on the extreme outside edge of the track, but by the end of the day's work I was too tired to care and placed my life in the hands – or rather the somewhat hesitant feet – of my mount, with more often than not half of me hanging over a sheer drop of several hundred feet. The exposed film unloaded and placed back in the drums, and the magazines reloaded for the next day's work, it was back up the track, into my 'bear costume' and so to dinner.

This was the routine for the next ten weeks or so, during which time I contracted dysentery and lost nearly two stone in weight. We were more or less incommunicado during this period as mail had to come from Malakand by runner, who I always felt discarded anything to which he took exception.

The highlight of our stay was dinner with the Mehtar in his 'Palace', a large building of hard-packed mud perched on a cliff high above the river. The interior rather resembled a pier-head funfair, with pieces of coloured glass set in the walls, and everything painted in garish reds, blues and greens. The meal consisted of dozens of small, highly spiced dishes, unrecognisable to European eyes and no doubt well-laced with various bugs waiting to pounce on the tender stomachs of the unwary visitor. Whatever it all was, it certainly did a power of harm to my dysentery.

The Mehtar's proudest possession was a 16mm projector, a gift from the British Government, together with some early silent films. This was operated by a water-driven generator placed in the fast-flowing river below, which also fed the bare electric bulbs hanging in profusion everywhere. To round off the evening we were treated to a nearly invisible film show which mostly dated back to the Chaplin era. Some years later I heard that there had been a severe earthquake in Chitral, and the entire Palace had ended up in the river below.

Geoff Boothby heard via a belated letter from the editor that Zoltan Korda, who was directing the main unit, had grown impatient at the lack of news from us and was away in the Welsh mountains shooting scenes which had to intercut with ours. It was rumoured that he had resorted to whitewashing sections of hillside to look like snow. Zoltan Korda, the principal director of the three brothers, was by far the least likeable. Dishevelled in appearance and given to ungovernable rages at the mere sight of actors or a camera, he failed to endear himself to cast or crew. He suffered from various ailments, numbered among which were indigestion and a slipped disc.

It was his habit to get the riggers in the studio to suspend him from the roof by chain tackle in such a way that his feet were just clear of the floor, no doubt in order to relieve the pain in his back. I remember once going on the set where he was working to find myself confronted by this hanging apparition in hat and long great-coat, screaming abuse at all and sundry in a patter of Hungarian-English few could decipher. He was unshaven and his lips were covered in a white foam, generated possibly by his indigestion tablets. Not an attractive sight, it made a deep impression on my mind, and I consider myself fortunate that our paths never crossed during the many years I worked at Shepperton.

Our work in India completed, we travelled to Bombay and thence to the P & O steamer *Chitral*, for the journey back to England. Most of our fellow passengers were either Army or Indian Civil Service and, since each appeared to feel in some way superior to the other, two separate social camps quickly became established and we were the pariahs in between. My clearest recollection of this voyage was an elderly ex-Indian Army Colonel with a lifetime of service to the Raj behind him. He had found retirement back in England totally unacceptable, had rid himself of his wife, either by divorce or other unspecified means, and had returned to a small island in the Seychelles, where he settled down and passed his time photographing fish, a subject in which he had built up a considerable international reputation. He was on his way to London to give a series of lectures and spent the journey through the Red Sea clad in a tweed overcoat and cap, complaining bitterly of the cold. His blood, as he was at pains to explain to me, was considerably thinned by a lifetime out East, and whisky in generous quantities, preferably paid for by other people, had been found to be the only antidote.

On our return, we anxiously waited for the film to be processed and were all delighted to find that it had survived the five months of ill-treatment, confounding the gloomy forecasts of that dreaded Hollywood dossier. Whether it would ever match Wales and the whitewashed hills was another problem which, luckily, was not my responsibility.

5

World windows

After a few weeks at home I was off again, this time to Italy with a newly formed company called 'World Windows' to make a series of travelogues. The company was owned by Count von Keller who, we were told, had escaped from the clutches of Hitler with only the clothes he stood up in, repairing, of all unlikely places, to Egypt. Here he met a blonde and rather ugly American widow, whose sole attraction was the fact that her husband had been a millionaire. This fact, in von Keller's eyes, appeared to transcend all the other drawbacks and they were duly married in Cairo. He was tall, blond and very handsome, with the stereotype duelling scar on his left cheek. His interests were travel in remote places and women, both of which were readily attainable with his newly found fortune. It had been suggested to him by a director of Technicolor that while on his journeys he should make travel films, much in vogue at the time, and so the company came into being. Being a film producer obviously lent an air of legitimacy to his two abiding passions, and he entered into the spirit of his chosen profession while dipping deeply into his wife's fortune.

Jack Cardiff was to be cameraman, and I was promoted to fully fledged technician. We made three films in Italy, and one of them, *The Eternal Fire*, about Vesuvius and Pompeii, won a number of awards.

Encouraged by this success, the next trip was to be Palestine and the Middle East. We took with us our own transport including a large Bedford truck equipped with tracks for the desert and a Calor gas-operated refrigerator for the film. On arrival at Haifa, we found a message awaiting us to meet him that evening at ten o'clock at a casino situated on the beach a few miles out of town. It transpired that the casino was run by a fellow German, who had imported a number of attractive girls of various nationalities to act as hostesses, and with whom conversation, other than of a very basic nature, was next to impossible. Count von Keller had discovered the existence of this establishment within hours of his arrival, and the conversational limitations had not proved an encumbrance to his aspirations. By a stroke of good fortune his wife had taken an instant dislike to the Middle East, and the thought of weeks of travel across the desert convinced her that she was suffering from an unspecified illness which required immediate attention in Switzerland.

We spent a week or so in Haifa unpacking the equipment and planning the order in which to shoot the six films we were to make, retiring most evenings to the casino where von Keller had more or less taken up residence. On one occasion he was dancing with a particularly beautiful Hungarian girl, and at the same time conducting a heated argument with her on a subject which can only be surmised at. Suddenly she pulled off the shawl she was wearing, ran to the balustrade and threw it into the sea. Turning to him she declared, 'If you are the German nobleman you profess to be, you will go in and get it for me.' Without more ado, clad in an immaculate dinner jacket, he dived off the balcony and, having retrieved the shawl, returned dripping wet and placed it around her shoulders. 'Now, if you are the Hungarian lady you profess to be, you will dance with me,' he said. She rose to his challenge and they spun off across the floor in each other's arms, leaving a pool of water behind them, the honour of Germany and Hungary now fully restored.

We spent four months out there, during the course of which we drove from Haifa up to the Lebanon and then via Damascus and Amman down to Petra. The final journey was across the desert, following the oil pipeline and a track marked out by a company who ran a bus service to Baghdad once a week. This venture was started after the First World War by an enterprising New Zealander called Nairn, with the aid of two ex-army trucks, and had been built up into a successful organisation operating large American-built coaches specially designed for the job and even equipped with air conditioning. We were supplied with radios by the RAF in case of breakdown and told to carry revolvers for protection. We had been warned of the presence of bandits on our route, and even, according to Shadwell, our truck driver, of the possibility of encountering lions.

Camped beside the route one night, we were sleeping in the rear of the truck with the rear doors open because of the heat when 'Shad' woke us with a subdued whisper. He pointed out through the door to where something was gently moving in the starlight. 'A lion, it's the tail waving.' We all took another startled look. He was right. Quietly reaching for his revolver, Shad slid towards the open door, then suddenly leaped out with gun blazing, emptying all six chambers in the general direction of the lion. We cringed inside the truck, waiting for an anguished roar from the wounded beast, but instead there was silence. Perhaps he had killed it outright or, if he had missed, he was now facing it unarmed and alone? Suddenly his face appeared in the doorway. 'It's all right,' he informed us with a sheepish grin, 'toilet paper in the breeze.'

The six travelogues completed, including one about a tribe of Bedouins with whom we lived for several weeks, we returned home by boat from Haifa to Marseilles. During our time out there Jack Cardiff had been given a particularly ugly and unpleasant dog by one of the Bedouin, no doubt glad to see the back of it, since its appearance was more than matched by its temper. It will forever remain a mystery to me why Jack accepted this dubious gift since he was no dog lover and, in spite of being bitten on numerous occasions during the ensuing weeks, he faithfully kept it with him on our travels, trying all the time to win its affections.

Being, like myself, young and impetuous, Jack had also collected a wife, a half-French, half-Syrian girl with whom he became enamoured in Beirut. He decided to drive back across France in one of the company Buicks, making this part of the homeward journey a honeymoon, a convention which had up until now been denied him. He also made up his mind to take the dog, in spite of warnings from us all about quarantine. He was firmly convinced that these problems could be overcome and we waved him goodbye as he set off with his two companions.

Some weeks later, sitting happily at home, I received a reversed charge call from Dover. Jack's rather faint voice poured out his story of woe. He had unearthed a vet in Calais who undertook to drug the dog, giving him time to clear customs at Dover. The plan was to put the dog between the back seat and the rear of the luggage boot in a special compartment which had been made for them by a carpenter in Paris. It had all become a challenge which Jack was determined to see through. All went according to plan. They drove to the vet half an hour before they were due to go aboard and the dog was put to sleep and hidden in his compartment. After a perfect trip across the Channel they were alongside in Dover. Then came disaster. In those days cars were lifted off the ferry by crane and the crane was out of commission. One, two, three agonised hours ticked away until at last the crane was repaired. Jack's turn came and the Buick was hoisted aloft. At this precise moment the dog recovered its senses and began objecting violently to its unfamiliar surroundings. The car was lowered slowly to the quay before the questioning eyes of HM Customs, accompanied by sustained howling from the region where one would expect the petrol tank to be. Having uncovered the dog and with minds filled with suspicion, the Customs officers carried out a thorough search of the car. As I have mentioned already during our time in Palestine we had been advised to carry revolvers when travelling by road at night. Owing to the the troubles then taking place, there was a curfew each night and I had been granted special permission by the police to ignore it when on my way to collect fresh film from the cold storage, as long as I was armed and informed them of each trip. I had inadvertently left the revolver in the door pocket on the driver's side, and it was the next item to be discovered. It also transpired that his brand new wife was without either passport or visa. 'You must come down at once,' said the now even fainter voice, 'I am under arrest in the Customs shed.'

I got straight into the car and on arrival found that Jack had told a most heart-rending story of his travels alone in the desert, the mangy dog his only companion. He explained that love for the dog and his own emotional nature had overcome reason. He was bitterly repentant. With, I understand, slightly moist eyes, the Customs man decided to overlook the affair of the dog on condition that it went back to France on the next ferry. A crew member gallantly volunteered to take it and the situation was resolved. I was able to explain the gun with the production of the permit issued in Haifa, and we gladly let them confiscate it. There remained the question of his wife, who appeared to be without status. By now in floods of tears, cold and bedraggled, she presented a figure of abject misery. Regulations once again gave way to compassion and they were released on the condition that they left their London address and reported to the police next morning. On that occasion I made a youthful resolution never to attempt to smuggle dogs, guns or wives.

The next World Windows location was to be India, where six travelogues were planned, involving travelling from Mysore in the

South to Agra, Benares, and Simla. This was to be my last experience of the now dying Raj. It was my birthday and I was travelling alone by train with all the equipment from Bombay to Mysore. Much of the line was single track, and the trains had no corridors, thus affording no communication between the European and Indian sections. There was no dining car and the custom was to order one's food in advance. A menu was produced several stops before a mealtime, and one's choice was telegraphed ahead so that the meal could be prepared and waiting for the train's arrival. It so happened that on this occasion I was the only European passenger on the train and, having chosen my lunch just after breakfast, I descended from the coach at the appointed stop to find a small station, little more than a halt, with a thatched verandah facing the track.

There in its welcome shade stood a solitary table and chair, the table impeccably set for one. Overhead swung a lazy punkah made of rush matting, operated by a reclining figure, his head covered by a shawl to ward off the flies and his big toe firmly hooked to the chord which operated the punkah. The entire Indian contingent of passengers, numbering several hundreds, squatted along the track beside the train, eating their equivalent to a 'Ploughman's Lunch' and gazing with Oriental inscrutability upon my efforts to nonchalantly consume the unappetizing meal. I tried in vain to expedite the lunch and cut down on the numerous courses. 'No hurry, Sahib, train will wait for you,' reassured the smiling waiter. After what seemed an eternity, the ordeal over, I rose to pay the bill. This was the cue for my fellow travellers to clamber back into the packed carriages, squatting in the aisles, on the roof and even clinging precariously to the outside. I hurried gratefully back to the anonymity of my compartment, having resolved to go hungry for the rest of the journey.

Some weeks later we arrived in Benares together with the 'Rains', a period of suffocating heat and high humidity, and my old travelling companion in the form of amoebic dysentery struck once again. A cooler climate was judged the only cure and I was sent up to Darjeeling to recuperate. A stifling journey followed across the plains from Calcutta under leaden skies, to arrive at Siliguri in the early hours of the morning. Here I transferred to an Emmett caricature of a train with carriages and a tiny wood-burning engine at either end. The gradient was so steep that conventional bends were out of the question and we progressed in a series of zigzags, each engine pulling in turn. Backwards and forwards we went, climbing through the foothills into the tree-clad lower slopes of the Himalayas. On each side of the track grew azaleas and rhododendrons in profusion, worthy of the finest tropical garden. The temperature fell with each change of direction.

As darkness came we drew into a tiny station, in scale with the train, and I was immediately aware of a great difference in environment. All around were small, laughing brown men with Mongolian features and heads crowned with battered felt hats. Every inch of platform space seemed to be taken up by small groups of excited, gesticulating gamblers, playing some form of local dice, to which they were all addicted.

We set off for the Mount Everest Hotel in a pony and trap, led by a small, bandy-legged man in ragged clothes, seemingly full of the joys of living. I will never forget the view from my bedroom window next morning, my first sight of Darjeeling in daylight. The town lay below, set on a range of hills between 6–8000 feet in height, complete with golf club and racecourse, and much of it looking like a Himalayan Tunbridge Wells. At the end of the valley stood Kanchenjunga, its massive 28,000 feet peak clad in shimmering snow as it caught the early morning sun – surely the world's most impressive mountain! During my stay I was taken to the monastery at Kalimpong, on the borders of Sikkim, from where one can see Everest. A peak among peaks, it had nothing of the spectacular beauty of Kanchenjunga.

Darjeeling, a Victorian county town 'on the roof of the world', was full of shops displaying Harris tweed, Yardley's lavender water. Huntley and Palmer biscuits, Burberry raincoats, hand-made riding boots and all that a well-bred Englishman or woman could ever require. The climate, not unlike that of an English summer, soon cured my ailment and, in spite of a determined effort to malinger, after ten days of bliss I returned to the heat and dust of the plains where the rest of the crew, including the same old drums of film, awaited me. The travelogues completed, I was once again homeward-bound by sea, this time on the *Ranchi*, sister ship to the *Chitral*. The passengers were the same as before, two tightly-knit groups, civil and military, and both faintly disapproving of the 'film wallahs' so rudely set in their midst.

6

Prelude to the war

THE YEAR WAS now 1938, and all Europe seemed on the verge of war. Along with thousands of others I rushed off in a moment of blind patriotism and joined the Territorial Army, welcomed with open arms by a friendly Sergeant Major seated in a seedy drill hall in Uxbridge. My immediate fears of conflict were removed by the return of Neville Chamberlain from Munich, clutching his piece of paper, and apart from a two-week summer camp under canvas, which had to be abandoned half-way through because of the weather, I was free to pursue my career. In a matter of days I was off to Sicily, once again with Jack Cardiff, to make a short film about the almond harvest for Cadbury's.

Soon after our arrival, rumours of war once again began to circulate, rapidly gaining credence in our minds as we saw anti-aircraft guns being mounted around the port of Catania. We watched from our hotel window as a huge steel net was placed across the entrance to the harbour as an anti-submarine barrier. These activities were coupled with a distinct cooling-off of our relations with the Italians, normally the friendliest of people.

At the end of the first week, a much-delayed telegram arrived from Technicolor instructing us to leave with all haste on the first available ship or plane, a request that proved almost impossible to comply with. The shipping agents had deposited a large sum of money with Customs, most of it returnable when the equipment was finally re-exported, and their representative, a rather unpleasant Sicilian gentleman with obvious Mafia connections, did everything in his power to prevent our departure.

We finally secured three seats on a flight to Malta. Baggage was severely limited, so we decided to leave everything behind, including our personal luggage, taking just the camera and lenses.

On the morning of departure we went to the store where we kept the gear to collect the camera, hoping to steal away unnoticed, only to be met by the gesticulating and by now highly emotional agent, who had obviously received a tip-off. With visions of his deposit being lost forever in the grasping machinery of Customs, or more probably in the pocket of a senior official, he gave way to tears, alternating with threats. His already limited English vocabulary fast disappeared as passion got the upper hand. The gist of his outburst was, however, abundantly clear. He would call the police and have us arrested because already, in his eyes, clouded by patriotism and emotion, we were enemy aliens. He followed me down to the vault where we kept the equipment, shouting all the time as I removed the camera and lens case. I returned once more to the vault as though to collect other items, luring him in behind me. With his cries receding in my ears, I locked the two doors on the way out and threw away the keys, leaving us free to make a dash for the airport and freedom.

We spent an anxious hour in the departure lounge, expecting any moment to see the police arrive, but all went well and we landed safely in Malta, catching what was, I believe, the last flight out. The agent's fate has remained a mystery to this day, although, I must confess, not one over which I have felt undue concern.

War did not break out for a further two months, and during this period I worked on the second unit of *The Thief of Baghdad*, which was in production in Denham. The director was Michael Powell and, apart from my sojourn in the dark-room on *Wings of the Morning*, it was my first chance to work on a big feature film with 'real actors', who in this case included Conrad Veidt, Sabu, and Mary Morris.

The set was an exterior of a harbour filled with ships straight out of *The Arabian Nights*, running on underwater rails and drawn by tractors by means of concealed cables. It was all built on the 'lot' with the Buckinghamshire countryside carefully hidden behind a cut-out facade of the city of Baghdad. This brilliant ingenuity on the part of the art department removed the necessity of a location in Baghdad and, mercifully, a second aquaintance with the Maude Hotel, whose facilities I was in a unique position to judge.

Naturally, to complete the illusion of Baghdad we needed bright sunshine and blue skies, conditions which are not usually prevalent during an English summer. Many hours were spent sheltering from the weather in large marquees where the crew whiled away the time with tea and cheese rolls, all provided 'free' by the company.

Various card schools were soon organised, consisting of the 'sparks', 'props', 'carpenters', etc, and little or no concern was shown for the schedule or budget – obscure matters unrelated to the reality of location shooting. Anyway, they were problems firmly in the producers' court who were, it seemed, well rewarded for shouldering that responsibility. The guiding philosophy among the crew was 'more days, more dollars'. The atmosphere in the tent grew steadily thicker and 'Wally', the camera grip, a thick-set cockney of indeterminate age who wore a greasy cap and muffler at all times, indoors and out, would from time to time draw back the tent flap and take a brief look at the weather, more often than not returning with his favourite line, 'A nasty patch of blue up there, mates.'

All this was a new world to me but it was doomed, however, to come to an abrupt and temporary close with an announcement on the BBC that all Territorials were to report to their units immediately. My only claim to military prowess was the abortive ten days spent in the camp and a dozen or so evenings forming fours in the Uxbridge drill hall endeavouring to master the inner secrets of the Vickers machine gun.

Whilst at camp we were taken to a nearby range, where we each fired five live rounds at a moving target representing a German soldier, with varying degrees of success, and the following day we were each to throw a live hand grenade. The significance of the safety pin was carefully explained; once it was withdrawn, the only thing that prevented the grenade exploding was the fact that you were holding the firing pin handle clasped to the side of the bomb. Once you let go, the handle flew off and the short time fuse was set in motion, marking a sinister point of no return. Once this fact sank in, we were overcome with visions of dropping the thing or making such a poor throw that it would come rolling back into the sandbagged trench, which was the throwing point and our only refuge.

'Don't panic,' said our cheerful instructor, 'you have all the time in the world before it explodes. Stay on your feet and watch where it lands before ducking down.' Driven by unreasoning fear, we all achieved throws worthy of Olympic shot putters. When my turn came, I produced a tremendous heave, the grenade arching high into the air, and, ignoring the time factor completely and any concern about where the grenade landed, I was safely prostrate behind the sandbags long before the missile reached the peak of its flight.

To return to mobilisation, I went straight home from the studio, collected together my few personal possessions, which I stuffed into a kitbag, and put on my uniform. Being a well-trained soldier. I cleaned my webbing and brass buttons and shined up my boots, for I was determined to at least start the war in a civilised manner. My mother, who was French, watched the preparation with an air of total gloom. With her country having been occupied twice during her lifetime by the hated 'Boche', the prospect of her child going off to war weighed heavily on her mind. Her feelings lent an air of drama to my departure, which was only added to by the atmosphere at the drill hall where I had to report.

A Victorian building draped with flags hung from the roof amid the festoons of cobwebs, and lit in the gathering dusk by flickering gaslights, it had all the ingredients for a scene from *All Quiet On The Western Front* and did little to allay my growing sense of foreboding. We were issued with rifles and 12 rounds of ammunition, groundsheets on which to sleep, which could also be worn as capes in the event of rain, and, finally, gas masks. A line of coaches drew up outside and we were told to say our goodbyes and be ready to board and move off in half an hour. We climbed in, peering through the steamed-up windows at the tear-stained faces of parents and girlfriends. Snatches of 'It's A Long Way To Tipperary' and 'Pack Up Your Troubles' broke out in a rather halfhearted manner from little isolated groups and the picture of nostalgia was complete. 'Don't worry, it will all be over in a month,' the more stout-hearted called out, but I confess that I did not share their optimism.

So this is it, I thought, as the coaches moved off into the night. Tomorrow morning it will be France and a mud-filled trench. The memory of the hand grenade swept over me. This time it would be in anger – and coming the other way, too! My dismay was complete, and even the thought of the Maude Hotel became appealing.

In about half an hour we came to a stop outside a Salvation Army hall in Ealing, where we were formed up in a ragged line on the pavement and told that we would spend the night there. After a miserable four or five hours trying to sleep on the floor without blankets or bedding, we rose, to discover that we had no feeding facilities whatever. We were finally marched in small groups to a nearby Lyons tea shop, where we had breakfast at government expense before returning to the hall in pouring rain.

The term 'raw recruit' was rapidly assuming significance for me as I looked around at my brothers in arms. Our officers were equally unversed in the martial arts, and the War Office, doubtless aware of our limitations, had recalled a number of retired regular officers to set things to rights. It fell to our lot to be allocated an elderly Captain, ex-Indian Army, who was greatly discouraged by our general appearance and demeanour, a fact which he was at pains to bring home to us. It was announced that before leading us into battle he wished to address the assembled company in order to stiffen up morale. Dressed in an old but immaculate uniform, with gleaming Sam Browne belt and boots, he climbed onto a trestle table erected for the purpose and with great enthusiasm, nurtured by a lifetime spent on the North West frontier with a Sikh regiment, explained the great virtues of serving with The Colours. He underlined the more than obvious fact that we were, certainly in military terms, a pretty worthless lot. It was his considered opinion that, as a start, an extended route march through the streets of London would do much to improve our fighting qualities.

'Fall in, 09.30 hours with packs and rifles. Steel helmets and gas masks at the ready.' We set off in the pouring rain, draped in the camouflaged groundsheets, on what was to be a 20 mile march around town. Every so often we had to don the masks for periods of ten minutes to ensure that we would remain equally efficient as a fighting unit under conditions of chemical warfare. As the gas masks appeared to be a job lot, rejected by a more worthy regiment, with straps and other vital parts missing, this assumption was very misplaced. We returned to the Salvation Army hall in the late afternoon, a disillusioned company of soaking wet cripples, the unfamiliar army boots having taken their toll.

We reported sick to a man, this being the Army procedure in case of illness, as our sergeant explained in unsympathetic tones. We were made to sit on the hall floor with our boots and socks removed and our feet held up in the air, while a very newly commissioned RAMC Captain, obviously straight from a junior partnership in an obscure suburban practice, examined our ailments. He walked between us, prodding here and there with a swagger cane, a look of total disgust on his face, mingled with an acute sense of his newly found superiority. On reaching me he asked, 'What's your trouble?' 'I have blisters on my feet,' was the obvious retort. 'Your problem, my man, is the way you walk,' he responded. 'Sir,' I replied, in my most deferential tone, 'I have walked the same way for the past 20 years without trouble, and I suggest that it's the silly bloody boots.' I was immediately charged with insubordination to an officer, and at the same time became something of a hero.

My indiscretion caused an unforeseen dilemma since nobody knew the formalities for putting someone on a 'charge'. After consultation with King's Rules and Regulations, I was marched in – 'Caps off, quick march, left right, left right – to stand before the Indian Army Captain. He lectured me at some length about showing due respect to my seniors. 'It's not the man you defer to, it's the King's Uniform', he pointed out, which in this case was a considerable relief, for to show respect to the former was stretching my powers of duty. After lengthy deliberation he announced that, bearing in mind my extreme youth and lack of experience of Army etiquette, he would let me off with a caution. I was a free man, and I left with the distinct impression that his decision was largely influenced by his intuitive dislike of the medical officer, a feeling shared wholeheartedly by myself.

So began my attempt to stem the German advance, and so it continued for a further four or five days, patrolling the streets of Ealing, with our activities masterminded from the nerve centre of the Salvation Army hall. Obviously our efforts had made little impression on those conducting the war, for we were returned to our drill hall in Uxbridge and divested of our greatcoats, rifles and webbing, urgently needed, it was explained, by those more able to defend 'our islands'. They also removed our gas masks, replacing them with civilian-type ones, and told us that we would be permitted to wear our civilian overcoats, for which privilege the War Office was willing to pay the sum of one shilling and sixpence per week. As no accommodation was available, we were allowed to sleep at home, reporting each morning for further route marching and talks by visiting professionals to encourage a more aggressive attitude. The prospect of marching round the town in semi-military attire in full view of friends and relations was a bitter anticlimax after the heroic farewell accorded us and it was with great relief that we were posted to the East India Docks in London to mount, so we were told, an anti-parachute guard at dawn and dusk each day.

With the recent bombing of Rotterdam fresh in everyone's minds, the skies full of diving Stukas and heavily armed paratroops, our unarmed presence seemed anachronistic in the extreme, but hopefully it brought a sense of security to our leaders.

After several weeks of guard duty, sleeping in a disused warehouse which was carpeted with half an inch of rotten floor, salvation in the form of dysentery came unexpectedly my way. I was admitted to Millbank Hospital, where by chance the CO happened to be a Colonel, ex-Indian Army. A man of fearsome mien, whose brick-red countenance was broken by a carefully tended snow-white moustache, it was his custom to carry out a daily inspection of all the wards. The nurses and orderlies were drawn up in parade ground fashion to undergo the closest scrutiny, including hands and fingernails. This completed, he would drop on one knee by the foot of the end bed and take a careful sight along the rail to ensure that all the beds were in perfect line. This was repeated for the opposite side of the ward, whereupon he would remove a temperature chart from the wall above the first bed and carefully measure the turn-down of the bed sheet, which had to exactly correspond to the chart's length. This was repeated for each bed in turn, the inmates lying to attention if their physical condition permitted. Perhaps this routine contained some magic panacea, gleaned from the plains of India. Who knows?

On this third or fourth visit he decided to read my chart, and the words amoebic dysentery brought a spontaneous gleam to his eye. Of course to him it meant India, for where else would one contract the disease? 'What regiment?' he barked. 'No regiment, sir, I was a civilian,' I replied. This was, of course, a disappointment. In fact I am not certain that he was aware that such creatures penetrated there. Nevertheless he was intrigued and the next evening he returned to find out more about me. Films had some sort of allure for him, and over the next week or so he came frequently to see me, striking up an odd sort of friendship, if that were possible. I took the opportunity of explaining my regret at impetuously joining the Territorial Army and the frustration of not being able to 'do my bit' in a more effective way. A creative chap like myself would be more at home in the RAF where traditions were not so deep rooted. His discerning though jaundiced eye quickly perceived that I was not military material and with the help of my father, who had rejoined the service, a transfer was arranged from the Army to the RAF.

Once cured, I was posted direct to Uxbridge to join the flow of volunteers, having achieved the near impossible feat of transferring to a junior service, an action much frowned upon at that time by authority. Barrack rooms with beds and sheets were like a four-star hotel after the East India Docks and a new world opened up before me, presenting a chance to do something towards the war effort in an atmosphere of relative comfort! We were formed into courses, and before commencing training in our chosen fields it was the practice to send everyone for two weeks 'square bashing' at Bridgnorth in order, no doubt, to instil the rudiments of military discipline before getting down to the more complex studies of aeroplanes and how to fly them.

The Orderly Room Sergeant, who controlled all our destinies, seemed a nice chap, so very different from his army counterpart. Full of feeling and understanding, I thought, when he said, 'Not much point in sending you on two weeks square bashing, laddie, if you have just come out of the Army. Where do you live?' 'Stoke Poges, Sergeant,' I replied, my voice full of grateful thanks. 'Northholt would be a good spot for a couple of weeks, then you can catch up with your course,' he suggested. 'Thank you, Sergeant, it would be fine,' I responded. Next day they posted me to Wick. I left that night by train carrying 'the unexpired portion of my day's rations', as King's Rules and Regulations put it, which in my case consisted of half a loaf of bread, a portion of butter, two potatoes, and some uncooked meat. Not the easiest thing to prepare in a crowded, blacked-out, second class compartment on the way from King's Cross to Scotland!

7

RAF film production unit

SINCE MY STORY is really concerned with movies, I don't wish to digress for too long over the period of the war, but one or two incidents seem to fit into the overall pattern of films. After a period in Bomber Command and then Coastal Command, where I spent several weeks at Abbotsinch endeavouring to drop torpedoes from a Beaufort aircraft onto targets supplied by the Navy, I was posted to the newly formed RAF Film Production Unit.

The Unit was formed, like those of the Army and Navy, because of the increasing awareness within the three services that full publicity for their activities was an essential part of the war effort. The headquarters were at Pinewood Studios, and people with a background of films, already in the service, were collected together to form the nucleus of the Unit. Our job was to chronicle on film the activities of the RAF, covering many operations which for reasons of security could not be filmed by civilian war correspondents. The scope of the work we became involved in grew as the weeks passed, some of it having only the most tenuous connections with the service.

My newsreel training served me in good stead as we were required to work very much as individuals. The Russian Foreign Secretary, Mr Molotov, paid a secret visit to this country to sign a treaty of alliance, and we flew out to a rendezvous over the North Sea with the Ilyushin bomber which was bringing him and escorted it to an airfield in Lincolnshire. The Russian crew, who had not a word of English and wore, to our eyes, the oddest of sheepskin flying gear, tackled the operational breakfast of bacon and eggs with great fervour. I later travelled with Molotov to London by train and filmed the signing of the treaty at the Foreign Office with Churchill and Eden. Many weeks after his safe return to Russia, the treaty was made public and my film issued in limited form to the newsreels.

During the later stages of the war the RAF was granted an airbase on the island of Terciera, in the Azores. This was made possible by invoking an ancient treaty we had with the Portuguese, the oldest military alliance in existence in the world. The airstrip had to be built from scratch, and a convoy sailed from Liverpool carrying everything needed for its construction. As far as I can recall, Coastal Command Liberators were operating within a week of the convey arriving, thus filling a gap in the central Atlantic, hitherto out of reach of anti-submarine patrols from either side. This turned out to be the turning point in the U-boat war and the early patrols, on many of which I flew, inflicted huge losses on the unsuspecting submarines while they were charging their batteries on the surface at night.

In the early days on Terciera there was no accommodation apart from tents, many people living in large packing cases which had contained engine spares and equipment. I managed to get myself billeted in a small and primitive farmhouse whose owners were kindness itself, in spite of having no means of communication. My room was small, with an earth floor, one tiny and very dirty window set high in the wall, a bed and a cane chair. I invariably left before dawn each morning and they called me without fail with a large and dirty tumbler filled with a potent homemade eau-de-vie, standing beside my bed to make sure that I drank it all. The often erratic mile walk to the airfield down the dusty track, lit by the predawn light, has remained my most vivid memory of Terciera.

Having completed what was virtually a one-man documentary of the operation, I managed to cadge a lift to Casablanca in a Transport Command Dakota, there to await a flight back home. Because of strong headwinds, the aircraft could not make the journey in one hop and the only refuelling possibility was Lisbon. The Transport Command aircraft was theoretically civilian, and the passengers of all ranks were kitted out in sports coats and flannel trousers of a remarkable similarity, together with identity documents to enable us to land in Portugal, a neutral country. It was a strange experience mixing in the streets with crowds of Germans who were perfectly aware of our identity, for Lisbon was a great clearing house for espionage.

After the Normandy landings and the breakthrough from Falaise to Belgium and Holland, all of which we covered, the attention of the Air Ministry was directed towards the Ruhr and the effects of our bombing. A small group of experts was formed whose job it was to get into what remained of German factories as our armies advanced, if possible before evidence of interesting military developments could be destroyed by the Germans or by looting. I was attached to this force, which had a small Commando escort. With us was Philip Sandeman, who had spent six months in hiding outside Paris after being shot down over Northern France and had escaped safely when the city was liberated.

Philip and I set out one morning in a jeep with Krupp's as our objective. We were dressed in khaki battledress as our RAF blue was deemed to be unfamiliar to our American friends, who tended to shoot on sight. The scene was one of total destruction, with hardly a building standing intact. The very outline of roads had disappeared amid the vast mountains of rubble, rendering the map we carried virtually useless. What civilian life existed was underground, the population having taken to the cellars. Here and there a temporary stove pipe emerged through the debris, a whisk of smoke indicating human life. I actually saw a German woman clad in an apron on hands and knees scrubbing the doorstep of a vanished house, indicating, I felt, either a great faith in the future or a total lack of imagination. Bands of half-starved immigrant workers, mostly Russian, roamed amid the ruins searching for food, friends, or a stray German on whom to exact revenge. All was chaos, and we had no idea which areas had fallen or where our troops were. A canal blocked our way with all bridges gone, the only way over being a large pipe across which we decided to crawl, having immobilised the jeep.

After scrambling across the rubble for several hundred yards, we were approached by a wild and ragged man who pleaded with us on bended knees to follow him, indicating in sign language that someone was wounded or ill. We followed him for about half a mile, growing steadily more concerned at the lack of friendly faces, until we came to the ruins of a small café. A large crowd of emaciated slave workers dressed in rags stood around the body of a man laid out on a broken door. We discovered that he had been severely stabbed in the stomach, and as we knelt beside him I suddenly became aware of the silent, staring crowd who were slowly closing in around us. Philip and I exchanged frightened glances as the attitude of the onlookers became increasingly hostile, or so it seemed. My eye was caught by a particularly villainous character who appeared to be the ringleader. His right hand was hidden in the front of his jacket and obviously held a gun or a knife. Drawing my revolver for the first time in anger, I ran across to him, pulling his arm roughly from his jacket, and there, grasped in his hand, was a teaspoon! The ending to this bizarre episode is that we were able to get the injured man back to the jeep and finally to an American medical unit.

As a consequence of our almost total air superiority, RAF Bomber Command, a force designed for night operations, was being used on daylight missions, and it had been decided to mount a mass raid on the town of Wesel, prior to the crossing of the Rhine. Wesel lay on a loop of the river, the west bank of which was held by us and formed a salient into enemy territory. The Air Ministry decided that this raid would afford an excellent opportunity to film at close quarters the effect of our 'blockbuster' bombs, and two of us were sent to make contact with the Army. At the very tip of the salient was a ruined farmhouse, used by the Army as an artillery observation post. Access was by a narrow road in full view of the Germans on the opposite bank and in range of numerous 88mm guns. The Army only used that road at night but because of lack of time we would have to make the trip in daylight. This struck the soldiers as a huge joke and we were advised to drive like hell along the mile or so. Never have two jeeps put up such a performance as we safely completed the trip, to be greeted by ironic cheers from the gunners, well dug in to the cellar of the farm. They impressed us with the fact that the slightest movement seen from the opposite bank would result in heavy shelling, causing their extreme displeasure.

With trembling hands we set about constructing 'hides' in two of the blown-out windows, using odd pieces of blackout material and anything else that came to hand. Crawling around on hands and knees and scarcely daring to breathe, we finally had the job completed and carefully cut two small slits to poke our lenses through. There across the river lay Wesel, so near that one could see every detail of the streets.

I fervently hoped that Bomber Command would be as accurate as their reputation. On the tick of time the drone of the first wave could be heard approaching, accompanied by a tremendous barrage of anti-aircraft fire. Undeterred, the Lancasters and Halifaxes, still in their black night camouflage, dropped the first load. The entire wall of our farmhouse collapsed in a cloud of dust leaving us 'naked and far from unashamed' with our shining aluminium Newman Sinclair cameras in full view of the Wehrmacht. Fortunately, by now they had other matters with which to concern themselves, as wave upon wave came in, completely obliterating the town in a matter of minutes but without dropping a single bomb on the west bank, where our troops waited to cross. We were able to get some unique film and make our trembling escape.

With our rapid advance, large pockets of resistance were left behind and it was very difficult to find out exactly what was happening. The BBC had a habit of liberating places in the hourly news broadcasts from the safety of Broadcasting House and were, at times, one jump ahead of our troops on the ground. One such case was The Hague, whose liberation was announced on the one o'clock news. I set off in a single-engined Auster spotter plane in the hope of getting pictures of our aircraft dropping food and supplies to the starving population of the beleaguered Dutch city. With my Australian pilot we flew for an hour or more over the flat, featureless countryside, following the paths of canals and railway lines, and hugging the ground in case of 'flak'. At last the outline of the town showed up on the horizon, but there was no sign of our conquering armies. We passed low over a couple of startled German sentries on a canal bridge and realised that all was not well. Almost out of fuel, we had no option but to carry on, but the airfield no longer held much appeal. There followed more bridges and more startled Germans as the tiny plane with RAF markings flew over, feet above their heads.

As we reached the suburbs we spotted a football field, with rows of neat houses on three sides, and phlegmatic Dutch cows grazing on our would-be landing field. There was nothing for it but to go straight in, bovine protesters galloping in all directions, to a perfect landing. We were quickly surrounded by a large crowd of cheering, waving Dutch people who appeared as if by magic from the surrounding houses. They fought with one another to shake our hands as they hurried us across the road and into the nearest house, crowded to bursting with people all talking at once. They explained that the Germans were still there and asked us what we were doing. While we explained what had happened, a German half-track full of troops appeared at the end of the road and halted on the edge of the crowd surrounding the Auster. They watched for several minutes without making any attempt to interfere, before turning and driving off.

The owner of the house spoke perfect English and explained that they had been waiting daily to be liberated and had thought that our arrival heralded the beginning of their freedom. We had to explain that we were not the spearhead of an Allied Army, but just photographers in uniform, and in a plane without petrol.

'The Germans will be back for sure,' he said, 'we must get you away as soon as possible.' With visions of the half-track returning, reinforced by several Tiger tanks, I wholeheartedly agreed with these sentiments, but I could not see how it was to be achieved. Fortunately the Auster would run on 80 octane fuel, and our host said he could get petrol for us through the Underground, of which he was a member, but not a moment must be lost. 'Wait in here,' he said, 'do not attempt to go out to the plane. I will be back in a very short time.'

As we waited in nail-biting anguish, a steady drone, getting louder all the time, filled the crowded room. 'The RAF!' everyone shouted, as we rushed out onto the tiny balcony. There, right overhead and no more than 500 feet up, were the Lancasters and already containers with parachutes were falling to the ground, filled with the food and medical supplies so desperately needed. As the crowd below surged out across the field to collect the supplies, I was able, with shaking hands, to get some marvellous shots of the whole incident. A scoop indeed in newsreel terminology – but where was the petrol? Our luck could not last much longer and I expected to see our German friends again at any moment. In a short while our host appeared with a group of neighbours carrying several large cans of fuel. We ran back through the crowd to the Auster and quickly poured it into the tank. During the half hour or so that we had been in the house, the Dutch crowd had autographed the fuselage on every available space and filled the cockpit with tulips. Somehow a path was cleared and we were away, cows and people running in every direction as the Germans appeared in force at the end of the road.

The appearance of the aircraft's fuselage caused quite a stir when we arrived back at base, and the story was given to the press by the public relations officer, making most of the London dailies. The General who had been amassing his forces for a formal entry into the town was much displeased and lodged the strongest possible protest with RAF headquarters, quite understandably feeling that our unwitting intervention had stolen much of his thunder. I was concerned about the fate of the Dutch family who had helped us, and a week or so later, when the town had been finally liberated, I made my way back by road to find out what had happened to them. They had been taken away by the Germans shortly after our departure, together with many others in the crowd, but thankfully, after two days in custody they were all released unharmed. The sequel came some five years later when I was presented with a beautifully engraved silver cigarette case by the Mayor and People of Voorberg, commemorating the 'gallant' landing of the first Allied plane. How very nice of them, I thought, but little did they know how very ungallant we were.

With the war in Europe over, I was posted back from Germany to await transport to the Far East, but, while incarcerated in a transit camp in Kent, the atom bomb on Hiroshima changed the whole complexion of the war. The Air Ministry decided that hostilities could now be pursued without my help and I was demobilised within a month. Clad in an ill-fitting demob suit, with an oversize grey raincoat over my arm and a meagre gratuity in the bank. I said goodbye to HM Forces in 1945 and set about resuming my career as a cameraman.

8

A Matter of Life and Death

JACK CARDIFF WAS working as director of photography on *A Matter of Life and Death* for Powell and Pressburger. and he asked me to photograph the second unit, subject to Michael Powell's approval. I approached the interview with much trepidation as 'Micky' enjoyed a somewhat fearsome reputation. He did not suffer fools lightly and I was not at all sure that I did not, in his eyes, fall into this category.

He had a special triangular desk on castors which followed him round from stage to stage and at which he worked tirelessly with his secretary. While lighting and other time-consuming jobs were going on, he constantly revised and refined the script and dialogue. Having rehearsed a scene with the actors and blocked out the various camera set-ups, he would dictate a list of shots together with any changes which may have arisen during the rehearsals from suggestions by artists and technicians. Autocratic in the extreme, he nevertheless listened to all ideas and when he rejected them, always had the courtesy to say why. The list of shots covering the scene was then issued to all concerned so that everyone was 'in the know'. He would insist on shooting in continuity if he felt this would help the artists, but on other occasions would say, 'I don't mind in what order we shoot.'

This, of course, was a great saving in time and labour, for usually a set-up meant 'floating', ie. removing a wall in order to get the camera in position, and lighting to shoot in that particular direction. A reverse angle meant putting the wall back and floating another, redressing the set and lighting in the opposite direction. Sometimes this could happen many times in one sequence, so, bearing in mind that some sets came apart more easily than others, it is simple to imagine how much time could be saved when it was possible to shoot out of continuity. It is of course only possible when the director has a clear idea how the individual shots are to be assembled in the final cut.

Micky was a past master at being organised and in organising others, in stark contrast to others I have worked with, who will remain nameless so that I may avoid libel. The latter flounder through a film, covering everything from every possible angle in the forlorn hope, I often feel, that something coherent may come out of the cutting room in the end.

My interview took place with me seated at the third and unoccupied side of the triangle, with all hell going on around as lamps, cameras and walls were pushed around. The secretary stopped work and, chin in hand, gazed pensively at me. She had seen it all before. I was just another aspiring cameraman ripe for a little disillusionment. After what seemed an eternity, Micky looked up from whatever he was writing, his blue eyes holding me with a piercing and unblinking stare. The silence continued while he willed me to speak first and say something silly. I had been warned of these tactics and somehow determined that I would sit it out, and if necessary leave without saying a word. Several 'hours' passed and suddenly a wan smile relaxed his pursed lips. 'I remember you on *The Thief of Baghdad* as an assistant. Tell me about the war.' I set about recounting my 'heroic' efforts to save the nation, but he cut me short with, 'When can you start?' Totally taken aback, I stuttered. 'Do you really mean you want me to photograph the second unit?' Out of the corner of my eye, I saw the secretary turn back to her work as he replied rather acidly. 'Naturally I do, or I would not have asked you here.' His attention returned to his desk and I realised I was dismissed, a second unit cameraman on a feature film at last.

* * *

The film was, of course, a brilliant, original script by Micky and Emeric. A piece of pure writing for the cinema, it used colour as it had never been used before, and my little part of it, be it ever so humble, made me very proud to be there at all. I did not see Micky again, apart from at the screening of rushes of our work, which he always attended. He discussed things with the second unit director but never spoke to me. I was reassured by those who knew him that he was never lavish with praise, and the fact that I remained was the most encouragement that I could expect.

The story stemmed from an original idea which was set half in

Heaven and half on Earth. Heaven was to be shot in black and white and Earth in colour. People travelled between the two on a giant escalator specially built on the largest sound stage at Denham Studios. As they progressed up and down, they slowly changed from black and white to colour and vice versa. This posed enormous problems for Technicolor, who experimented for months to perfect the process. Micky and Emeric were on their way home from New York on the *Queen Mary* and the nucleus of the idea grew so fast that, after five days aboard, they stepped off the ship with a more or less completed script. So original was the idea that J. Arthur Rank gave the go-ahead at once, showing great courage on what was a step into the unknown.

Emeric Pressburger was the perfect partner and foil for Micky's flamboyant and at times 'boy scout' approach to things. Born in Hungary of Jewish parents, he was an accomplished musician at an early age. It was felt that a German University was where his future lay and his family begged and borrowed German currency to send him on his way. His ever-prudent and tearful mother carefully sewed the marks into the lining of his jacket, enough to keep him for a year.

Within weeks of arriving in Germany, the great slump set in and his hard-won nest egg would scarcely buy a cup of coffee. Undaunted, and with the help of some Hungarian friends, he worked with his violin doing the rounds of the cafés, ekeing out a meagre living which was just sufficient to get him through university, but with little money for food or clothing.

Cooking was one of Emeric's fortes and he always maintained that he mastered his art learning to make meals out of discarded leftovers. On graduation he got a job with UFA Berlin as a junior script writer, where he worked with all the great names in German films. Hitler's rapid rise to power posed a threat to numerous talented Jews and many of them decided to leave, Emeric settling on England, where he had a friend in fellow Hungarian, Alexander Korda. Here he met and teamed up with Micky and one of the great film industry partnerships was formed. Gentle and quiet by nature, with a wry sense of humour, he was a man with an iron will and limitless patience. Speaking slowly with a great economy of words, he retained his atrocious Hungarian accent to the end. At times I thought he kept it intentionally in order to take refuge behind it. He became naturalised and was intensely patriotic. He once said to me,

'You know, Chris, I am more English than you. You were born here, but I *chose* to become English.'

I remember one day in the theatre after rushes, a particular and apparently insolvable problem arose and deep gloom descended on all present at the thought of reshooting the previous day's work. Breaking the heavy silence, Micky suddenly sprang to his feet with the air of a Kipling hero urging on his thin red line, saying, 'What's the matter with everybody? It's all perfectly simple. We'll do this, that and the other, and it will go bang, bang, bang!' Again an unenthusiastic silence, this time broken by Emeric. 'Michael, it sounds so easy, but the trouble is that when you do it, it will be BOOM-BOOM-BOOM.'

Many years later, after they had amicably parted, Emeric decided to live in Austria, where he built a house. However, soon he was back and living alone in a 'Hansel and Gretel' cottage in Suffolk, complete with thatched roof and roses round the door. 'What made you come back?' I asked him. 'Well, Chris, you know how it is in Germany. You never find anyone who was a Nazi or even was aware that they existed. Well, in Austria it is the same, except that when you ask anyone, they reply, "No, I was never a Nazi, but *he* was". That is why I am here, back in my true home.'

* * *

But to return to my interview, or rather the results which stemmed from it. I was busily engaged with shooting the sequences delegated to the second unit. The completion of this work, which included the killing of Roger Livesey in a spectacular motorcycle crash in order that he might appear as advocate for David Niven in the High Court of Heaven, coincided with Geoffrey Unsworth, the camera operator, receiving an offer to become director of photography on another film. With six weeks of shooting still remaining, Micky characteristically agreed to release him and it was decided that I should take over. Geoff left to photograph his film and went on to a distinguished career.

I now found myself working directly under Micky, forewarned of what I might expect by the lurid stories told me by all and sundry of his short shrift for indecisive and dithering 'new boys'. My moment of truth came early on the second day. I was perched up on a camera crane, which in those days was a cumbersome affair pushed by a gang of stagehands, gardeners and anyone else who was strong and happened to be at a loose end. As an operator trying to carry out a creative and complicated shot, you were entirely in their horny and not exactly sensitive hands. A long shot to begin with, looking down on the High Court in Heaven, all white with the aurora borealis shimmering in the background, we slowly moved across the sea of faces, sinking and closing in on a close shot of Kathleen Byron and Roger Livesey, with the camera now down to the floor level. After numerous lumbering and painful rehearsals, during which I sensed the tension mounting and Micky's impatience growing, I announced in a shaky voice, which somehow seemed to belong to someone else, that I was ready. 'Turn over, action!' shouted the assistant director.

Luck was with me and all went perfectly, a fact which I proudly announced in a very loud voice, which again didn't seem to be mine. Micky walked over and looked through the viewfinder. Fixing me with the same unblinking stare he asked, 'Is that the way you framed the end of the shot?' His voice conveyed complete disgust at what I thought was a very good composition. Plucking up my courage, I explained my reasons. 'Oh, don't give me all those old worked-out theories,' was his acid retort. Every worm has its turning point and, shaking with righteous anger, I shouted, 'Well, why don't you do the next one yourself?' Absolute silence reigned on the huge set which, for me, had turned from heaven into hell. After what seemed several hours, during which he stared at and through me, he turned on his heel, calling over his shoulder to the continuity girl, 'Print it.' Life resumed its normal tenor and the incident was never mentioned again. It marked the beginning of a lifelong friendship with them both, which I treasure above all else in my working life.

Following my baptism of fire and what seemed a successful weathering of the storm, I once again was camera operator for Jack Cardiff on *Black Narcissus*. This was an adaptation by Powell and Pressburger of a book by Rumer Godden about a group of Anglican nuns in a convent set high in the Himalayas. I mention it only because it shows their diversity of style and original approach. It was decided to make the whole film in the studios at Pinewood. The sets and wonderful painted backings, often with several layers of gauze between, were incredible and, once carefully lit, looked completely real. Out in the studio lot, ranges of mountains were built in plaster and tilted back so that the sunlight struck them at the right angle and, when viewed from the camera angle, stretched away in perspective for hundreds of miles. The only location we had was Leonardslee Gardens, at Horsham in Sussex, where they have a valley of exotic Himalayan shrubs and plants. The final result was so realistic that old Indian 'hands' wrote in to say they recognised many of the views and knew just where we had photographed them. All this was designed by Alfred Junge, the art director, who was also a refugee from UFA in Berlin. Jack Cardiff won a well-deserved Oscar for his outstanding work.

9

A 'DP' at last

DEREK TWIST, AT one time an editor for Michael Powell on *Edge of the World* had risen to be CO of the RAF Film unit, and on returning to civilian life planned to direct for the first time. This was a not uncommon aspiration among editors and cameramen, no doubt driven by frustration and a firm conviction that they must be able to do it better than a lot of the people they have to work for. His chosen subject was a book called *The End of the River.* Set in Brazil, it told the story of a simple young Indian boy and girl from a primitive tribe in the North who marry, and via a series of adventures drift into civilisation, ending in the town of Belem, at the estuary of the Amazon, where the boy kills a man in a fight. He is finally set free because the court decide that civilisation, so-called, has exploited him and he is not responsible for his actions.

Powell and Pressburger agreed to produce the subject under their 'Archers' trade mark and, unlike *Black Narcissus*, it was to be shot on location. This would entail several weeks in Belem followed by a trip by boat 1000 miles up the Amazon to Manaus. The sequences with the tribe were to be done with the Arecunas who live on the borders of Brazil and British Guiana, as it then was, and Venezuela. The idea sounded wonderful, and every detail was discussed at great length, each of us creating a mental picture of what it would be like. Enthusiasm was rife among all of us and we couldn't wait to be off. In the light of experience, I now know that every film is in fact two films. There is the one you dream about, plan, cast and write the script for, in a cosy office somewhere in Mayfair, and the grim reality of the one you shoot, assuming that you are fortunate enough to raise the money, full of compromises brought about by weather, lack of time and money, clash of personalities, difficult actors and often sheer incompetence. Forward planning is necessary and there cannot be too much of it, so long as it is coupled with the ability to adapt and change when faced with the reality of production. Inflexibility, principally on the part of directors, often with little experience, has been the cause of many a film going wildly over budget and schedule, with nothing to show for it on the screen in the end.

* * *

The moment of disillusion must come to all directors and is well illustrated by a story told to me by a close friend who was camera operator on *Nine Hours to Rama*. Mark Robson had worked on the script for some years and the subject had become a mission in life for him as the time passed. At last, after countless problems and pitfalls, and months spent in India, the picture was on. The crew arrived from England, tired and thirsty after their long flight. Jet-lagged and already sweating in the unaccustomed heat, they were greeted by an excited and jubilant Mark with the request that they all got together in an hour in order that he could 'fill them in' about his 'dream'. To the jaundiced company, who had seen and heard it all before, he told with moving passion of his struggles to complete the script, raise the money, obtain permission, and overcome the many vicissitudes and frustrations attendant upon all 'would be' film producers. At last all the battles were won, and they were about to embark together on the greatest film ever about India. They must look upon the teeming masses as their brothers, and try to identify themselves totally with the script (which, incidentally, most of them had not read) and merge into the noisy, hot, dusty background that was India so that, unnoticed, they could faithfully document the epic story that meant so much to him.

The very next morning they were to shoot a simple pre-production shot of a car driving through the crowded bazaar in Lahore, past the open-fronted stalls, the beggars, the rickshaws, and the demure, sari-clad women. A simple shot to start with; no actors and just a skeleton crew. An early start would avoid the heat, with the smallest unobtrusive camera set up in a doorway. Immediately a large crowd of betel nut-chewing passers-by gathered around, in no hurry and ever on the look-out for free entertainment. Mark arrived, immaculate in white linen suit, and a way was cleared for him to reach the camera. He immediately took exception to a luridly coloured shirt worn by the camera assistant, which he felt was causing the disturbance. 'Ginger' was a very large man with bright red hair and a massive beard to match, much given to exotic clothes, which in this instance took the form of serpents entwined with large brightly coloured tropical flowers. Ginger was sent off with an Indian assistant to purchase a more sombre garment and the rest of the assistants, together with the police, attempted to control the now enormous crowd, pleading with them to go about their business – in the unlikely event of their having any – and not to look into the camera.

Take after take went by, each ruined by a curious face thrust into the lens. The heat increased rapidly with the passage of time and Mark's immaculate attire began to show signs of dust and perspiration, with the odd splash of betel nut juice for good measure. Ginger returned, clad in a more sedate shirt, and immediately set about opening a bottle of Coca-Cola on the tripod leg. Probably due to the heat and excessive agitation, the bottle exploded, spraying the director with sticky brown liquid. After many more attempts to drive the car through the street and at the same time achieve the finer points of direction in terms of crowd action, Mark decided to watch yet another rehearsal, this time looking through the finder while operating the camera himself. In the middle of panning the camera round while endeavouring to follow the car, the heavy cast metal sunshade on the viewfinder fell down, taking the skin off Mark's nose, which slowly dropped blood onto his shirt and jacket. It was past noon, everyone was hungry, the heat unbearable. Mark Robson was covered with dust and sweat mingled with blood and Coca-Cola, and already, I am sure, he could sense his dream slipping away. 'OK fellers,' he said wearily, 'take the goddam car back down the street, turn it round, drive it back past the camera and let's get the hell out of here.' I must add that, in spite of this inauspicious start, they went on to make a fine film.

* * *

To return to *The End of the River* and its pre-production planning, Derek Twist set off with the production manager on an extended trip to Brazil and British Guiana where they were to meet the author of the book, which was largely based on fact, and reconnoitre the proposed locations. A first-hand view of the terrain and the people would greatly help to finalise the script and assess the difficulties we might encounter working in such a remote area. After some six weeks they returned with a well documented survey of all the possible alternatives, accompanied by dozens of still photographs. These clearly illustrated the incredible background of the Amazon and the surrounding jungle, and the fascinating old Portuguese colonial towns of Santa Maria de Belem and Manaus. Unfortunately Derek also brought back a leading lady for whom he had developed a great attraction during his short stay in Rio, where she was a cabaret singer of some repute.

A lady of considerable personality, vivácious and with, I believe, a very good voice, Bibi Ferreira was between 35 and 40 years of age, with a decidedly unconventional shape and unphotogenic face. She was to play the part of a 16-year-old Indian girl with nothing to hide her shortcomings but a simple cotton shift. For me, embarking on my first feature film as a director of photography, she rapidly assumed the proportions of a cinematic Calvary. The well-established convention that all females should be beautiful and all males tall, suntanned and handsome, stemming from between the war years when most films were escapist in concept, still largely held good. The era of stark realism and total fascination with the seedy side of life, warts and all, lay ahead. It was believed that a film had to entertain, and did not necessarily have to contain a message. Producers of the old school still expected their stars to look more beautiful, more handsome, taller and more suntanned than they did in real life.

If one pauses for a moment to consider that a close-up on a large screen produces a face 30 feet across, the problem becomes readily apparent. Every small imperfection is a 'crater on the moon'. A shiny nose, a hairy upper lip, the slightest of casts in one eye, a hair out of place, all assume unrealistic proportions at rushes. Unlike a still photograph, which can be heavily retouched in the later stages, moving photography has no such recourse to darkroom fiddling. Photography has been described as 'painting with light' and, although rather ostentatious an expression, it is nevertheless a fairly accurate one. To photograph someone to the best advantage there is the choice of the correct lens, the ideal camera height, and the perfect position of the 'key' light, all of which can be controlled in a still picture. But in cinematography, by definition, the subjects have to move, and what is ideal for one actor is anathema to another.

To overcome these problems there exists an elaborate system of diffusion on lights and camera lenses, gauzes and false shadows cast by small pieces of wood held in stands to cover strategic positions, fondly known as 'Charlie Bars' for obvious reasons. For these things to work it is essential for the actors to hit 'marks' accurately as they move around during a scene, otherwise a shadow cunningly arranged to hide a double chin might end up across the eyes! This imposes considerable limitations on the artists, but they are generally accepted as necessary, for artists are well aware that their faces, and in many cases their bodies, are their fortunes. The more professional among them quickly become adept at hitting their marks and soon realise where the keylight should be for them to look their best. Woe betide the harassed cameraman, doing his best to please three or four actors at the same time, if it was not in the right place.

Some, more conscious of their appearance than others, would borrow a mirror from make-up and check each position for themselves. Skilful make-up, dentistry, and even plastic surgery all played their part as 'improvers', and costume design covered many a scrawny neck of a figure considered to be lacking in essential curves. Many artists became convinced that they possessed good and bad sides to their faces, and were prepared to go to great lengths in order to present the more favourable side to the camera. There was a certain degree of truth in these beliefs, but in practice the crunch came when two actors appeared facing each other in a 'two shot' and their good sides were not compatible.

Men had, in principle, to be taller than women, and male leads taller than their fellows, a theory which more often than not proved to be unsubstantiated in real life. To rectify this error of nature, many a scene has been shot with one actor standing on a box and wearing 'high lift' shoes, and in some cases even the contour of the ground was used to set matters right. The moment of truth came when their feet had to be seen, but the use of carefully chosen angles, coupled with judicious editing, usually overcame the problem.

In studio shooting, once a scene had been rehearsed to everyone's satisfaction, each position was carefully marked and the lighting went ahead with stand-ins, the object being to effect the best compromise between the various conflicting elements and care being taken to give principals the best 'deal'. Newcomers treated the marks with varying degrees of abandon, some progressing round the set with downcast eyes until the next mark was safely reached. It was a rigid approach made necessary by the size of cameras and the amount of light required, and the sort of results expected by the 'front office', whose attitude was conditioned by the firm belief, built up over many years of box office analysis, that the public paid to see the 'stars'. In all but the most experimental and adventurous cases a conventional, glossy look was the order of the day.

From the preceding observations it will be apparent that I had a problem on my hands with the leading lady. Fate, coupled with affairs of the heart, had dealt me a cruel blow. Direct sunlight is the harshest of photographic task masters in relation to faces and our film was to be shot on location without the aid of booster light, since it was quite impossible to take generators to the jungle and river situations. My only hope was to manoeuvre as many scenes as possible into backlight or shadow.

The next four months of my life were entirely taken up with the creation of artificial shadows, cast by pieces of palm frond or other handy foliage. These had to be nailed to long poles since the sun was so high, in order to create a gently moving shadow over the lady's face. A close observer of the film will notice that she existed in a private world of dappled sunlight, in contrast to the stark reality of the surroundings. Wherever she moved, the shadows went with her, the mobile undergrowth carried by Indians who stoically accepted my directions, feeling, I am sure, that they stemmed from a mind deranged by the heat and humidity of equatorial South America. They soon became adept at following her, occasionally walking into the shot when creative art overcame their natural shyness. Of course they had no idea what we were doing, but the work was a giggle and the money good.

Sabu, who played the young Arecuna Indian boy, had progressd far from the day when Robert Flaherty discovered him in Mysore, the son of a mahout, and used him as the lead in *Elephant Boy*. He now lived in Hollywood, possessor of considerable wealth and the awareness that he was an Indian and a world-famous star. These facts brought him great advantage for it was a 'niche' with little competition. He was very well aware of the strength of his appeal but, perhaps with an increasing sense of 'colour', he had no wish to be too dark an Indian. With the help of his make-up man, a light foundation had been devised which met the occasion admirably – that is, until he met up with Torin Thatcher, who played the white villain. Torin suffered from a skin complaint, greatly aggravated by the heat, which necessitated a very heavy make-up to cover the marks on his face, and we were confronted with the interesting phenomenon of the Indian boy being several shades lighter than the white man.

10

The End of the River

THE FIRST STAGE of our journey out was by air to New York, uneventful apart from the time it then took, via Prestwick, Iceland, Newfoundland etc. From New York to Belem we had a charter flight, or rather we thought we had, but on arrival we discovered that, due to a slip-up somewhere along the line, it did not exist. We spent four days in New York almost destitute, since in the late '40s one could only take £12 out of the country.

Derek Twist and I were ensconced in Arthur Rank's suite, which was retained for him permanently at the Sherry Netherlands Hotel. Surrounded by extreme luxury, we quickly discovered that when we rang for room service, which seemed a way round our predicament, the waiter made it clear that he expected a substantial tip, in cash, word having reached him of our already crumbling Empire. Our slender resources were soon used up and we lived a sort of hermit existence amid astonishing plenty until our flight was finally organised.

It turned out that our flight was booked with a one-plane airline, run by a couple of ex-US Air Force pilots and a very attractive South American girl, who among other duties acted as hostess. The aircraft was an ex-Air Force Dakota, its new paintwork barely disguising its old wartime markings. After another enforced delay in Miami due to lack of landing permissions, we finally made Belem. During the three days of the flight, Sabu had embarked on a violent love affair with the air hostess, sitting hand in hand on the very back seat, or alternatively completely hidden from view in, we presumed, either the toilet or the galley, both of which must have placed severe restrictions on the art of love making. Apart from restricting cabin service to the minimum, it did not appear to bother anyone, least of all the crew, who being part, or rather all, of a small and individualistic company, saw nothing untoward in the situation.

The location divided roughly into two parts. The first was the journey by boat up the Amazon to Manaus, nearly 1000 miles through the jungle, and the second the Indian village where scenes of the young couple's early life were to be shot. The Arecuna tribe were chosen as the most suitable, being unwarlike and not particularly given to the collection of heads. We were introduced to a Spaniard named Orella who lived in British Guiana and knew the Arecuna country well, having served on the Boundary Commission with Brazil and Venezuela when he had explored the territory and made friends among the Indians. The script called for a village on a river bank, and since the area where they lived was unapproachable except by canoe, taking several weeks to accomplish and with endless rapids to negotiate, he suggested that the best thing to do would be for a small party to carry out a reconnaissance by air to find a suitable site. He felt it unlikely that such a village existed, but if we could choose the location he would be flown in later and landed on the nearest suitable section of river. He would then go on foot to find the Indians and get them to build the village.

The savannah country in which they lived was beyond the jungle belt, and mostly flat for countless miles except for huge termite heaps. It could easily be levelled to make a landing ground for a Dakota. He had discussed the plan with Major Williams of British Guiana Airways, who also knew the country well, and they both thought it entirely feasible. Derek Twist and I flew up to Georgetown, where we joined Orella and Williams and next day flew low over the tree tops which blocked the end of our 'runway'.

Only from the air can one really appreciate the silent immensity of this South American jungle, stretching below for hundreds of unbroken miles like a giant parsley bed, with no glimpse of the ground in any direction. From time to time the silver thread of a river wound its tortuous way through, the white foaming water of rapids breaking the line every few miles. It made one wonder how men ever succeeded in passing this way on foot and by canoe, beset as they were with malaria and beri-beri fever. With these thoughts running through my mind, the idea of a landing strip on the savannah, which had not appeared to me all that reassuring, grew more attractive by the minute. On we flew, pausing to spiral down into the bowl of the Kaiteur Falls, higher than Niagara, their beauty seen by few men. Circling through the cloud of spray, we climbed again over the rim and on towards the Pakaraima Mountains and the flat topped Mount Roraima.

The jungle was giving way to the savannah and a perfect spot for the village was found and carefully pin-pointed by Orella on his map. A short distance away was an Indian village, and a suitable stretch of water where he could be landed. Williams felt the terrain was ideal for bringing in the Dakota, and we had complete confidence in his opinion, his whole life having been spent bush flying. At the start of the war, already operating his small airline with a single-engined Ireland flying boat with an open cockpit, he claimed the unique distinction of dropping a home-made bomb on an unsuspecting U-boat that was charging its batteries on the surface and soaking up the Caribbean sunshine.

Back in Belem, the production manager had been busy chartering a highly unsuitable steamer for the trip to Manaus. A man of severely limited nautical experience, and much overcome by the heat and humidity, both of which he sought to combat with large quantities of fierce local gin, he concluded a deal for a vessel which looked like something out of *Huckleberry Finn*. Reputed to have been a Mersey ferry in the distant past, it had somehow found its way to this corner of South America where it had undergone adjustment of its former shape by, I would imagine, a firm of local housebuilders. It was on offer complete with a nondescript crew and an unshaven, intoxicated 'Captain' who assumed the unconventional attire of pyjamas topped by a Naval cap, with enough gold braid for an Admiral of the Fleet. General dismay was countered with the hard fact that nothing else was available. Designed to burn coal, the vessel's wheezy reciprocating steam engine now had to function on a diet of wood, which it consumed in vast quantities, necessitating every square inch of available space being used for its storage. Ready for departure, it closely resembled a floating timber yard. It boasted a range of small boxlike cabins, giving the impression of an early broiler house, but as these too were stacked with wood, sleep was to be arranged in mosquito-net draped hammocks, slung wherever a space could be found. There was, of course, no refrigeration, and just one shower which, if persevered with, would eventually disgorge a trickle of dirty brown water, straight from the river and well laced with numerous bugs.

The river of course flowed against us, which reduced our effective progress to a crawl, and wood started to disappear at an alarming rate. The crew had the habit of using it all from one side so that we rapidly assumed an unseamanlike list to port and, with the low freeboard, the deck was soon awash. According to the script, we were meant to be travelling in the opposite direction and with the current. The purists among us insisted that, when filming, we should turn around so that on each occasion when we shot a scene, we raced downstream with the current, losing several hours of painful steaming in as many minutes.

The first night on board I selected what appeared to be a likely spot among the wood piles and rigged up my hammock to a couple of rusty iron hooks in the roof. The mosquito net was then fixed to canes attached to the hammock lines, an operation that proved next to impossible. After several abortive attempts I at last managed to climb in and tuck the net around me. This enraged a cloud of mosquitoes who, already wise to the white man's device, had taken up their abode inside. It seemed pretty clear that the net, far from keeping them out, was doing a fine job of keeping them in. A crew member appeared, armed with an ancient Flit gun, and suggested that once safely settled with my defences in place. I should give the interior a thorough spraying. At last, lying on my back in the form of a banana, and shrouded in evil smelling mist, I attempted to sleep. I fell in and out of the hammock at regular intervals, on each occasion going through the ritual of securing the net and spraying. To say that the night passed fitfully would be an understatement. The ritual gradually assumed the proportions of a nightmare and towards dawn I gave up the unequal struggle. Putting my trust in the anti-malarial tablets that we were all taking, I fell into an uneasy sleep. After what seemed minutes, I was rudely woken by something crashing into my hammock, to the sound of much frenzied shouting. In the grey light of dawn the shape of a large and startled pig darted between the wood piles, hotly pursued by two of the crew, armed with large knives and intent on breakfast.

Food was a disaster. Fresh meat was truly fresh, in the sense that it was on the hoof. We carried chickens, pigs, and even a couple of steers and several sheep, who one by one met the same untimely fate as the pig. Because of the climate, the meat had to be consumed on the day of slaughter, resulting in the toughest joints I have ever encountered. We all took refuge in the large stock of tinned food we carried, leaving the crew to eat the fresh variety, which they did with apparent relish.

It quickly became clear that our boatload of timber would not last long and, sure enough, in a couple of days we pulled into a suitable spot on the bank and the crew disappeared ashore armed with saws and axes. The refuelling took two days and once again we resembled a wood yard, the cabins and deckspace so tightly packed that one moved about only with great difficulty.

We pursued our tedious way, leaving behind small clearings in the jungle to mark our progress and the remains of our disembodied livestock swirling in the muddy waters astern, to be snapped up gratefully by shoals of piranhas. The river is navigable up as far as Manaus by quite large ships, and one British company still maintained a dock and freight service there. In many places there is a generous choice of channels, the river at times being over a mile wide and dotted with islands. Our 'Captain', proud of his seafaring Portuguese ancestry, scorned the use of all charts. His English was meagre, and his command over his native tongue decreased in direct ratio to his intake of booze. His navigational eccentricities usually occurred after a session on the bottle, when he would indicate by sign language that he knew the river like the back of his hand, a revelation which brought little comfort since it was obvious that even this member was obscure to him.

We survived many strandings and our unconventional course enabled us to see sections of the river rarely on view to ordinary travellers. The nightly search for a place to sling one's hammock turned into a game of one-upmanship at which we became adept as the days passed. On one occasion two of us hit upon a clever idea. Why not the roof of the wheelhouse, which was in the bows of the boat? Up there we would get the benefit of whatever breeze there was and take advantage of the stanchions which had once supported an awning and were ideal for bearing the hammocks.

All seemed perfect. It was relatively cool, the gentle movement of air kept the mosquitoes away and, adopting the usual banana shapes, we were soon asleep. The frantic ringing of engine room telegraph bells from the bridge below, accompanied by shouting and the sound of running feet, woke us. We suddenly found ourselves in the midst of trees which overhang the bank all along the river. Startled monkeys, their night as rudely interrupted as our own, gazed at us through the mosquito netting. It was one more grounding, this time straight into the bank. We extracted ourselves from the tangle of broken branches and went below in search of a strong drink, while, with the engine hard astern, the crew furiously fed wood into the boiler to raise a bit more steam.

A half-way stop was made at the small town of Santarem,

where we decided to film the wedding sequence. The location was a charming, crumbling small Portuguese colonial church, and a crowd of locals were taken on as extras, all highly delighted to receive payment for doing nothing but standing and waving in the sunshine. We needed to use all our three cameras, placed at different vantage points, to make the most of the colourful scene and, since we had only one camera crew, other members of the unit were called in to operate them. Bob Lynn, the second assistant director, was allocated a position in the belfry of the church, reached by a decaying spiral staircase in complete darkness. The heat at midday was unbearable and once clear of the eyes of the clergy he stripped to his shorts and set off on his climb. He emerged ten minutes later, screaming with pain, and collapsed in the road outside. He had disturbed a nest of hornets and had been bitten unmercifully all over his body. He was rushed to a nearby convent hospital, where for 24 hours his life hung in the balance. I went to see him that evening as he lay in a coma, his normally lanky body swollen to twice its normal size. With careful nursing he was back with us in a week, completely recovered and resolving never to enter a church again.

For some days I had been suffering from toothache which grew hourly more acute and it was felt that I should avail myself of this last contact with civilisation and have it attended to. There was but one dentist in town, who turned out to be a Chinaman, and to whom I presented myself in some trepidation. His surgery was small, dark, unbelievably hot, and strewn with the evidence of past extractions. Communication was by sign language, and after a cursory examination he indicated by waving a pair of pliers before my startled eyes that removal of the offending tooth was the only cure. I cheered up considerably when he produced a hypodermic needle, for at least I would be spared pain. This quickly proved to be a false illusion, for the injection had no effect whatsoever. After several attempts, the needle broke in my gum and had to be retrieved with the pliers. He disappeared, muttering to himself, into the darker recesses of the room and returned in triumph with another bottle of anaesthetic, probably only two years out of date, and a comforting sense of numbness spread over my apprehensive features as it took effect. He set to work and soon encountered problems which necessitated the use of a scalpel and a hammer and chisel, for it transpired that the trouble was an impacted wisdom tooth. Sweat dripped from his face onto mine as, beyond caring, I resigned myself to an early death from blood poisoning and a jungle grave. At last it was out and the stitches inserted. I rose from the torture chair so saturated in the sweat of abject terror that I could well have been under the shower. Somehow I got back to the boat, drank half a bottle of whisky and collapsed into my hammock and a troubled sleep, haunted by dreams of being chased by hordes of grinning Chinamen brandishing knives and hypodermic syringes. Miraculously, next morning the pain had gone and in a week's time, with the stitches removed in the convent hospital by a sympathetic nun, I was completely cured.

I have carried with me for the rest of my days an inborn hatred of all dentists who, I feel, carry a collective responsibility for my experience.

During these days on the river I came to realise just how difficult it was to convey to the screen any idea of the immensity of the Amazon and the surrounding jungle. The river bank looked like any other, lined with trees to the water's edge, and a shot of it could not show that the forest extended unbroken for 1000 miles, mostly unexplored and fever-ridden. The width of the river made it look like the sea or a vast lake. Only from the air could one appreciate the scale of it all, but flying did not feature in the script.

* * *

Months later, back in England, when the film had reached the editing stage, this shortcoming became very apparent and it was decided to shoot some extra scenes on the Thames near Hurley. Having by now a clear idea of exactly what was wanted, we got some of our best Amazon footage in these gentle surroundings. With the camera set up in the bows of a sleek river launch, we followed a large dug-out canoe, made in the carpenter's shop at Pinewood, manned by dark-skinned men, courtesy of the make-up department, clad in loin cloths, and armed with blowpipes and bows. We paddled our way through overhanging branches into the most secluded and secret places, causing consternation and panic to many a courting couple hidden beneath the canopies of their punts in what they thought was complete seclusion.

* * *

At last we reached Manaus, capital of Amazonas. Once a flourishing city at the height of the wild rubber boom, its site carved out of the virgin jungle, its only line of communication was the river. Vast fortunes were made selling the rubber to the outside world, hungry for this newly found substance. Indians were sent into the jungle to bleed the trees, smoking and rolling the latex into large balls which they somehow managed to get down to the river bank. With little food and no medicine, they died in their thousands of malnutrition and disease as their masters grew rich. The new millionaires, almost overnight, built a fantastic city, the streets lined with magnificent houses in stone and marble, designed and built by craftsmen brought in from Italy and France. The streets were paved and a tramway system installed equal to anything in Europe. A beautiful opera house was commissioned and cafés and restaurants abounded. Everything was brought in by ship up the 1000 miles of river from Belem and at the height of this opulence the Rubber Barons even sent their laundry to Lisbon.

Now, in 1947, all was decay. The speed of Manaus' growth was only matched by the rapidity of its decline. With the advent of cultivated rubber in Malaya, the bubble burst. The houses were in ruins, the opera house a shell, the trams long since gone. Beautiful wrought iron balconies hung rusting in the corrupting humidity of the jungle which was slowly but surely taking back what had been wrested from it. At the end of each avenue of stately houses, the road surface full of potholes, the paving stones cracked and broken, one came face to face with the advancing forest, closing in to reclaim what was rightly nature's.

We spent about a month in Manaus shooting the scenes of our young Indian couple making their first contact with civilisation. Hotels were scarce and mostly on the lines of the Maude in Baghdad. I was fortunate to be offered a room with the English manager of the Booth Line, who still ran a cargo service and maintained part of the dock area. His apartment, complete with a Peruvian cook carefully trained in the art of English cuisine, was an escape to paradise after the weeks on the boat. He kept a high-powered outboard speedboat for pleasure trips on the river and of an evening he took me on crocodile-hunting excursions. At last light they would lie just below the surface with only their snouts showing, looking for all the world like floating logs amid all the debris which floated by. He was an excellent shot and knew just where to aim below the water in order not to spoil the skin with bullet holes. The one good restaurant was, of course, run by a French family. Set in a delightful courtyard, the tables grouped around a large artificial pool, its outstanding attraction, apart from the food, was the fact that the pool contained a crocodile of no mean proportions. This reptile was a veritable Houdini, frequently escaping from its man-made habitat during the course of dinner, whereupon discretion overcame gastronomic desire. The diners abandoned their meals in varying degrees of panic until the cause of the commotion had been safely returned to the pool by the restaurant staff, who were as accomplished at this as they were with conjuring up first-rate French food in the middle of nowhere.

Our next move was to Georgetown in British Guiana, where we were to meet up with Orella. The village and airstrip had been completed and Major Williams had already made a trial landing in the Dakota. The unit was to be reduced to a minimum as no actors were coming; only the camera crew, director and assistants, and a construction manager would be going. It had transpired that the location chosen was just within the boundaries of Brazil, and the authorities in São Paulo insisted that we must be accompanied by a government representative in the form of an army Colonel. His function, apparently, was to insure that we confined ourselves to filming and did not branch out into a little private prospecting for gold and diamonds on the side, as the area, as yet unprospected was thought to be rich in these materials. The Colonel arrived in Georgetown some three days late, dressed in full ceremonial uniform. He carried an impressive personal arsenal in his baggage, including a dress sword, all of which was immediately confiscated by an unsmiling British Customs Officer at the airport. After several days of high level negotiations with São Paulo, it was agreed that he could have his possessions back when we took off for the Indian territory, so long as it was seen aboard the Dakota by a Customs representative. Our Colonel, in spite of his Gilbert and Sullivan wardrobe, turned out to be an extremely nice fellow. After overcoming his initial disappointment that our party did not include Dorothy Lamour, he entered into the spirit of things and gave us very little trouble. During our four weeks' stay with the Indians he spent most of his time wading waist deep in the rivers, armed with a prospector's pan with which he had equipped himself. I am sure he looked upon the experience as a 'golden' opportunity to supplement his meagre army pay and make possible a more attractive retirement, always assuming he was able to avoid implication in possible forthcoming coups.

At last all was ready, with the gear loaded into the Dakota, including a cricket set without which our construction manager, a stalwart Yorkshireman, refused to travel. We made an excellent landing on our 'Savannah' airstrip, now cleared of termite heaps, and were immediately surrounded by a large crowd of Arecunas, who were making their first acquaintance with this large and noisy bird. Indeed most of them had never seen a white man before, yet they showed no fear as they gathered round clad only in G-strings, and armed with blowpipes and bows. We learned later that the arrows and darts were dipped in a home-made poison which caused almost instant death. Not a warlike people, their weapons were used purely for hunting game, which could be safely eaten after a few hours. They had been living in the specially constructed village for some time and it all looked completely authentic. They had built us a long open-sided hut to eat and sleep in, the roof thatched with branches. Along the side was a long bench of rough hewn timber on which to spread our sleeping bags. The climate was mild, and being away from the jungle there was no need for mosquito nets.

On the recommendation of Orella, we had brought with us a 'safari' cook, a large and very black negro with a perpetual grin spread across his ugly face. He came complete with two large empty oil drums which had until now been a mystery to us. They were to be his ovens, and he proceeded to dig them into the ground, lying on their sides. One end was removed and made into a door, and a hole scooped underneath for the fire. With this simple equipment he produced some excellent meals from the game and fish brought in daily by the Indians. A favourite was a sort of wild hog which tasted as good or better than anything from the high street butcher. After a few days sampling his cuisine we abandoned the large supply of tinned food we had with us in favour of the fresh variety. Standards of hygiene were, judging from our cook's clothes, general appearance and strongly personal aroma, not particularly high, but we all survived five weeks of it without a single upset, which is more than can be claimed for Cairo or the Costa Brava.

We had with us a camera 'dolly', a flat platform with a wheel at each corner, two of which could be steered from a position at the back. This 'go-cart' proved a great attraction for the Arecuna, as the wheel was unknown to them. In no time the village lads were careering around, ten at a time, with 20 or so pulling or pushing, the object being to tip each other off as rapidly as possible. We soon had to ration its availability for fear of it being rendered useless. In the meantime, Tom Howe had laid out his cricket pitch on the hard earth. They quickly grasped the basic idea and, equipped with a natural ability for judging the speed of objects in flight, mighty boundaries were hit from every ball. Batting and bowling were highly unorthodox and scoring of little consequence, the bowlers looking upon the infliction of painful personal injury as an hilarious added bonus. Cricket became the success story of the location, and I am sure it is played there to this day, no doubt with a substitute for the English willow.

Our stay passed all too quickly for me. With no leading lady to contend with, I was relieved of the task of creating artificial shade, which was just as well since the area was treeless. I was able to concentrate on photographing the Indians about their daily tasks against the most magnificent backgrounds of river, rapids, and distant mountains. Doubles were chosen for Sabu and Bibi, only to be seen at a distance, the closer shots to be added later in the safety of Pinewood Studios. We covered every aspect of their lives, one of the most interesting being their method of fishing. This was done with a bow and arrow, standing on a suitable rock in mid-stream. The fish were easily seen in the clear water and, without being aware of the scientific explanation, they knew exactly how to allow for refraction when taking aim. Without the need for clothes or permanent houses, and the pangs of hunger met by an abundance of game, life was simplicity itself. No attempt was made to cultivate land and gourds cut in half were the only articles of crockery.

A potent drink made from cassava roots was their only means of escape from the pressures of society. This was produced by the simple means of chewing the tough, unpalatable root and spitting the proceeds into a large gourd, where it was allowed to ferment. Carried out by the women on a production line basis, with a large group sitting cross-legged on the ground round a central bowl, it seemed a happy alternative to knitting. The resulting liquid, which seemed to have the power of producing oblivion without aggression, remained for all of us an untried experience, with the intimate knowledge of its brewing method proving an unsurmountable deterrent.

Major Williams had provided us with a short-wave radio and an arrangement whereby he would listen out each day at a predetermined hour back in Georgetown in case we were in any sort of trouble. Our work completed, we called him up and arranged the flight out. It was a sad day for us, saying goodbye to these short, potbellied people, their faces wreathed in permanent broken-toothed smiles, and their hearts full of goodwill towards visitors from a world totally beyond their comprehension. There are few places or societies that one genuinely regrets leaving and, for me, this was certainly one of them.

A unique experience behind us, we faced ten weeks of studio shooting, where scenes with the actors would be dovetailed into the Amazonian backgrounds. The stage was filled with tropical vegetation, some of it real and some made from plaster and cleverly painted. Native huts hid amid the 'jungle', peopled by brown-painted extras in loin cloths. The illusion was broken when one saw them in the queue for tea and bacon rolls at break time. Once again I was in the shadow business, although it was now more controllable, with the bits of palm leaf on adjustable stands and the sunlight movable in terms of height and direction at my slightest whim. Slowly the weeks passed, a poor substitute for those of us who had been fortunate enough to see the real thing. The smell on the stages became more realistic with the passage of time as the heat from the lights got to work on the foliage. The real wilted and died and the paint peeled off the unreal. One area after another became unshootable despite watering and spraying. We were nearly through, with just a few close-ups left to be done against a background of potted plants from Kew Gardens. Our jungle had died around us and, in spite of everyone's endeavours, so had our story, as we were to find out later when it was screened before the disapproving eyes of the London critics.

With a full feature film to my credit, I was now an established director of photography. I had learned invaluable lessons about getting along with actors and directors in the closely confined world which is a film unit. I had also picked up a number of useful tips in the realm of photographic subterfuge which helped to make the subject matter, at least in a conventional sense, better to look at than nature had intended.

11

The Red Shoes

POWELL AND PRESSBURGER were about to start production on *The Red Shoes*, to be photographed by Jack Cardiff, and I decided on voluntary demotion to become camera operator. It was a decision I have never regretted, for the picture turned out to be one of the most memorable I have ever had the privilege of working on.

This was a wonderful period for British films, and the loosely-knit group known as Independent Producers, financed by the old Rank Organisation, were able to function in exactly the way that their name implied. Although technically a formidable project, entailing for those days a very high budget, support was quickly forthcoming, enabling one of the greatest of British films to become a reality. Sadly, in the years to come, this freedom for the really creative people who made up the group was slowly eroded as the accountants took over, and one by one the producers and directors went their separate ways. No one would deny that financial control is necessary, but when the people dealing with money spread their field of influence into the realms of taste and choice of subject, the old magic quickly disappears and is replaced by a second-rate, dull mediocrity.

The Red Shoes was very original in concept, for within the web of a conventional story ran the parallel one of the ballet, complementing what was to happen in real life.

Again the technical problems were enormous, and this time they were approached in an unusual way. Hein Heckroth, the production designer, came from a background of theatre and opera and sought to solve the visual effects in a theatrical way, using stage techniques like painted gauzes which when unlit were transparent, but when front lit became solid backgrounds. Double exposures were made in the camera, and many photographic tricks of the early days of cinematography were resorted to in order to avoid using special effects and laboratory optical printing later. Hein was a man of great visual imagination and boyish humour and, apart from his ability as a theatrical designer, was also an excellent painter. Not versed in the many special effects processes of the film medium, his approach to film design was original and exciting and quickly caught the imagination of Michael Powell, ever on the look-out for something different. After exhaustive tests it was decided to shoot the whole of the ballet in the camera, as it were, without recourse to laboratory effects. This, I suppose, could be looked upon as a step back, for this is how the earliest movies were made, but the results had a quality which was unique and in a strange way more believable. One great advantage was that the results could be viewed next day at rushes instead of waiting months for the combined prints to be made, by which time it would be too late to have second thoughts.

The ballet was unique in that I believe it to be the first truly 'film' ballet. Once the score was written, Hein did a series of paintings illustrating every scene, which were photographed to the correct length and cut together to the music so that we had a 'still' film of the whole sequence. This gave a very clear picture of what we were trying to do, easily understandable by everyone including the dancers and much easier to comment on, and if necessary alter, than mere words on paper.

Once the 'straight' part of the film was completed, the whole unit went on holiday while the ballet sets were built and the dancers rehearsed, so that on our return we could work straight through in continuity. Our 'still' film was run each day after rushes, with the previous day's work replacing the appropriate painting so that, day to day, it came to life. It is the only time I have seen this done, and the effect was incredible. Word quickly spread that something unusual was afoot and the theatre was packed with every member of the crew, electricians, plasterers, carpenters, and even the office staff, everyone gladly forsaking their lunch break to feel a part of it all. This sort of enthusiasm is rare, quite understandably, because what we were doing was experimental and one could see it clearly taking shape each day. The whole film was a long slog of about 24 weeks but it passed like a few exciting hours, led along as we were by Michael Powell's infectious enthusiasm and tenacity. No matter what the problems were, we had to get it right, and the reward was there each day to see.

I have worked on many a film with a schedule of eight weeks or less, whose titles are best forgotten and whose days seemed like years of uninspired drudgery, yet the five months or so we took to make *The Red Shoes* passed like an enchanted hour. With the approach of old age, I look back on the days of *The Red Shoes* with the fondest of memories, a habit no doubt common with the lapse of time.

It was also an experience to work with a ballet company, many of whom were dancers of international repute. Unlike many actors, particularly the ones referred to as 'stars', their lives are highly disciplined and their dedication to work total. Moira Shearer was a marvellous choice for the principal role. A dancer who had succeeded by dint of sheer hard work, coupled with much talent and startling beauty, the offer must have been one of great personal trauma for her. Should she give up all she had worked for to become a 'film star' overnight, and perhaps never again dance as a *prima ballerina*? With international acclaim would come money, something which I always felt did not greatly influence her decision, and, of course, the possibility of another career as an actress, which probably did. Her decision was our good fortune, for with her ability as a dancer, her looks and her wonderful red hair, she looked a sensation on the screen. How I envied Jack Cardiff, for there was no need for palm frond shadows this time. She looked marvellous wherever she went and whatever she did. She was great fun to work with and quickly picked up all the little tricks of movie making. Having a great sense of fun, she taught the camera crew the basics of the dance of the cygnets from *Swan Lake*, and we used to do it each morning before shooting, as a gag.

Robert Helpmann, Frederick Ashton, Leonide Massine, they were all, of course, outstanding in the world of ballet, and equally so as artists to work with. Helpmann and Ashton were friends of long standing and shared a marvellous sense of humour. Members of the *corps de ballet* told us that often in the middle of the most serious part of a classical ballet, when they had their backs to the audience, they would clown around and have the whole company on the verge of collapse. One of Robert's favourite stories was of the famous but unpopular *prima ballerina* who had to make an entrance from the wings executing a series of rapid pirouettes. With little room to spare between the flats, her tutu caught in a nail and neatly stripped off her skirt as she twirled her way onto the stage. Knowing Robert's sense of humour I could imagine him having engineered the lady's discomfort.

Massine was a dour character who did not approve of hilarity in any form and consequently there was a considerable amount of 'needling' between him and Helpmann. Perhaps it would be better described as bitchiness, and everyone made the most of it, never losing an opportunity to stir things up between them for a diversion. Any preconceived ideas we may have had that dancers were a bit 'cissy' were quickly dispelled, and by the end of the picture nobody needed convincing that ballet was synonymous with extreme hard work, both mental and physical, coupled with great self-discipline. Due largely to Michael and Emeric's enthusiasm, and a generally held conviction about the film which was shared by everyone concerned with its making, we grew in some unaccountable way, artists and film crew alike, into a closely-knit company, all working together towards a common goal. I have experienced something of this kind on other pictures all too rarely, I regret to say, and never again to quite the same degree. In spite of being very hard work, it was certainly not without its moments of humour. One such incident remains very clearly in my memory, though countless others are forgotten.

In the story of *The Red Shoes*, the artistic director of the ballet is consumed with the idea of introducing live animals into the decor, an idiosyncrasy firmly resisted by Lermantov, the impresario. As the result of a wager between them over whether the girl will make the grade as a dancer, the art director, having won, arranges for a donkey to be among the crowd in the market square scene. A donkey was duly called by the property department and reported to Pinewood Studios on the appointed day at 6 a.m. complete with its owner, a diminutive cockney from Covent Garden Market. Immediately on arrival he was taken to wardrobe and fitted out with a ballet costume, tights, shoes, etc. Then followed make-up and hairdressing, where he was given the full classical look. This he endured without comment or complaint, being a man of few words who had prepared himself for the peculiarities which he might have to face in a film studio. His donkey, equally phlegmatic, grazed on a patch of grass outside the window. He was then taken to the crowd dressing room where he sat, silent, in the farthest corner, surrounded by the other male dancers with whom he was totally identified in looks, if not in spirit. He waited patiently for something to happen, all the time keeping his own counsel, apparently unmoved by all that went on around him. At last, his patience rewarded, the dancers were called onto the set with him leading his donkey, which by now must have become his only link with the outside world. The market square sequence had been fully rehearsed the evening before, so all that was required was a quick run-through before shooting. 'Quiet, everybody, for a final rehearsal,' shouted the assistant director. 'Playback, please,' and with the magic word 'action' and to the sound of the recorded music, the crowd leaped and twisted their way across the stage with pirouettes and *entrechats*, all perfect apart from the 'dancer' with the donkey, who stood immovable and expressionless. 'Cut, cut!' shouted Michael above the sound of the playback, never endowed with great patience on these occasions. 'What's wrong with everyone? It was all rehearsed last night. Pull yourselves together and let's go again.' And so we did with exactly the same result. With the third attempt 'cut', Michael strode angrily through the crowd to confront the dancer with the donkey. 'What's the matter with you? Everyone else knows what to do. It was all rehearsed last night. You can hear the music like the others, you're a dancer, aren't you?' 'Of course I f. . . . g ain't! I just brought the f. . . . g donkey.'

The Red Shoes is now a part of film history, and all the fun and anguish that is a part of every movie is long since forgotten by me. What remains is the sure and certain knowledge that I did the right thing when I went back to camera operating. If I had decided otherwise I would have missed one of the great experiences of my career and the pleasure of working again with Jack Cardiff, and with artists like Marius Goring, Esmond Knight and Anton Walbrook. It also marked the beginning of a long period with Michael Powell and Emeric Pressburger as director of photography for their production company, The Archers.

And what of Moira, who had also made a decision? She went on to make several other films, including *The Tales of Hoffman* for The Archers where, once again, she was able to bring the magic of her dancing to the screen. As far as I know her other films were of no particular merit, and I am not certain whether in fact she continued her career as a dancer. She was soon to marry Ludovic Kennedy and raise a family. Years later, we met again at Michael's 80th birthday party and in spite of the passing years she looked unchanged, with the same red hair, the bubbling sense of humour as ready as ever to surface. Time has undoubtedly dealt lightly with her, so maybe for her, too, *The Red Shoes* was a good decision.

12

Korda

In 1949 I made my first film as director of photography for Michael and Emeric. *The Small Back Room* was shot in black and white from the novel by Nigel Balchin, and is worth recalling if only for the sequence on the beach when David Farrar dismantles a booby trap bomb. This illustrates as well as anything Michael's original approach and visual imagination. These bombs were being dropped by the Germans and had killed a number of people, among them several children, and nobody had lived to describe what they looked like.

In the film, two are at last discovered lying close together and Michael Gough, who played an Army bomb disposal expert working with a scientist, David Farrar, decides to tackle the first one while waiting for his partner to arrive from London. Michael Powell chose Chesil Beach as the location, with its heaped-up banks of shingle which cascaded in a miniature pebble 'Niagara' each time anyone moved. With a group of experts sheltering behind an old concrete tank trap some hundred yards away, Michael Gough begins to dismantle the first one, describing every move he is making over a field telephone to an ATS stenographer, played by Rene Asherson, who takes it all down in shorthand. Finally, at a crucial stage when he is attempting to remove the fuse, the bomb explodes, killing him instantly. Farrar arrives and decides to tackle the second one immediately, the girl reading back to him in detail each step of the first attempt.

We started the sequence in extreme longshot, first with Farrar a small figure in the immensity of the sweeping line of the beach, then the reverse of the tank trap, again in longshot from his point of view. Throughout the sequence we got progressively closer, until, when the moment is reached when the first bomb exploded, we were shooting just eyes, fingers undoing screws, pebbles slipping from under the clamps which were holding the bomb steady, a tear trickling from the girl's eye. One cannot describe on paper the terrific tension which was built up in what was, I think, the best sequence of its kind ever to be filmed. The choice of the location was really at the heart of it all, and only Michael had the imagination to see exactly how it could be used.

In 1950 came *The Elusive Pimpernel*, my first full-length picture in Technicolor as lighting cameraman, and a remake of *The Scarlet Pimpernel*. The project was the result of a deal between Alexander Korda and Sam Goldwyn, starring David Niven, Margaret Leighton and Cyril Cusack. Not a good idea, these remakes, particularly if you happen to be following in the footsteps of Leslie Howard and the great success of the original version. It was certainly not Michael and Emeric's 'cup of tea', and quite why they decided to undertake it only they know. A somewhat tongue-in-cheek approach was decided on, at times a bit of a send-up of the original. As the locations in France and the studio sequences in England were cut together, the feeling that we had a disaster on our hands spread through the unit as rapidly, and as accurately, as the sense of euphoria had spread over *The Red Shoes*. Beautiful to look at, with the wonderful locations among the chateaux of the Loire valley, and the interiors to match by Hein Heckroth, it did not add up to success. We finally ground to a halt, and the results were shown to Korda, who obviously shared the general opinion. Undismayed, he decided to reshoot a major portion of the film, in the hope of some form of cinematic redemption. Meanwhile the press had got hold of the story and articles appeared accusing Korda of extravagance, and the wasting of other people's money. It was a situation not entirely new to him and in true Korda style he called a press conference before shooting started. In an atmosphere pervaded by exotic food, champagne, and the haze of cigar smoke, he explained to everyone the difficulties as he saw them, together with the action he proposed to take which, overnight, would transform this manifestly 'lesser' Pimpernel into a winner. He was immediately attacked by one eminent critic, his courage and sense of injustice fortified by abundant free food and drink, who demanded, 'Sir Alex, will you please tell us the cost of these retakes?' 'About thirty per cent of the original budget,' was the ambiguous answer. 'And what was the original budget?' asked the critic, sensing a scandal.

Sir Alex regarded him for a few minutes in silence, and then with all his considerable charm replied, 'One hundred per cent.'

* * *

Alexander Korda was to me the only truly great film impresario we have ever had. Others have settled for a while and, using our talents and our theatrical tradition which has produced a pool of so many wonderful artists, have made numerous, excellent pictures which, I suppose, could be looked upon as British, only to return home again when the tax climate became less auspicious. Korda came to stay, and at a time when British films were of a largely domestic nature and made on a shoestring to fill quota regulations. He imported leading directors from the continent and America, together with cameramen and art directors from whom we all learned a great deal. Budgets became larger and productions more ambitious and lavish. Starting in 1933 with *The Private Life of Henry VIII* which he directed himself, a foothold was gained in the international market. All his films were financed with money he had been able to charm from other people, and much of it wasted in the process, which seems to be an inescapable part of making films. He built Denham Studios, at that time the only studio in Europe to compare with those in America. At the outbreak of war he left for America in order to complete *The Thief of Baghdad,* and Denham was sold to the Rank Organisation.

On his return to England he took over Shepperton Studios, where many more outstanding films were made. He had close personal contact with all who worked for him, down to the humblest carpenter and electrician, and made a great point of knowing them all by name together with details of their families. His uncanny judgement for as-yet unrecognised talent in young artists and technicians gave the industry many of the famous names we have to this day.

In 1953 I was working on *The Story of Gilbert and Sullivan,* a Korda production by Frank Launder and Sidney Gilliat. Hein Heckroth and I were both loaned by The Archers, to whom we were under contract, to Sidney Gilliat, who both wrote and directed the film and had a string of successes to his credit. He was a charming and very down-to-earth man. If the script called for a scene with a door and a window, he expected to have both there and both working. Dear Hein, who came from the world of opera and ballet, saw things in an entirely impressionistic way and produced a set of delightful sketches which Korda took with him to the States and on the strength of them managed, while exercising his great charm and persuasiveness, to extract from the dazzled money men a large number of dollars. I don't think Sidney ever seriously thought that his sets were going to look like the impressionistic sketches and, when the reality confronted him, all hell broke loose.

We encountered tremendous problems with set design and artistic concept which bore little relation to what was required by the script. Hein had inherited an art department comprised largely of Hungarian emigrées, presided over by Vincent Korda. Their collective mastery of the English language was minimal, and only matched by their patriotism. For that matter, Hein's English was not that good, so communications were, to say the least, confused. Vincent interfered with everything that Hein did and was busily engaged in producing alternative drawings as fast as Hein could draw the originals. Each tried to outdo the other in creative ideas, while all that Sidney Gilliat wanted was a set with a door and a window in the right place, so that he could play the scenes. He would throw his beloved pipe on the ground in sheer exasperation as row followed row. Apart from artistic conflict, I suspect that nationalistic feelings played their part since Hein was German in a Hungarian ambience. The situation was further aggravated by the lack of a common tongue and degenerated to the point of incomprehensibility as tempers were raised.

The situation reached its climax one morning when Hein's wife telephoned in great agitation to say that he was out on the roof of his studio in Chelsea with a gun, threatening suicide. With a keen sense of the dramatic, stemming from his background in grand opera, he felt this to be the only way out. Vincent, who understood everything, gave the impression that he rather hoped the threat would be carried out. Fortunately, reality gained the upper hand and Hein was back in his office within the hour. The story had reached the ears of Sir Alex and that evening, after shooting, I was called to his Piccadilly office. Veiled in the smoke from a large cigar and with brandy set before him on his very large and intimidating desk, he asked, 'Now, what is this trouble down at Shepperton?' I tried to explain without being partisan when, after a minute or so, he cut me short with a wave of his hand and in his heavy Hungarian accent said, 'You know, the trouble with this bloody art department is that none of them speak English!'

13

The Tales of Hoffman

THE TALES OF Hoffman, produced in 1951 by Powell and Pressburger, was the first attempt to adapt a full-length opera to the screen. A way had to be found of avoiding the straightforward photography of a stage presentation with close-ups of overweight *prima donnas* dying robustly in the arms of harassed lovers. The sight of someone singing, when enlarged onto a cinema screen, is rarely a pretty sight and the attendant problems of make-up and dentistry become more apparent.

These moments of operatic drama and passion are better seen from the conventional distances of an opera house. Without the limitations of a stage, the canvas could be wider and, with the experience of *The Red Shoes* ballet to draw on, it was decided to adopt a similar technique. There would be no exteriors, everything being shot in the studio. The sets were vast and stylised and all the effects were achieved in the camera or by stage techniques using gauzes and changing light effects. Most of the action was choreographed so that the final result in many ways resembled a ballet. The entire score was pre-recorded and no direct sound was used during the shooting. As the artists mimed the singing to playback, it meant that dancers like Moira Shearer and Leonide Massine could be used in the principal roles.

Hein Heckroth once again designed the production, taking full advantage of the unique opportunity afforded to his highly original talents. Most of the picture was shot on the so-called 'silent' stage at Shepperton. Originally built by Korda for the 'special effect' shots on *The Shape of Things To Come*, the studio stood on a site at the old Isleworth Studios. Without any form of sound proofing, it resembled a large aircraft hangar. It was decided to move it to a new site at Shepperton, where it was re-erected, again without sound proofing, to become the largest film stage in Europe.

As we did not intend to shoot live sound it was the ideal situation for us. The acoustic properties left much to be desired, with the sound of the recorded playback reverberating around the cavernous interior, but this unusual method of shooting a sound film meant that we could talk to each other during filming. As things went wrong during a complicated 'take', we could shout instructions to the artists and to each other, presenting to the casual onlooker a scene of total anarchy. The electricians, perched high up in the roof on the wooden spot-rails, discovered a new-found freedom. Normally during shooting they had to remain perfectly still, since the rails creaked at the slightest movement. Now they could move, and even join in the odd aria or chorus if they felt so inclined. As with all new freedoms in this life, there were attendant hazards. Instead of a scene being ruined by the creak of a protesting spot-rail, we would occasionally be confronted with a copy of the *Daily Mirror* gently fluttering to earth against the exotic background of a Venetian canal. Naturally enough, this apparent lack of discipline was strictly controlled, and the freedom to talk during shooting proved a great help in the technically complicated shots we were attempting. Much of the camaraderie which existed during *The Red Shoes* again expressed itself, most of the artists being dancers or singers, and once again there was a feeling of being united in an exciting experiment.

Sir Thomas Beecham had agreed to supervise the musical side of the production and over a period of several days had played the entire score on the piano, interspersing the music with comment as to how he thought things should be done, and even singing many of the arias in a decidedly unmusical voice to illustrate a finer point. This was taped in its entirety and made fascinating listening. I often wonder what happened to it. It would make a wonderful record for the countless admirers of this great and humorous man.

For another story about Sir Thomas, I must set the scene. At the back of the studio there was a huge wood pile where the old sets were broken up. It was a custom, every Thursday evening, to allow employees to take away as much wood as they could carry, at a cost of five shillings. There had been a protracted discussion with Sir Thomas over the idea of him appearing in *Hoffman*, something which he strongly resisted. Perhaps he would agree to just one shot of himself conducting the final bars of the work, to be followed by a close-up of a hand closing the score and a stamp imprinting the words 'Made in Britain'? This idea seemed to appeal to him, but he would only agree if it could be done at a time of his choosing, without make-up and with the understanding that we would drop whatever we were doing at the time of his arrival. A separate little set was constructed and lit so that on arrival all that would be necessary was to switch on the lights and shoot. The much-discussed moment arrived, lookouts were stationed at the studio gate to warn us of his approach, and in silence we waited for him to appear on the set. Bill Wall, the cockney chief electrician, was a legend in the industry, both for his humour and the lurid language with which he purveyed it. It was a Thursday. As Sir Thomas was ushered on to the silent and expectant set by a group of obsequious 'front office' underlings, Bill Wall's irreverent and strident voice rang out for all to hear. 'Cop a load of this, blokes, the old bastard's come for his f. . . . g wood.'

The overall design by Hein Heckroth was the most imaginative I have ever encountered, conceived as it was in terms of pure theatre. Its originality inspired Micky to ever wilder stretches of the imagination, for he could see the final result as perhaps nobody else could. Somehow he managed to communicate a necessary sense of reality to us lesser mortals who had in our various ways to translate it in terms of lights and camera. Light levels in the theatre are extremely low, since the human eye can adapt to seeing even by moonlight, but light levels needed for colour photography in those days were enormous, necessitating the almost exclusive use of arc lights, each one of which took two or three men to lift. The cameras, too, were huge and unwieldy compared to what exists now, and camera cranes were manually pushed about by a squad of explicit cockneys in caps and mufflers whose artistic aspirations were limited to beer and sex, together with an acute awareness of the approach of 'knocking-off' time. When a crane shot was required, all the fine artistic nuances of a scene, discussed at great length beforehand, were suddenly, in the final analysis, placed firmly in their horny palms. Musical cues, which we had learned to use like the dancers on the *Red Shoes* ballet, were to them communications from outer space, and had to be translated into crude English which, fortunately, we could shout at the appropriate moment. The artists, both dancers and singers, grew accustomed to this background chaos and continued serenely about their business in another private and ethereal world.

Sequence by sequence, by trial and error, we discovered how to translate Hein's ideas and Micky's development of them into film terms which were possible to achieve, bearing in mind the limitations of the equipment available at the time. There were disasters along the way and often it was 'back to the drawing board' and the search for a new approach.

Korda, under whose aegis the film was being made, wisely left us well alone. Conscious, I am sure, that a great experiment was taking place under his roof, he gave Micky and Emeric complete artistic autonomy, much to the dismay of the more mundane inhabitants of the front office.

On this occasion Emeric had a different role to play. The script, which was largely an adaptation of the libretto, already existed. With little creative writing to do, his main preoccupation was to control Micky's wilder extravagancies and retain a sense of logic and order in what could have become a madhouse. His wise, pertinent and wry comments from day to day contributed more than can ever be accurately assessed. Exercising all his charm and wit, he staved off the unwelcome enquiries of the money men and the 'front office'. He convinced them that they knew what was going on when, of course, nobody really did, apart from Micky, in whose quicksilver mind the images would form and change with the hours and the circumstances. He treated the 'management' with total disdain, assuming them to be idiots of the highest order, which of course they were – at least artistically.

The 'silent stage' had been re-erected in a far corner of the studio lot, surrounded by weeds and long, dank grass, with old discarded sets from past glories stacked in hapless fashion all around; a long walk from the main studio with the bar and club, and the excellent restaurant, we felt in every sense social outcasts. Micky and Emeric hit upon the marvellous idea of putting up a large marquee, with our own caterers, where we could all eat together. Since the food was provided free, it proved a huge success with the electricians, carpenters, etc, and provided an excellent opportunity for the exchange of ideas and opinions about the day's difficulties, all of them encouraged by Micky, who believed in drawing everyone into the innermost secrets of his thoughts. It was normal to see the top table littered with Hein's sketches and set construction drawings, all mixed up with lasagne and salad, while a heated discussion raged over what to do. The dancers would group together, discussing the problems of the hard concrete studio floor, and each other when the opportunity arose, whilst it must be admitted that the intellectual level of the conversation descended to beer and overtime as one moved further afield.

A sense of happiness and a feeling that what we were doing was different and creative once again spread through the unit, as it had done on *The Red Shoes*, and the feeling that we were very much a team was accentuated by our isolation from the rest of the studio and the other films in production.

The notorious Bill Wall, who had been with The Archers long before I came on the scene, enjoyed the privileges of a court jester, and was always on the lookout for a laugh or the telling of an outrageously crude joke. He discovered that by tearing a sheet of windowlite, a material used to diffuse lights, he could produce a sound closely resembling that of splitting tights. With a perfect sense of timing, he reduced the most complicated leaps and lifts to a shambles. The gag was repeated *ad nauseam*, to the huge enjoyment of the 'sparks' in the spot rails, and the chagrin of the dancers, until they got used to the idea. His humour knew no boundaries and Moira Shearer, Helpmann and Ashton all suffered the same fate.

To illustrate the sort of technical difficulties I was facing, I will try to briefly describe the last act. This is known as 'The Tale of Antonia' and is set on an island somewhere in the Aegean. The four walls of the vast stage were covered with a backing from floor to ceiling, stretched taught on a framework of tubular scaffolding and painted to represent a stylised view of sea and sky. The house in which the action took place stood on an island in the middle of the stage, and was formed of Doric columns and statuary, open all around to the view beyond. In the middle distance were cutouts and plaster models of islands and trees, with gauzes in between to give the illusion of infinity. Overhead was a vast network of cradles on which were mounted the hundreds of arc lamps, each one set to a precise position for every shot, with adjustable flaps on the front to control exactly where the light fell. Various types of chiffon were placed in front to control the intensity of the light, and each was measured with a photocell meter to ensure the correct light level. Because of its size and the fact that it was in colour, the set needed the biggest collection of lamps ever used in a British studio. Extra electricians and mobile generators were brought in to supplement the output of the studio's main power house.

The most difficult shot ran for over four minutes continuously, the camera tracking and panning a full 360° while the lighting changed from brilliant Mediterranean day to a star-studded night with a crescent moon. As conventional dimmers cannot be used on arc lights, we used remote controlled shutters rather like venetian blinds. As day faded the shutters opened on lamps with blue filters to obtain the night effect. The key lights were operated manually in cues given by me and, as can be imagined, the whole thing was a nightmare, relying as it did on so many people and so many bits of machinery which needed to operate exactly as planned. The arcs would flicker, the shutters jam, and the operators doze off with the heat as the studio slowly filled with a smoky haze produced by the burning carbons in the arc lamps. The point would be reached when the fog started to flatten out the lighting and the individual beams of the lamps would start to show like a hundred searchlight beams from above, destroying the whole illusion. Then it was 'cut', open the doors and start the extracter fans and extra wind machines to clear the air. The air had also to be cleared in a more metaphorical sense as tempers became frayed. After half an hour or so the atmosphere would be clear, so it was 'Shut the doors, kill the extracts and start all over again', by which time people had forgotten their cues and everyone wanted lunch. This was the mechanical reality of the imaginative artistic idea, so inspiring to discuss creatively and so very hard to achieve in practice.

At last, unbelievably, it was over, after what seemed an eternity. A large section of one's life, with moments of intense anguish, still leaves the memory of a wonderful creative experience shared with the very best of mortals. The lamps came down from above, the generators lay silent, the sets were consigned to the vast heap outside, to be burned or taken home on Thursdays for firewood. After months of editing came a Royal premiere before Queen Mary, critical acclaim, and total disinterest on the part of the fee-paying public.

Only now, so very many years later, is the film accorded the sort of praise I feel it deserves. This is true of many of The Archers' pictures, always before their time, always interesting, but not always appreciated when they first appeared.

14

Gone to Earth

AN EARLIER PRODUCTION for Michael and Emeric was *Gone to Earth*, in 1948. 'Have you ever read any of Mary Webb?' asked Micky on the phone. 'Well, not really,' I hedged, vaguely knowing that she was a sort of rural mystic who wrote about Shropshire, a female Thomas Hardy. 'Come into the office. I want to give you a book to read,' he continued, then he rang off. A typically cryptic conversation with him, but at least I was spared the piercing eyes which would have revealed my ignorance. He in fact gave me a pile of books, several by Mary Webb and a delightful edition about the hill villages of Shropshire. 'Go away and read them all, then you and I are going up there for a few weeks to find the places she wrote about. Bring some boots and waterproofs, because we are walking.'

Unlike many directors and producers I could mention, who choose their locations from the back seat of a Rolls Royce, preferably fitted with a cocktail cabinet, he believed implicitly that the only way to see things was on foot.

With boundless energy, he strode the hills of Shropshire as I followed in his wake, trying hard to keep up with a man 15 years my senior. This sort of mini-adventure brought out all the boy scout in him and he loved it. On evenings around a pub fire, discussing the day's 'finds', I got to know him as never before. He had a deep love of the English countryside and a wide knowledge of its literature. He seemed at one with Mary Webb, all so very far removed from Offenbach and his *Tales of Hoffman*. Due to the size of the camera and lighting equipment at that time, some of the more remote places proved impracticable, but the final result was, I think, one of the most beautiful films ever to be shot of the English countryside in all its moods. Hours of patient waiting in rain, cold and sleet for just the right angle of sunlight across a landscape, 5 a.m. calls day after day to catch the early morning mist, it was all so very worthwhile.

Sadly, even with bigger and bigger budgets, the opportunities to film in this way grow ever fewer, overheads and huge salaries using up so much of the money which should be used on the production.

We began filming *Gone to Earth* on location in Shropshire, but in order to overcome the vagaries of the English climate we had obtained permission to use an aircraft hangar on a nearby disused wartime airfield. Here we could build 'sets' just like a studio, in which we could take refuge when the weather became completely impossible.

It was decided that the ideal sequence to put in our 'studio' would be the fairground, which was to be shot at night anyway. The huge hangar was filled with period steam-driven roundabouts complete with organs, tents, marquees and all the paraphernalia of a country fair. The floor was covered with turf which had to be watered daily and the set was peopled by some 200 volunteers of all ages, dressed in period costumes and all from the surrounding countryside.

Lit by gas lamps and flaring torches, it was to be one of our more spectacular scenes. For the introduction, a complicated crane shot had been planned, lasting four minutes or more, with the camera drifting through the colourful throng, picking out the sword swallowers, fire eaters and so on, as we followed our artists across the length of the hangar, with the camera finally coming to rest in close-up on a gipsy sitting on the steps of his caravan, smoking a long clay pipe. At the psychological moment, he was to remove the pipe from his mouth and spit with deliberation on the ground to mark his disapproval at all the goings-on. All went well apart from the fact that he was unable to spit. Take after take ended the same way. We had chosen one of the few people in the country who, either through mounting fear or physical disability, was quite unable to rustle up any saliva. We could not change the poor unfortunate for someone else more versed in the art of expectoration as he had already been established in the previous scene. The more often the shot ended in disaster, the more determined the director became not to relinquish this little human touch which had become increasingly dear to his heart. No, he would not settle for the man just removing his pipe without spitting. Eventually the props put something in his mouth, I hesitate to speculate what, and the crisis was over.

Jennifer Jones was cast as the wild gipsy girl – perhaps an unlikely choice in view of the very Englishness of the story. She did her level best to cope with the Shropshire dialect, spending hours each day with a coach, going over every line a hundred times. Possibly the reason she was chosen was the fact that she was married to David O. Selznick, but one did not enquire too closely into these matters. Being extremely pretty, she presented no problems for me and her serious approach to acting enabled her to give a good performance despite the difficulties. An extremely nice person, bordering on the verge of eccentricity, she insisted on cycling everywhere, in preference to the back seat of a Rolls-Royce. This habit caused consternation in the production department as they were responsible for getting her to the locations on time. On a number of occasions she was lost among the Shropshire lanes, blissfully unaware of the unit waiting to shoot, and more often than not riding on the wrong side of the road. Being a devotee of the method school of acting and much given to yoga as a means of relaxing, she had the disconcerting habit of standing on her head for several minutes just before a take while the assembled company waited in expectation. She and David were married just a few days before shooting started and a clause had been inserted in her contract giving her several days off during the location so that they could spend some sort of honeymoon together. Selznick chartered a private DC3, special permission being given for it to land at a nearby RAF airfield so that they could make the most of every minute.

At the time we were all living in a large hotel in Church Stretton, recently reopened after the war. Food was still rationed and we were more than fortunate in having with us a firm of location caterers which consisted of two brothers by the name of Hobbs, newly demobbed from the airborne forces and still wearing their red berets. The idea of mobile catering was then a novel one and, equipped with a battered old van, they scoured the countryside for provisions, putting to good effect their army training in initiative when faced with living off the land. Many a shady deal was struck with local farmers in which ration cards did not feature too prominently, resulting in the food produced from their van being very much better than that in the hotel. In no time they were asked to take on the hotel catering, a responsibility gladly relinquished by the management who faced endless complaints and impossible competition. An 'Archers' atmosphere quickly developed and in the evenings after dinner we all played games together, artists and crew alike, with much general ragging and practical jokes. In retrospect it sounds rather childish, but we were young and full of high spirits, and it proved a wonderful safety valve at the end of what might well have been a frustrating day.

At first Jennifer seemed rather bewildered by it all, certainly not accustomed as a Hollywood star and wife of David Selznick to being treated as 'one of the boys'. She quickly adapted, however, and took her full part in everything. The day arrived for her 'exeat', and she departed from the location at lunch time, leaving us to work on until last light. We returned to the hotel around seven, to be greeted by two forlorn figures sitting side by side in the hall, the dusk gathering around them. David and Jennifer, of course. 'What's happened?' we asked, sensing some minor tragedy. 'Well,' replied Jennifer, 'David and I can't decide where to go, Paris, Rome, Naples or any place else.' They decided to join us that evening for dinner – pheasant, if I remember correctly – followed by the usual evening's hilarity.

David Selznick, one of the most feared men on 'the coast', turned out to be a great gamesman, introducing several new versions of dumb charades. And so they remained for the next few days, exploring the countryside and joining in the fun of an evening, while their DC3 sat on the airfield, its crew totally disenchanted as visions of an escape from ration-ridden England faded by the hour. I am sure that David Selznick, a sort of demi-god back home in Hollywood, had never experienced this sort of relationship with a film crew before and he was more than fascinated by it all.

Several months later, with shooting completed, Selznick decided that the story should be radically changed for the American market, necessitating several weeks of further work. Michael Powell declined to have anything to do with it as he did not agree with the proposed changes, but he and Emeric agreed to Selznick's request that I should go to Hollywood to photograph the new scenes. After much telephoning and the exchange of numerous telegrams, and in spite of attempts on my part to delay my departure for a few days, it became clear that the great man required my presence immediately.

When I arrived in New York the following day there was a message waiting for me to telephone Arthur Fellows, his personal assistant, who would be waiting for my call at the studios in Hollywood. 'Welcome to new York,' Arthur greeted me, 'things have changed a bit out here. We are having problems with the script. Why don't you stay over in New York and have a good time? I will arrange some money from the office and phone you in a couple of days.' More than a week passed without word from the 'coast' and, with the money running low and the attractions of New York wearing a bit thin, I telephoned to find out what was going on. 'Come on out,' said Arthur, 'we still have script problems but you might as well be around. I will fix a hotel and arrange a rented car.' Installed in the Chateau Marmont on Sunset Boulevard and in temporary possession of a large Pontiac convertible, I ventured forth on the freeway in search of the studios. There it was at last, the white-painted, barge-boarded building with the sign swinging in the breeze, so familiar as the trademark on so many distinguished pictures.

Arthur Fellows met me with the news, not uncommon in the world of movies, that the script was proving difficult. Reuben Mamoulian had been chosen to direct the changes and he had made it clear that, since it was not his picture, he could only offer to carry out Selznick's wishes, thereby disclaiming any personal responsibility for the results. His only stipulation was that Selznick should not come on the 'floor' during shooting, if indeed we ever reached that position, as he felt Jennifer would become emotionally upset and impossible to direct.

Arthur Fellows lived in a world bounded by fear of Selznick and losing his job, coupled with a strange dogged devotion which made him accept any insult that came his way. As I sat in an outer office, day after day, watching the drama go on around me, it appeared that this feeling of fear and trepidation was shared by everyone else. The small group in the inner sanctum of Selznick's office appeared to live on black coffee by day, followed by a diet of various tranquillizers by night, as they wrestled with the insoluble problems facing them. From time to time pages of script would emerge, hot off the press, to be duplicated and distributed to all concerned, only to be cancelled before they were delivered. Hand-delivered sheets were pushed under my hotel room door at all hours of the morning. At last the agonising was over and a starting date fixed. During this whole period, I never spoke to Selznick, contenting myself with an occasional view of him through the office door as he sat surrounded by his haggard 'committee', the room littered with half-drunk cups of coffee and the blinds closed to ward off any suggestion of the lovely weather outside.

My crew were all American and I quickly sensed that I was not over-welcome. The camera operator, who was old enough to be my father, wore a trilby hat at all times and chain-smoked cigars, a habit only interrupted during a 'take', when he would place the smouldering butt on the viewfinder. He did his job with mechanical precision but offered no comment or help whatever. I felt very much alone in this strange atmosphere, so far removed from the spirit of co-operation I had grown up in. The one bright spot was Henry Imus, my old friend from India, who had been allocated by Technicolor as technician. He bore no resentment that I was now a lighting cameraman, while he still remained in the same job, and did everything he could to help me. I was regaled by everyone with frightening stories of the way Selznick treated cameramen, replacing them with monotonous regularity as his fancy changed.

The moment of truth came on about the third day of shooting. Each evening we had a long discussion about the following day's work, at which Selznick would explain at length how he wanted it to look and be played. On this occasion it was a shot of Jennifer entering her bedroom at night, carrying a candle and kneeling down by her bed to pray. He made a great point that it should be very low-key, with the solitary candle the only source of light. Next morning I was in the middle of lighting with the stand-in when Selznick appeared on the set and beckoned me over. 'You are using too much light. I want it to look like candlelight.' As if by magic, the crew melted away into the background, all finding things to do which would save them from implication in what promised to be a tricky situation. I must emphasize at this point that Selznick, in common with many other producers and directors, had a natural intuition for how a scene should be played or how it should look when photographed, and supreme ability to judge the result on the screen, yet he had little or no knowledge of how it was achieved technically. 'I'm afraid I don't agree with you, David,' I replied. 'We discussed in detail last night how you want it to look and that's the way I'm doing it.' 'It's not what I want!' he shouted. 'Turn off some of the lights.' 'Look, David,' I replied, 'you have brought me all the way here to do the job when you have dozens of first rate cameramen available. You have explained exactly how you feel it should look, so why don't you get off my back and let me get on with the lighting? Tomorrow, if it's not what you want when we run rushes, I can go home.' There was complete silence on the stage while he stared at me for what seemed an eternity, then he turned on his heels and walked off without another word. Slowly the crew appeared from their various hiding places and we got on with the scene without anyone mentioning what had just happened. Next day at rushes we had a full house, many of them hoping to witness my final discomfort. As the lights came up in the theatre at the end of the screening, David stood up and, turning to me, said, 'You were quite right, Chris. It looks fine and I apologise.' A great producer, he was the only one I ever worked for who, in similar circumstances, had the good grace to admit he could be wrong. This incident marked the beginning of a very close relationship between us as I think he liked constructive opposition and argument on which to sharpen his own thinking. Sadly, these were qualities completely lacking among his entourage.

In the days that followed, bearing in mind his undertaking not to come on the set during shooting, David would go to elaborate lengths to creep on unseen, gradually working his way behind the flats so that he could watch rehearsals. He was a perfectionist and could not resist the temptation to interfere. 'Pst, pst,' I would hear from behind the wall of the set, and there he was, beckoning me over. 'Suggest to Reuben that Jennifer does this or that,' he would whisper, 'and make it seem to be your idea.' I unwittingly became a sort of undercover intermediary and he successfully avoided detection. On the other hand, perhaps Mamoulian was well aware of what was going on and had decided that discretion was the easiest course to take.

Long after it was over and I had returned home, I heard that Arthur Fellows, in the course of some sort of argument, had punched David on the nose, an action which resulted in much litigation and the termination of their association. As I liked Arthur very much, I hoped sincerely that my successful opposition to David's will had not emboldened him to resort to physical violence. Upon reflection, I think it more likely that what happened was the result of many years of utter frustration, coupled with a total inability to cope with David's strong personality.

15

Genevieve

ONE DAY, WHILE having an overdue holiday with my family in Cornwall, I was contacted by George Gunn of Technicolor, who told me that he had a very interesting project to put before me and asked if I would care to come up to a meeting on the following Monday. Reluctantly abandoning one of the rare chances of a normal break together, I decided to find out what it was all about. Henry Cornelius had been for a long time trying to raise finance for a picture called *Genevieve*, written around the veteran car race from London to Brighton. He had approached in turn all the major distributors, who had turned it down, expressing the general feeling that it was a subject with little appeal to the average cinemagoer. Finally, the Rank Organisation had agreed to back it, but with the minimum investment, and on condition that Henry Cornelius put up the completion money himself. In order to do this, he had mortgaged his house and sold every tangible asset and here he was, with the absolute minimum of finance, on the verge of turning his dream into a reality.

George Gunn had persuaded him that, in spite of the money problem, the extra cost of filming in colour was more than worthwhile as, at that time, it was still a great attraction at the box-office. Planned to be filmed almost entirely outdoors, with a starting date in mid-October, weather was obviously a big hazard and Henry explained that he could not afford to wait for ideal conditions. 'If there is enough light to get a bare exposure, I just have to shoot. I know it's asking a lot, but there is no other way I can make the picture. Go away and read the script and if you feel you want to take it on under these conditions, I will promise that if any money is left at the end, I will try and retake anything that is a particular disaster.' He had written the script himself in collaboration with Bill

Rose and of course it was marvellous. I knew immediately that I had to do it, no matter what the problems, and to this day I do not understand why the backers could not see its potential.

Photographically, it represented a complete break with tradition. Convention dictated that, just as actors should look flawless, so should the world in which they lived be bathed in eternal sunshine. I had felt for a long time that colour photography looked very much better than black and white in flat light conditions and that the high contrast between highlight and shadow in sunlight was often a disadvantage. There was no time or money available for extensive tests. It was a straight 'yes' or 'no' to the offer, and with the challenge and the opportunity, it had to be 'yes'.

This period coincided with the ascendancy of the accountants and the management had become deeply involved with a process known as 'independent frame'. Briefly, the idea was to replace conventional sets with a projected background, both still and moving. A small piece of set was then constructed, where the actors performed, which interlocked exactly with the projected background. In theory, the need for large sets was over. You just went along and photographed the drawing room of a stately home or the interior of a church and all that was needed was a pulpit or a foreground settee to complete the illusion. In practice it meant tying down the camera height, movement and choice of lens months before filming commenced, which was obviously impractical and totally unacceptable to any creative director. Several million pounds were spent on rear projection equipment, hydraulic towers and lighting rails, yet only a few significant films were ever made using the process and a great deal of the equipment was finally scrapped.

The spin-off was the rear projection system, which was by far the best in Europe. In *Genevieve*, nearly half the script consisted of scenes between two people driving along in the old cars; the perfect situation for back-projection. We were unable for reasons of internal accountancy to use the facilities which were standing idle in the studio financing the film. The same situation existed with regard to the sound stages and our interiors had to be cut to a bare minimum on the basis of cost. As an example, the garage scene in Brighton was shot in two adjoining lockup garages belonging to the studio transport department, a communicating hole being knocked through the wall and a large tarpaulin extension erected to keep out the light and extend the area.

The travelling scenes in the cars were resolved by loading the whole unit into a large flat, open trailer, known as a 'Queen Mary'. It was a relic of the war and had been used to transport military aircraft. We all piled in – camera, lights, crew and small generator – and on the back was perched a mock-up of the car in which our actors 'drove'. The whole circus was at the mercy of the driver in the cab of the Queen Mary, who often proved difficult to communicate with. Another truck followed with mock-ups of the other cars, ready to be switched at a moment's notice. For forward-looking shots, another flat truck was used. The driving cab was removed, further mock-ups made to disguise what little we saw of the bonnet and a period steering wheel and windscreen fitted, all of which had to be changed each time we switched cars. For the forward-looking shot, the unit perched on the back and the actor in question had to drive. A slight drawback occurred on the first day, when it was discovered that John Gregson could not drive and, anyway, needed a goods vehicle licence. He was rushed off on an intensive driving course while we occupied ourselves with Kenneth More for a couple of days, and the question of the goods licence was overcome by ignoring it.

Everything was shot within a few miles of the studio because of the short days and the expense. We would set off each morning, whatever the weather, and take advantage of whatever turned up, often stopping to ask an astonished local if he or she knew of a watersplash, a sharp left-hand bend or a small pub with a courtyard, depending on what requirements had been forced on us by the weather and ever-changing schedule. Henry asked me every few minutes if there was still enough light to shoot, a situation I resolved by giving him an exposure meter on which I drew a red line indicating the point of no return. More than half the scenes were shot with the needle hovering over the line, or even a bit under it, for we all shared the will to make it work.

The artists, Kenneth More, John Gregson, Dinah Sheridan and Kay Kendall were all wonderful, more often than not being pitchforked into an unscheduled scene after waiting for hours on the back of the open truck in rain and wind. Not a single shot was taken on the Brighton Road and, in purely academic terms, nothing matched photographically because of the wildly fluctuating light conditions. Yet, when the picture came to be shown, I received some of the best notices ever and not a voice was raised in protest about the geography. There must be a moral here somewhere, and it surely is that what matters most is the script.

Genevieve became a big success at the box office and brought a well-deserved reward to Henry Cornelius who, I am glad to say, was able to get his house and other possessions back with interest. The Rank Organisation, at last aware of the film's potential, tried to buy out his interest, but he steadfastly refused all their offers. The first showing of the completed film was in the preview theatre at Technicolor. As the lights came up at the end, Earl Saint John, the American head of production, who had expressed little interest in the film during its making, rose to his feet and observed to Henry, and the rest of us who made the movie, 'We may get a few car nuts to go along and see it in this country but it won't do business anywhere else.' What a typical attitude from one who was supposed to be the arbiter of public taste – but, then, what could you expect from someone with a name like that?

16

Saadia

Saadia is a name I will remember when all else has slipped from my fading memory. The title of a book by Francis D'Autheville, a Frenchman living in Morocco, it had come to the notice of Albert (Al) Lewin, who proposed to make it into a film. Before proceeding further, I feel a thumbnail portrait of Al is appropriate in order to fully appreciate what follows.

Of diminutive stature, with white hair and mischievous blue eyes, he was something of a rarity among Hollywood producer/directors. A man of taste and education, a Harvard professor of English, he had an extensive knowledge of modern painting and music. By profession a writer, he had headed the Metro-Goldwyn-Meyer script department for many years under Dore Schary where he was affectionately known as the 'Metrognome'. Dressed immaculately at all times, all his clothes were made for him in England, down to his diminutive shoes. Whether in the studio or on location, he made no concession whatever to informal attire. In common with most people in the industry, he cherished the ambition to direct, in his case fired by the bitter experience of seeing so many of his scripts butchered by others. This ambition came to fruition with the making of *The Picture of Dorian Gray* for Metro. The production got more and more behind schedule and consequently over budget, largely due to Al's search for perfection and refusal to accept any form of compromise. His favourite story, which he liked to tell of an evening over dinner, concerned the time when, under great pressure from the 'front office' to speed things up, the end of the sixteenth week of shooting arrived, and with it the end of the planned schedule. Less than half the film had been shot and the money was spent. 'You know what I did?' he would ask with a chuckle, 'I gave a great big end-of-picture party. Everyone got very drunk and nobody showed up next day for work.' This attitude was, of course, completely incomprehensible to a conformist organisation like MGM, who were fortunately quite unable to deal with him. Undaunted, and in spite of them all, he went on to make a hugely successful film which has gone down as a yardstick in cinema history.

To return to *Saadia*. Al spent several months in Morocco with the author, working on the script and visiting all the places referred to in the book. He returned triumphant with his completed script and MGM were persuaded that it was a good idea. On the opening page he had written, 'I have toured throughout Morocco, choosing every location with the help of the author. It is all standing there ready and waiting to be photographed.' With these seemingly innocent words, he had unwittingly condemned us all to seven months of a kind of hilarious hell.

The film was to be shot entirely on location, with no studio facilities whatever. Among other things, it meant that all sound had to be recorded live, with no recourse to post-sync-ing later. The interiors were all to be in authentic places, with just a little embellishment here and there by the art department. Al, in common with so many producers and directors, had little idea of the practical problems, which in the early Fifties were considerable. Sound cameras were large and unwieldy, the film stock very slow, entailing high light levels, particularly when balancing Moroccan sunlight. Very few, if any, major colour films had been made this way, so there were no statistics for the studios to fall back on. But, on paper, the project looked attractive to the 'moguls' back on the coast, particularly in terms of cost.

The production supervisor was Henry Henigson, an American of venerable years and great experience, who had worked with Al on a number of previous occasions back at MGM. Henry had a basic and very direct approach to life and shared one thing in common with Al, they were both almost completely deaf. Al wore a deaf aid which crackled and whined alternately and suffered battery failure from time to time, usually at moments of crisis, resulting in only a limited amount of what was said getting through to him. Being a man of resource and wisdom, this fact presented him with limitless grounds for claiming not to know when in a tight spot with the studio. Henry, on the other hand, was made of sterner stuff and scorned all artificial help for his ailment, with the result that he heard even less than Al. During the course of the pre-production meetings, it quickly became apparent that the understanding between them as to what had been agreed during their trip to Morocco was tentative at best.

The crew were to be drawn from England, France and Italy, with equipment coming from all three sources. The lights and generators were to come from Italy, and Henry wanted a detailed list of all my requirements as soon as possible. As I had not seen any of the locations, this was not easy. I tried to strike a compromise between covering every possible eventuality, while bearing in mind the question of economy. The final list looked rather like the contents of a fair-sized studio and I submitted it with some trepidation. Henry, who had pictures like *Quo Vadis* and *Ben Hur* in his repertoire, did not bat an eyelid. 'Make sure you're well covered, kid,' he advised, 'once you get out there you'll have your arse on the desert, with not a goddam thing available locally.'

These words of wisdom proved to be prophetic from the day of our arrival. The centre of operations was to be Marrakesh, with secondary locations spread far and wide throughout the country. The first job on arrival was for all the heads of departments to visit the chosen locations, an exercise that proved more difficult than anticipated since Al had forgotten where a lot of them were. The interiors consisted of hospital wards and offices, palaces, and Berber village houses. Without exception, apart from the humble village interiors, they were tiled from floor to ceiling, ranging from pure white in the hospitals to elaborate Moorish designs in the larger buildings. The French sound recordist descended deeper into gloom and despondency. His first reaction on walking into a room was to clap his hands, not to register pleasure, but to check for reverberation or 'echo', which invariably continued for several seconds. 'It is no good for sound,' was his invariable comment. These were the only words in English that passed his lips during the next six months, possibly due to very little knowledge of our language, or perhaps because he had decided, like Al, to take refuge in a private world from where it was best not to understand. 'What'd he say?' Al would ask, tuning in his aid and sensing objections. Henry, also sensitive to trouble, would shout, 'What the hell's wrong now?'

Our very first scene was a conference between medical staff and the doctor in our story, played by Mel Ferrer. There were some fifteen actors involved, all with speaking parts, and the chosen loction was an office in the hospital. By the time we had moved in, complete with camera, lights and sound, there was hardly enough space left to fit in the actors. The room was so small that it was physically impossible to get an all-encompassing shot of the scene and keep the lights and crew out of the picture. Al also insisted on seeing out through the open window onto a white-painted courtyard in full Moroccan sunlight. The amount of light needed in the room to create any sort of balance with the exterior quickly pushed the temperature up over the 100° mark. Every lamp we set was reflected in the highly glazed tiles and, in fact, so were the camera and most of the crew. These reflections were dealt with by the standby painter, who sprayed them with a matt paint which had the habit of drying in different colours. An Italian, whose enthusiasm was matched by his total lack of English, he was difficult to restrain, with the result that our Moorish set, with its tiles by which Al set such great store, was transformed into a room with mottled, painted walls.

While all this was going on we became increasingly aware of the roar of low-flying aircraft at regular 30-second intervals, which blotted out the noise of our generator and the strident voice of the local muezzin, whose crudely amplified tones called the faithful to prayer. Even Al had to admit defeat as we retired to lick our wounds and reassess the problems. The art director and I tried to convince Al that an office in which a hospital doctor could comfortably carry out his day-to-day tasks did not fit the bill when it had to accommodate a Technicolor camera, sound equipment, lights and a crew of 30 or more technicians, not to mention the actors. 'But what about the atmosphere?' replied Al. 'The whole point of making the film out here is that it should be authentic in every detail.' Patiently we explained that what we needed was an area at least three times the size of that required to play the scene, so that physically we could all get in.

'Then it won't look big on the screen, Al. We shall only ever see a part of it, and the part we do see can be dressed with props and made to look exactly like the room you have chosen.' 'Then we are building a studio, and that is just what I want to avoid,' he replied. It did occur to me that it was precisely because of this sort of situation that they had indeed built studios in great proliferation all over Hollywood, but I decided to keep this observation to myself.

Beneath his gentle exterior, Al possessed a will of iron and, being first and foremost a writer, any challenge, in whatever form, to a single word of the script, savoured of treason and compromise.

'A bad movie is the sum total of all the compromises you make with the original script,' he would say. Of course, there is a great deal of truth in this remark, but when faced with the truly impossible, something has to give. He fought a bitter rearguard action, and only gave way under sheer weight of numbers, and then only to the extent that if alternatives were found they must resemble in every detail his original choice.

Henry sat through all this, completely unruffled, no doubt catching the odd word here and there and not caring overmuch where we shot as long as we shot somewhere. He had a wry sense of humour, and in times of stress loved quoting from his great fund of stories accumulated during a lifetime of movie debacles.

His favourite was of the bit player in *Ben Hur,* who had to gallop up to Caesar, clad in helmet and shining breastplate, with the whole Roman Forum in the background and say, 'I come with a message for Caesar.' After years of silent walk-ons, his break had finally come. In a state of great emotional stress, with the huge crowd cheering in the background and the cameras rolling, he galloped up, tried to rein in, and fell off his horse in front of a startled Emperor. 'Cut, cut!' shouted the assistant. 'Everybody back to the start.' With patience the director, William Wyler, explained that his final position was critical, as he would end in a big close-up for his lines. Intended to encourage, this information only served to create further anxiety and after several more takes, each ending in the same way, his shining armour began to resemble a battered sardine tin. 'Take it easy, take it easy,' said the director, trying hard to control the burning hatred he had by now developed for the demoralised wretch standing before him. 'Just one more time, and it's going to be fine.' Back to the start, roll the cameras, action. In galloped the messenger and, more by luck than judgement, came to a halt right on the mark. 'I come wi . . .' At this precise moment, the visor on his helmet fell down, totally obscuring his face.

* * *

We had many locations in and around Marrakesh, and of course they all shared the common sound problem of the aircraft noise, something of which Henry and Al were blissfully unaware, immunised as they were by their deafness. We discovered that there was a large military airfield just outside the city which was used by the French Air Force as a training base for fighter pilots, with continuous take-offs and landings around the clock. 'It must be stopped,' said Al, showing little concern for the future defence of the country. 'Get on to the American Consulate and tell them to fix it.' The request was received with considerable disbelief, followed by a very definite No. 'Then we must have a meeting with the Pasha of Marrakesh and get him to help,' said Al. 'We are going to spend thousands of dollars in his country and he will have to use his influence.'

An audience was arranged and a group of us were requested to attend the palace in two days' time. The delegation consisted of Al, Henry, Mel Ferrer, Cornel Wilde and his blonde and very attractive wife, the art director and myself. We were met by a male secretary who spoke perfect English and escorted us past the guards and across the vast courtyard, in which were parked an array of highly polished limousines, including several large Cadillacs and at least three Rolls Royces. I had the distinct feeling that many eyes were watching our progress from behind the shuttered windows. The area to the left was where the Pasha's numerous wives had their abode and no doubt the lady in our party was receiving critical scrutiny.

After travelling endless corridors, we were finally ushered into the Pasha's study, furnished in predominantly Western style. The Pasha sat in a large, red leather chair which rather dwarfed his ageing figure at the far end of the room. Behind him on a bookshelf was a signed photograph of Winston Churchill, a memento of his painting holidays spent in Morocco. We were invited to be seated by the secretary and without more ado got down to business. Al tuned in his deaf aid and at some length set about explaining the story, together with a long list of all the permissions we would need and the great benefits our picture would bring in terms of dollars to the country. Pride of place among our problems was of course the question of the aircraft, about which the French were proving so uncompromising. This speech, which at times became quite impassioned, was interpreted by the secretary for the Pasha's benefit. Henry, who no doubt heard very little of it, was nevertheless well aware of its content. Being a man with considerable experience of similar predicaments, and with a firm conviction that a 'deal' could always be struck provided that enough dollars were on offer, he interrupted Al's diatribe with numerous hard-headed financial suggestions, all made in a hoarse and penetrating stage whisper. Throughout this lengthy exhortation, the Pasha remained completely impassive, without uttering a single word of response. His gaze remained firmly fixed on Cornel Wilde's wife, who became increasingly uncomfortable under this unflinching stare. It may well have crossed her mind that she could become part of a 'deal', a suggestion which I am certain Henry would have had no compunction in agreeing to, had it been suggested. Abruptly the Pasha rose to his feet, indicating that the audience was at an end, and in excellent English said, 'Thank you, gentlemen, for your visit. My secretary will deal with all the matters we have discussed.'

He graciously stood by the door as we trooped out rather sheepishly, shaking each one of us by the hand, and giving Mrs Wilde a final penetrating look.

* * *

True to his word, most of the necessary permissions were granted, but the aircraft proved an intractable problem. It was finally proposed that whenever we were shooting in the city, the French authorities would lay a field telephone line to our location, connecting us directly to the control tower at the airfield. Whenever we were ready to 'turn over' we were to call them and ascertain the position. This routine rapidly developed into a complete farce. Once a scene was rehearsed and the lighting completed, Al would say to the French assistant director, 'OK, Jean, call them and say we are ready to shoot.' There would follow a lengthy conversation in French, largely drowned by the roar of aircraft, and Jean would return with the information that there were 20 Harvards lined up on the runway waiting to take off. 'How long will it take?' Al would shout. 'About half an hour.' 'I can't wait,' Al would respond, patience by now exhausted, 'give me the phone.' Tuning in the deaf-aid he would place the receiver over the microphone of the deaf-aid and shout into the other half. His command of French was minimal and conversation rapidly degenerated into a bilingual slanging match, neither side understanding what the other was saying. All this was accompanied by the steady roar of planes taking off and the tragic demeanour of the sound man, who had long since given up protesting. At last came a brief lull, by which time the artists had forgotten their lines and the make-up had run in the heat. Progress was painfully slow and Al as unwilling to compromise as ever.

In the script, the French doctor is called out to operate on a girl who has appendicitis. Berber houses are built around a courtyard and the living quarters are all on the top floor, with a sort of platform running around to give access. Beneath this platform the family livestock are tethered amidst considerable dirt and smell.

The outside walls of the houses are totally devoid of windows, all openings facing on to the courtyard. In his script, Al had conceived the idea of the operation on the girl being carried out amid the animals tethered below, an unlikely and extremely unhygienic proposition which, nevertheless, appealed to his sense of the dramatic. The artistic seeds of this idea had been planted in his mind during his reconnaissance trip with Henry many months before, and he could no longer remember where the house in question was. Henry, who probably could, but cherished a fond hope that the whole idea would die a natural death, kept his own counsel.

We spent several days looking at Berber houses, all of them exactly alike, but none of them turning out to be the scene of Al's inspiration.

One evening on our way home, driving along a narrow rocky valley, we spotted a small village upon the hillside, some 15 minutes walk up a boulder-strewn track. 'That's it!' cried Al, his face aglow with success. 'That's what?' said Henry, who had conveniently put the whole question from his mind. 'That's where the house is, right there in the village,' replied Al. 'We can't get the goddam transport up there, Al,' said Henry, who had doubtlessly known this all along. 'We can build a road, Henry. It wouldn't cost much out here,' was the uncompromising retort.

We set off up the hillside with Henry muttering under his breath, explicit and, no doubt, well-founded criticisms of directors in general. The house for which we had so long been searching stood right in the middle of the village, which was built entirely of hard-packed, brown mud with absolutely no means of approach apart from a narrow alley, down which it would have been impossible to get any of the equipment. Apart from Al, who was overjoyed at finding his persistence rewarded, we all stood silent, with feelings of unbelief tinged with insanity. Henry, beside himself with exasperation, committed a fatal error. 'It's no goddam good, Al, we can't shoot here,' he shouted, while Al fiddled with the deaf aid which was emitting a continuous whine, denoting, as we were by now aware, an imminent battery failure and even greater problems of communication. 'We can't shoot here,' Henry repeated, 'there's no way we can get in here without knocking down a couple of goddam houses.' 'That's the way then, Henry,' replied Al with a smile, as he went off the air. By what seemed a miracle, we were saved from the prospect of road construction and entry into the demolition business. The local Caid objected on religious grounds, against which there was no appeal, even to the Pasha. We all retained an impression that Henry was not entirely unconnected with this decision but, if so, he had covered his tracks well and Al had to settle for something a little more accessible.

The days passed with only slow progress, and we fell further and further behind schedule. The conviction that I might well spend the rest of my life in Morocco slowly gained credence in my mind and apparently similar ideas began to occur to the people back at MGM. Many abortive attempts were made to telephone Al, who adopted the same technique with them as he did with the man in the control tower. He professed not to understand a word that they said and suggested that they write. As a letter took at least two weeks, this gave him ample time to reschedule any scene they suggested cutting, so that, by the time the letter arrived, he could reply that it had already been shot. In the evenings he would always recount the story of these telephone calls with a mischievous twinkle in his eye.

The next difficulty concerned a horse. According to the script, having successfully saved the life of the Berber girl, played by Rita Gam, the doctor goes with her one day to a horse market. By now, of course, they are in love and when she sets her heart on a magnificent Arab stallion he buys it for her and she leads it away, as yet unbroken. Being a Berber, and consequently a marvellous horsewoman (as Al explained in the script), she quickly curbs its wild habits and in no time at all trains it to do circus tricks. In other words, what we were short of in order to continue production was a white Arab stallion able and willing to perform tricks at the bidding of Rita Gam, who was not over-conversant with the ways of horses. Every detail of what it was expected to do was there in the script.

Like the search for the house, the quest for a suitable horse went on for many weeks and the chance of finding a white stallion capable of performing tricks became increasingly elusive. After 'interviewing' countless hopeful candidates, it became clear that no such animal existed. Not even the Pasha, or for that matter Ali Baba, could conjure up such a creature. The longer the search continued, the more determined Al became. If he couldn't knock down houses, at least he could find a performing horse. Henry became suicidal when all his attempts at compromise were fiercely rejected by this otherwise benign little man. Suddenly, out of the blue, a French army officer appeared on the scene who claimed to have knowledge of such an animal. It belonged to a brother officer, at present stationed somewhere in Algeria, and he was quite confident that it would fit the bill. Henry informed Al, who said it must be brought to Marrakesh, no matter what the difficulties. Difficulties there certainly were, for, after finally tracing the owner, it became clear that it would have to be transported by special horse box some thousand miles, together with an army groom, its constant companion since birth, who was the only person for whom it would perform. To Henry, expense was no problem if only he could keep Al quiet, and the improbable operation was set in motion. Three weeks later the horse arrived, complete with 'keeper', and Al ordered a parade next morning of all interested parties to witness a demonstration of its prowess.

We all assembled on a patch of open ground behind the Mamounia Hotel, where the horse box was parked, and out of it was led a magnificent white stallion, in appearance beyond our wildest dreams. Al, in spite of the heat still dressed in his beautifully tailored camel coat and trilby hat, with a handkerchief across the lower part of his face, appeared pleased, in so far as one could see. 'OK,' he said, 'let's see it do its tricks.' The groom stepped forward and responding to a series of commands in Arabic, the horse went through a routine which even Barnum and Bailey would have been proud of. One sensed a feeling of profound relief for the unbelievable piece of good fortune. Complete silence followed as we all waited for Al to pronounce his blessing. 'Someone give me a script,' he said, tuning in the deaf-aid once again. In silence he thumbed through the pages, searching for the relevant passages. Everyone waited in trembling expectation, with just the sound of the deaf-aid crackle for comfort. 'It's no good, Henry,' he finally volunteered. 'What the hell did he say?' asked Henry, who may or may not have heard. 'I said it's no damn good,' repeated Al, adding for explanation, 'it says right here in the script it has a long flowing white tail.'

With one accord, all eyes turned to the horse, which had a carefully docked appendage. 'What the hell difference does it make what sort of tail it has?' shouted Henry, but Al, sensing another compromise, dug his heels firmly in. 'We could have a false tail made, which could easily be attached to the existing one,' said the Italian make-up man. This slender ray of hope was readily grasped by the assembled company. Much correspondence followed with the studios back at Elstree, and exact dimensions of the horse's relevant anatomy were sent back to them. In a matter of weeks they returned a selection of tails of varying lengths, some made from real hair, others from nylon.

Considerable difficulty was experienced in attaching the false tail, as it had a tendency to move in the opposite direction to the real portion, but after much experiment this problem was finally overcome. As I explained earlier, our unit was composed of numerous nationalities, and a problem in the shape of inter-union rivalry suddenly manifested itself. Whose job was it to fix the tail? A strike was threatened as the battle raged between props, make-up and hairdressing, there being no apparent precedent to fall back on. Henry intervened with offers of dollars and hairdressing finally won the day.

The next morning our call was a location some 30 miles out of Marrakesh. A small rocky hill, set in a flat, barren plain, contained a cave, which was the object of the location. We were to be in position ready to shoot at 8 a.m. in order to catch the early morning light. A perfect day dawned and we were ready on time. Just one snag remained – there was no sign of the actors! Nine o'clock came, then ten, and still no sign of the approaching convoy of make-up, hairdressing and cast. 'What the hell's going on?' demanded Al. 'Send a car back and get them out here.' In an hour or so the car returned with the assistant director. Great problems had arisen over fixing the horse's tail. The stallion had decided that enough was enough and had kicked the hairdressing department all round the yard. Swallowing their inter-departmental pride and the union lines of demarcation, make-up had rallied to the call for help, and had suffered the same fate. The groom was called in and finally met with success, but the actors had as yet to be made-up. Make-up and hairdressing were in first aid and it would be at least another hour before we could expect them. They finally turned up around midday, full of woe and covered in plaster, anxious to pass on lurid stories of their ordeal to anyone with the time to listen.

Another minor difficulty had arisen over transport because Cornel Wilde had refused to travel in the same car as Mel Ferrer, claiming that Ferrer picked his nose all the time.

The horse was led out of the horsebox by the groom. It looked splendid, with long white tail flowing in the breeze. The reins were passed to a somewhat apprehensive Rita Gam, and immediately a new difficulty became apparent. As soon as it came anywhere near her, being a young healthy stallion, it got a very large erection, making shooting quite impossible. Several times it was led away to cool its passion, but on each occasion its return produced the same dilemma. 'Get the groom,' shouted Al, 'he must know how to deal with it.' And sure enough he did. Having been acquainted with the problem, he grabbed a nearby piece of cactus and struck the offending organ a sharp blow, achieving instantaneous results. This crude but effective treatment successfully curbed the stallion's eccentric sexual ambitions during the rest of our stay in Morocco. It did, however, result in Rita Gam being thrown on a number of occasions when the enthusiastic groom rushed in, unbidden, with his piece of cactus, and the horse, wise to the situation, took violent avoiding action.

Al, among the nicest of men, never mastered the technical problems of movie making. With a background of the mighty MGM behind him, he had a childlike faith in the script and the written word. No matter how unrealistic it might be, on no account would the script ever be subjected to technical limitations. If you went to him with a problem, his reaction was always the same. 'Fix it, Chris,' he would say with a smile, and it never mattered how long it took. The interiors of the palaces were a photographic nightmare with their shiny tiled walls and open windows. Al always wanted to link some sort of action outside, no matter how trivial, with what was going on inside. This entailed using a vast amount of light on the interior to achieve some sort of balance with the exterior sunlight. No way would he consider avoiding the windows and the little bit of inconsequential background action that he had dreamed up.

On one occasion, we were in a very large room, tiled from floor to ceiling. There was a large four-poster bed, the only article of furniture, and Rita Gam, who had a rather complicated scene to play. Al wanted to see every inch of the room, which necessitated the camera being in a sort of cupboard in one corner in order to get back as far as possible. This meant that there remained no space to put the lamps, which were anyway all reflected in the tiles. There was, of course, the inevitable bit of action outside, this time a dog crossing during the scene, and the prime cause of taking us all day to get the one shot. What with waiting for aircraft and the dog, not to mention Rita Gam, who became progressively more incoherent, our chances of a complete take were minimal. During a moment of total despair, I sat on the edge of the bed, wondering if there was any way at all that I could possibly light the scene, no matter how crudely, rejecting all pretence at art, in order to make it just visible on the screen. I felt a hand on my shoulder and found Al standing by me. He was aware of my total dejection and had come to offer help. Perhaps a slightly closer shot, or even the possibility of breaking the scene in two. 'Chris,' he said, 'I want to talk to you about this shot before you get too advanced with the lighting.' I had already been struggling with it for several hours! 'Take great care over it and don't hurry. I want it to look like an early Dutch interior.' My comment to the effect that he would be lucky to see it at all no doubt went unheard.

* * *

During our stay in Marrakesh, Al had heard of a strange, erotic dance, performed on the knees, by a group of dancers known as 'The Blue Girls of Goullimine.' Its origins, stretching back into the distant past, were unknown, but it was presumed that the reason why it was performed on the knees was the lack of standing headroom in the Berber tents. Whether the girls were prostitutes or not was never quite clear, but Al became intrigued with the reports he had heard about them, and determined to include them in some way in the film. He thought up the idea of them giving a performance during a party in the Officers' Mess, something which had apparently happened from time to time. Since they could not come to us, we would have to go and see them perform in their own habitat. This entailed a trip south, via Tiznit, to the small village of Goullimine, on the borders of Spanish Ifni and the Sahara. Al, Henry, the art director and I set out in two cars with an Arab guide, having been granted permission to visit this remote part of the country, highly sensitive politically at that time and apt to break out in guerrilla warfare at the drop of a hat. The guide, a particularly villainous-looking character, not much given to personal hygiene, had about him an individual aroma which became unbearable in the heat and the confines of the car. He had no luggage with him, which ruled out the possibility that he might change his clothes in the near future.

The only accommodation in Goullimine was the Foreign Legion fort and we had kindly been invited to stay there by the Commanding Officer. We found, on arrival, that, owing to limitations of space, we would have to share rooms and immediately the question of who was to share with the guide dominated our thoughts. We could not possibly ask Al, so the rest of us decided to draw lots for the doubtful privilege. Henry was the unfortunate winner. After a courageous attempt on the first night, he gave up at around two o'clock in the morning and, adopting Arab convention, packed his 'tent' and stole off into the night. He settled for a couch in the dining room, selflessly claiming, to avoid any breach of protocol, that he was concerned that his snoring would disturb his unwelcome partner.

Next morning we were taken to a primitive mud hut, consisting of one large room with only the door for ventilation. Lit by crude oil lamps suspended from above, there was a bench round three of the walls, leaving the earth floor clear. The ceiling was low, making it impossible to stand upright, perhaps in order to create the atmosphere of the tents for which the dance was originally 'choreographed'. Led by Beshara, the 'Madame' of the troupe, they came coyly in to face the scrutiny of Al and Henry. They had elaborate and identical hair-dos, consisting of coils and plaits held in place by long silver pins and a liberal dressing of, so we were told, a mixture of camel dung and olive oil. Judging by the smell, I had no reason to dispute this analysis. They wore an all-enveloping costume made from some sort of shiny cotton material, dyed a deep blue, hence the name 'blue girls'. The whole attire was held in place by an elaborate silver buckle, through which was a silver pin. The 'orchestra' arrived, consisting of five or six men clad in loin cloths and carrying small drums and a one-string fiddle, and without more ado the performance began.

To the slowly increasing tempo of the drums and the plaintive but unmusical notes of the fiddle, the girls swayed back and forth on their knees, the hand and arm movements precise and graceful. The 'orchestra' gradually worked themselves into a trance, perspiring freely as the dance became ever more erotic and suggestive. The girls whirled faster and faster, their hair brushing our faces as we crouched back against the walls. The blue dye, which came off on contact, quickly covered our trousers and shirt fronts and the mounting atmosphere of passion was more than matched by the smell of dung and sweat, mixed liberally with garlic, to which the Arabs were addicted. The leader of the troupe worked her way across the room to a position in front of Henry, seemingly giving him her individual attention. The guide whispered to him in a hoarse voice, charged with emotion, 'Pull the pin from the buckle and all her clothes will fall off.' Since she was by far the least attractive of them all, and Henry was suffering from a bad night's sleep, he visibly recoiled from this prospect. 'Go on,' said Al, 'you can't offend them. They'll never come to Marrakesh if we don't go along with it.' Henry, his sense of duty to MGM overcoming his personal distaste, seized the pin, and her clothes fell off as promised, revealing a henna-stained body, sweaty and streaked with blue from the clothes. To the frenzied beat of the drums and a rhythmic chant from the 'orchestra', each girl in turn got the same treatment as they swayed ever faster in the dim light of the guttering oil lamps. Suddenly it was over and, the clothes back on, the girls resumed their demure appearance. A dance of great originality and beauty, it would have been that much more enjoyable seen from a distance and divorced from the smell of our guide and the assembled company! They duly came to Marrakesh and performed a modified version, more in keeping with Metro's sense of propriety, in the setting of Al's Officers' Mess.

At last the impossible was happening! We were finally getting to the end of the schedule with all the battle honours going to Al and not a compromise made. We had just two sequences left, both with that wonderful French actor Michel Simon, who spoke not a word of English. He was to play the part of a bandit chief, with a fair amount of dialogue to cope with, and Al decided that the best way to overcome the difficulty would be for him to learn his lines phonetically. To this end, Cornel Wilde kindly recorded them on tape for him so that he could rehearse in the privacy of his room. The first scene took place in a bedouin tent at night. In the centre was the carcass of a large goat, around which Michel and his fellow bandits were seated cross-legged. Beneath the carcass was a fire on which it was slowly cooking, as the diners selected choice portions with their fingers. Due to the height of the tent, the best any of us could do was to progress on bended knees, apart from diminutive Al, who was able to get by with a stoop. For various reasons the scene had to be filmed during the day, which meant covering the tent with several extra thicknesses of heavy material to keep out the sunlight. We had in turn tried to persuade Al that, since we could only ever see a very small section at any one time, it would be easy to shoot the sequence against a small piece of tent material hanging in the comfort of the studio we had rigged up in a disused cinema for just this predicament. 'No,' said Al, sensing further compromise instigated by Henry, 'people will know it's not real.' So the tent it was, with ten actors, camera, crew and lights all packed in and fighting for room.

With the sun beating down outside, the temperature in the tent rose by the minute as we struggled painfully, shot by shot, to complete the scene. Since one side of the tent looked exactly like another, the easiest thing would have been to leave the camera and lights where they were and move the actors and the carcass around, but Al would have none of it. Round and round the tent we went on hands and knees, with the smell from the deceased goat getting ever stronger, until we reached the point where an Arab messenger had to burst in with news for Michel Simon. Chosen at random from the crowd outside, he had no idea what he was doing, and Michel, who had several lines of dialogue, had no idea what he was saying. The messenger's name was Calipha. During the countless takes which followed, while Al tried to extract a performance from the Arab which bore some semblance to sanity, Michel's dialogue became more and more incomprehensible, until finally he was calling the Arab messenger Halifax.

The ultimate debacle was a sequence where Rita Gam, with the French doctor, the Caid and a group of ten or so followers, was being chased by the bandits. Being a resourceful lady, she decided to lead them into a cave she knew, the cave having a narrow entrance that could be easily defended. The search was on for a suitable location, and it followed the usual pattern. All the likely places were inaccessible and, as the interior would be in darkness, the scene would involve using lights and a generator. We found a disused quarry on the outskirts of Marrakesh with a good access road. It seemed perfect and looked exactly like a cave to me and the rest of the crew. 'It hasn't got a roof,' objected Al. 'You will never see the roof,' said Henry, once again on a losing wicket. 'You can either shoot it at night or we can cover it over with tarpaulins and black it out.' 'It will never look the same, even if we don't see the roof,' replied Al. 'It's a low-key sequence, it should be so goddam dark in there that you can only just see the actors,' said Henry. 'All you will have in the background, if you see it at all, is a pile of bloody rocks.' 'I want the real cave, Henry,' Al countered with a gentle smile, and we all knew that the battle was lost.

The floor area in the cave was very limited and, since it had to accommodate about 15 horses and riders, every lamp had to be hung from an iron spike driven into the rock wall. The camera was on a wooden platform built just inside the entrance and to one side, so that the way was clear. Most of the actors were only fairly competent riders at best, and they had to gallop full tilt from the sunshine into the gloom, which was not an easy task. Each horse was led in turn through the entrance to accustom it to the situation and, after six hours of preparation, we were ready. Everything had been taken care of, except for one small item. Rita's horse was a stallion and all the others were mares. As they got inside, all Hell broke loose and most of the actors ended up on the floor, together with the camera and crew as the wooden platform collapsed. The light cables were pulled out and everything was plunged into darkness. By some miracle, nobody was hurt, and slowly the tangle of people and horses was sorted out. 'What are we going to do, Henry?' queried the totally undaunted little Al, 'I must have this scene, and we have to go on until we get it.' The horse experts were consulted and they offered up two solutions. We either changed the stallion, or all the other horses. 'We'll change the bloody mares!' shouted Henry, very near to breaking point – and with the vision of another search for a white mare with a long tail that could do tricks.

17

MGM

WORKING AS A freelance, there always seems to be a tendency to be asked to do several films in a row for the same company, for no better reason than that one's name happens to be in circulation. This was the case after *Saadia*, when I was asked to photograph *Quentin Durward*. A very different proposition, it was to be shot mostly in the studios at Elstree and on location in France. One of the last big historical films to be made by MGM, it came at a time when the influence of the major studios was very much on the wane. For so many years they had controlled every aspect of film production, owning studios and laboratories, the distribution chains and the theatres in which to screen the final product. Artists, directors, writers and technicians were all under contract and artists in particular were subject to discipline in respect of behaviour and time-keeping. It was a period when the industry came as near as it ever will be to a rational organisation, with powers to check wild excesses of expenditure and irrational behaviour by directors and producers. Films certainly did not get the go-ahead until they had an approved script, which is certainly not the case any longer.

It is often claimed that it was a system which stifled all creative thought, turning out a stereotyped product, tailor-made for an assured world market. There is a great deal of truth in this accusation but, to be fair, one must judge the films made during this period in the context of the time. The cinema-going public world-wide wanted escapism, as opposed to reality. It was still a novelty to see foreign lands or the way the rich lived, neither of which appeared to create envy in the hearts of the moviegoers. Artists were often chosen for their looks, put under contract, and carefully groomed for stardom. Special projects were built around them, turning unknowns into valuable studio assets and international box office attractions. The odd thing that has always struck me is the fact that, in spite of the 'glamour' sausage machine and the often dubious quality of what went into it in terms of artistic ability, a number of good actors emerged over the years to confound the harshest critics of the system. All this, of course, is a generalisation, for within the confines of the system there operated a number of outstanding producers and directors, who were able to assert a degree of independence which resulted in so many wonderful films.

Many factors joined together to bring about the end of this era. The decline in cinema-going, so easily attributable to the advent of television, is, I feel, only part of the story. The war had changed public taste and people's aspirations and, oddly enough, a more prosperous society did not mean more cinema-going. People now had holidays abroad, homes, gardens, cars, boats, in fact an endless list of alternative attractions to compete with the old habit of a twice-weekly visit to the cinema to escape from the dull reality of their lives, which hitherto had contained none of these symbols of prosperity. The cost of operating the major studio complexes became prohibitive and the advent of modern equipment freed the producer from the necessity of being tied to one. Films could be made anywhere in the world, entirely on location. This newly found freedom was quickly grasped by many producers, tired of the restrictions of the past, and there were independent sources of finance available worldwide, ready to back them in what could still be a highly lucrative market. The main guarantee for the distributors and financiers was the cast, the story taking second place in their calculations. With carefully kept statistics, they knew, or thought they knew, precisely what a film would gross worldwide with certain actors in the cast. Sadly, this fact put unlimited power in the hands of actors and their agents, resulting in astronomical deals which took more than half the budget of a picture, and very often included powers of veto over the script and the choice of director and crew.

The director of *Quentin Durward* was to be Richard Thorpe, a product of the old studio system. Starting, I believe, as a property master, he had worked his way painstakingly upwards to his present position by dint of faithfully adhering to the script with which he was presented. His chief concerns were the schedule and the budget, a careful daily check being kept to ensure that we were not an hour or a dollar over when the overnight report was telexed to the 'coast'. My purpose is not to denigrate him, for he made many successful films for MGM, but to sketch in the background of the world he came from. A sad, dour man, totally without humour, his life was dedicated to producing, without innovation, a verbatim representation on film of the approved script which it was his duty to complete on time and, if possible, under budget. Worthy aims indeed, so long as anyone wanted to see the movie.

One of the first tasks was to visit all the locations in France, already chosen on a previous visit by Dick Thorpe and Pandro Berman, the producer. One location was in the woods at Fontainebleu, where each selected position had been marked by a stake driven into the ground and by careful cross-reference with surrounding landmarks. I had the temerity to suggest an alternative to one of the positions, a proposition which caused endless discussion. 'Pandro stood right here,' said the head of special effects, an observation which drew a chorus of approval. 'But Pandro isn't here,' I countered, 'and, since he chose the spot, spring has arrived and with it the leaves on the trees, which make it impossible to see the action.' The irrefutable truth had to be faced up to, necessitating a cable to Pandro explaining the difficulties. Perhaps they felt that he might be unaware of these vicissitudes of nature which had overtaken us, insulated as he was in the fastness of his air-conditioned office in Los Angeles. Anyway, the matter had been put on record and, in the event of future repercussions, the blame could be laid at my door. Over the years I have known other natural phenomena, like the rise and fall of tides, to cause equal consternation among the makers of schedules.

The reconnaissance completed, Dick Thorpe and I, accompanied by the art director, Elliot Scott (Scottie), were in a car together on our way back to Paris and a flight home. 'Would you mind if we went a little out of our way so that I could take a look at Chartres Cathedral,' asked Scottie. 'Sure, why not?' replied Dick, hat drawn over his eyes and immersed in the *Hollywood Reporter.* Drawing up outside the main door, Scottie and I jumped out, at once overawed by the reality of this Gothic masterpiece. Dick remained unmoved in the rear of the car, completely absorbed by the latest box office returns. 'Won't you join us, Mr Thorpe?' asked Scottie. 'Go ahead, fellas, take your time, I've already seen a cathedral,' was the reply.

Some weeks later we were working at the chateau of Chenonceau, the scene being the arrival of the King of France, played by Robert Morley, on horseback and heading a large contingent of mounted soldiery, there had been a number of delays while the assistant directors tried to sort things out. The weather was also being difficult, with the sun in and out of cloud every few seconds. Dick was growing more and more impatient as we waited for a break long enough to shoot the scene. A patch of blue sky came up on the horizon. It looked promising and Dick shouted, 'Let's go, let's go!' as the cortège started to move. I anxiously watched the racing clouds, hoping against hope that the gap would last long enough to get the King to the entrance and dismounted. We were lucky, apart from the fact that Robert Morley fell, rather than dismounted, in a distinctly unregal fashion. 'OK, print,' said Dick, the schedule heavy upon him. 'But, Mr Thorpe, didn't you see what happened to Mr Morley?' came the worried voice of the continuity girl. 'Sure I did, so what? The king don't ride so good,' replied Dick, already on his way to the next set-up.

Very little that happened brought a smile to his face, or broke the air of unemotional sadness which seemed to engulf him. The one exception was the mention of 'special effects', for which he bore a pathological dislike, no doubt rooted in some incident in the past. With little or no confidence in their ability, he insisted on seeing a full rehearsal of anything before we attempted to shoot. One scene was set at a castle wall and ramparts, which completely filled one of the large studio stages. The castle was under attack by a group of soldiers, led by Robert Taylor. The 'special effect' in this case was a large cannon ball, which was to slide down an invisible wire and, on impact with the wall, set off a small charge, blowing an already-prepared hole in the wall. Inside was a complicated array of chutes, down which the prop men would pour a mass of stones and rubble at the right moment. 'OK, let's see a rehearsal,' said Dick, and down the wire came the cannon ball, only to bounce harmlessly off the wall, followed several seconds later by a small muffled explosion from inside. Apart from a puff of smoke, the wall remained completely intact. 'What the hell's going on? There has to be a goddam great big hole in the wall large enough for the men to climb through. Get your act together and let me know when I can see a proper rehearsal!' Turning to me, his dour countenance unbroken by even the slightest trace of a smile, he said, 'You see what I mean about these bastards? You can't trust them an inch.' Two or three days later, all was ready once again. Down came the cannon ball, followed by the most enormous explosion, demolishing half the castle wall and revealing the scaffolding behind it. The explosion also revealed the chutes, down which came the masonry, together with the prop men, who were ejected onto the set like children on a playground slide.

* * *

Before embarking on *Quentin Durward*, I had been called in to see Ben Getz, head of MGM in England. 'I have a problem on my mind, Chris, and I think you can help. We are going to make a picture over here called *The Flame and the Flesh*, starring Lana Turner. The director is Richard Brooks, who has a reputation back home of having a very bad temper. He's a nice fellow and doesn't mean most of what he says, but at times his fury reaches such a pitch that crews are refusing to work with him. I am very concerned about how he will go down with a British crew and I think you could well be the one to get along with him and perhaps smooth things out a bit. Could you meet him for lunch tomorrow and see how you make out?' Of course I knew of Richard Brooks, though not of his reputation as a fire eater. He had some wonderful pictures to his credit and a big reputation as a writer, which was more than enough to make me say yes.

Next day we met in the studio restaurant and I was immediately struck by his personal charm and calm manner. Dressed in an entirely conventional way, apart from a thin black cord suspending a medallion round his neck in place of a tie, he outlined the story to me in a voice so quiet that I had to lean over all the time to catch what he was saying. He also explained in detail how he wanted the picture to look photographically, quickly making it obvious that he also had a keen pictorial sense, which was a big attraction to me. The director, after all, is the story teller and must have control over every aspect of the production. It must be made 'his way', the rest of us contributing what we can with our various skills. Wonderful sets and beautiful photography can only embellish; they can never redeem a bad picture. It has been my experience that very few directors discuss in detail the visual approach to a subject, more often than not leaving it entirely to the cameraman. We have the knowledge and experience to achieve different styles, things which the director does not need, but a clear lead from him as to how he feels the visual aspect can help, and be part of the story, is essential. How many directors are there whose personal imprint is so clearly on the film in every department, with a style so distinctive that their work can be recognised at once? Not very many, I would suggest.

The story was set in Naples, Lana Turner playing a young woman of the streets. The cast also included Pier Angeli and Carlos Thompson. The deal was set, I wanted to work with Brooks and he appeared to want me. It did occur to me that Lana was not the obvious person to cast from the point of view of looks, with blue eyes and blonde hair, not to mention a very fair skin. This, of course, had also occurred to Joe Pasternak, the producer, who felt that her following at the box office far outweighed any minor disadvantages in respect of looks, which could easily be taken care of with make-up and a wig. She was described in the script as having a warm olive skin and black hair, so priority number one was to test a large range of make-ups, wigs and hair styles, all carefully catalogued and sent to Hollywood for approval. This made very good sense, apart from the fact that we had no Lana Turner.

It appeared that she was emotionally involved with Lex Barker, the 'Tarzan' of the moment, with whom she had departed on holiday to an undisclosed destination. She would not be available until the first day of shooting in Naples. Joe Pasternak, the discoverer of Deanna Durbin and Mario Lanza, with a name famous throughout the world as a big Hollywood producer, was far too afraid of her to insist on her return. A double was found with the same head measurements and after several days of exhaustive tests a combination was arrived at which received universal acclaim and approval from the studios in Hollywood, who were the final arbiters in all matters.

The first morning of shooting in Naples arrived, and I was busily engaged in lighting a complicated tracking shot through a restaurant overlooking the bay. Suddenly Joe Pasternak appeared in obvious distress, rushing up to me with the news. 'Lana won't wear make-up or the wig.' 'What are you going to do then?' I asked. 'If you want her to look the way she is described in the script, she has to.' 'I know, I know,' he replied, almost on the verge of tears. 'She's sitting over in make-up and refuses to let them put it on. You will have to go over and talk to her.' 'Why me?' I replied. 'You're the producer, surely it's your job to sort it out? And anyway, I haven't even met her yet.' 'She refuses to talk to me about it and won't even have me in the room. You will have to convince her that it's all been tested and looks wonderful.' Dropping my mantle of cameraman, and assuming that of a diplomat, I went over to the make-up room and introduced myself. 'You must have thought about the part,' I began, 'how do you imagine you should look? You are going to be a pretty odd Neapolitan with your usual make-up. I have seen all the tests we have done and I think the chosen one is very good. Why don't you give it a try? If you don't like it, you can blame me. I would just as soon be at home sailing, anyway.' Without a second's thought she replied, 'OK, we'll give it a throw,' and sealed the bargain with a big smile.

From that moment onwards, I had the best of relationships with her. Like most artists with a background of the major studios, she was very professional and, from my point of view, extremely easy to work with. Getting her anywhere on time was always a problem, fortunately one which did not come within my realm of responsibility. Once on the set she could not have been more co-operative. Any difficulties which did occur were behind the scenes, mostly between her and Joe Pasternak, for whom she appeared to retain an intense dislike. He tried hard to establish a more loving relationship and formed the habit of coming on the set as soon as he had viewed the previous day's work, announcing to everyone in his loud guttural accent, 'I've just seen the dailies, boys. Lana's never looked lovelier.' If I happened to be standing anywhere near her, she would mutter under her breath, 'Listen to the bum. Who is he trying to convince?'

During the first few days of shooting, Richard Brooks remained the epitome of calm good manners, completely belying his fearsome reputation. The moment of truth arrived at the end of the first week. We had to get a shot of Lana walking alone through the large out-door market in Naples. A route was worked out between the stalls and we went over it with her on the previous day. The camera was to be hidden in the back of a small truck, the rear of which was covered with a tarpaulin with just a small slit for the lens to shoot through, and at first light we parked on the chosen camera position before the market got busy. Secrecy was the key to success, for if the crowd became aware that we were filming it would be hopeless to control. With just the camera crew and Richard in the back of the truck, we took up our position and, with half an hour to wait, all seemed well. Soon the market was alive with people as Lana casually approached her starting position, unnoticed in the noisy, gesticulating crowd. A minor triumph for the olive make-up and the wig, I thought. One or two loiterers leant against the truck, talking and smoking and rocking it around, but of course we could do nothing about it.

For the first time Richard started to show signs of stress, obviously finding it hard to restrain himself from dealing with the offenders. One of them, with a more enquiring mind than the rest, pulled open the flap and peered in at us, a huge smile spreading across his face as he made the motions of cranking a camera by hand, a universal sign, it seems, whenever a movie camera is spotted. Quick as a flash, Richard grabbed a copy of the script (bound in a hard board cover) and hit the cheerful interloper smartly across the head. He followed up quickly by jumping out of the truck and setting about the other loungers, as yet unaware of our presence, and in no time at all we were surrounded by a large crowd happily joining in the fray without any clear idea of its origins. The truck was nearly overturned before we managed to retrieve Richard and make our escape, leaving Lana to find her own salvation.

This incident heralded the emergence of the true Richard, who, unable to bear fools lightly, suffered many paroxysms of rage during the next few weeks, though never resorting to physical violence. He genuinely could not help himself, more often than not being, I felt, fully justified. Whether it was the best way to achieve greater efficiency is debatable, but it certainly added zest to life. More often than not he regretted his behaviour and would come to us at the end of the day and ask, over a drink in the bar, 'How was I today?' He was fully prepared for the answer, 'Bloody awful.' He became so conscious of his behaviour that if one of us caught his eye in the middle of an outburst, he would slowly dry up, a sheepish grin spreading across his face. An excellent director, it was a privilege to work for him. I liked him a lot and I hope very much that he liked us. The realisation that nobody was frightened of him but, rather, looked upon his outbursts as a bit of fun, resulted in a rapid relaxation of tension.

Among the many odd practices and regulations which, by tradition, were a part of working in a British studio, Richard's *bête noire* was the morning and afternoon tea break, which always seemed to come at a moment of great emotional stress, announced by the arrival of the cockney girl with the trolley. On one particularly acrimonious day, I arranged for a special trolley to be prepared, complete with large silver tea pot, matching hot water jug, plates, cups and saucers, napkins and a large Dundee cake, which took pride of place. We waited patiently for the moment to arrive, as sure enough it did when Richard was involved in a violent slanging match with the 'props' over some minor indiscretion. In came the girl, carefully rehearsed by us, breaking into his tirade with, 'Here's the tea you ordered, Mr Brooks.' The whole stage broke up, including Richard, who to his great credit thought it very funny.

Several more pictures followed at MGM, none of which have left significant memories apart from *Twelve Golden Hours*, with Ernie Kovaks in the lead. Ernie was one of the funniest men I have ever worked with, and life on the picture was a constant riot. We were on location in a small town in Italy and Ernie had purchased in the duty free shop at the airport one of the first cordless rechargeable electric razors. On the first morning, he joined us at breakfast and asked the waiter for a large bowl of sugar. He pushed the end of the charging lead into the sugar and started to shave, while the fascinated waiter stood by, open-mouthed. He kept this up for the three weeks that we were there, each day surrounded by an ever-increasing crowd of hotel staff, together with others from further afield to whom the news had spread. He must have been a great distraction to his fellow actors, extemporising with his lines and changing the action as he went along. With his large rubber features he was the complete clown, playing as much for the crew as for the final cinema audience. On another occasion, in the middle of a serious scene with Cyd Charisse, who was wearing a low-cut cocktail dress, he walked behind her in the middle of her dialogue and, with his enormous tongue, licked her back from top to bottom. Sadly he was killed in a motor accident shortly after returning home to California.

The director on *Twelve Golden Hours* was Mario Zampi, a charming, small Italian, who had settled here before the war. The Thirties had seen an influx of directors from Europe, seeking refuge from Hitler, Mussolini or the management at UFA. Some were talented, most were not, but there was work to be had on the cheap quota pictures still being made. There is the story of a little German whose name, I believe, was Klein, his future hampered by a limited ability and an even more limited vocabulary. As the threat of war grew ever nearer, so did his concern over his request for British nationality, gathering dust somewhere in the Foreign Office. One morning he rushed breathlessly onto the stage where he was working at Elstree, brandishing above his head a sheet of paper. 'Boys, boys! It is good news that I have. Since a week that is now past, I am British.'

The industry is as famous as the Stock Exchange for its stories, many legendary and others apocryphal. Sometime in the Thirties the King and Queen of Greece were on a visit to this country and had expressed a wish to visit a film studio. The old BIP Studios were managed by a wonderful cockney character, renowned for his wit if not for his sense of decorum. He proudly conducted the royal party around the stages, cutting rooms and theatres, ending up in the electrical department, where he demonstrated the latest arc lamp, imported from America and the only one in the country. He elaborated at some length on its virtue to an increasingly bored audience, when, sensing the lack of an enthusiastic response, he remarked, 'I have carried on a bit too long about this. It's a bit technical, and anyway I expect it's all Greek to you, your Majesty.'

Monty Banks, a great practical joker, was directing a picture in the early days of Denham. The studios were to be visited by an American producer with the view to making a picture in England. Monty heard that the gentleman in question was a confirmed isolationist, with ideas about the 'little old mother country' set firmly in the Middle Ages. Monty arranged for everyone on the stage, including the electricians on the spot rails, to be dressed in morning suits while exercising medieval courtesy towards each other when shouting orders. It is reputed that the visitor accepted it all as perfectly normal, returning home with all his preconceptions fully confirmed.

18

ABPC

FATE, AND THE need to earn a living, decreed that my next three or four pictures were to be for the grandly named Associated British Picture Corporation. The ABPC Studios, just across the road from MGM in Elstree and under dour Scottish management, were well-equipped and meticulously kept, but the outer cleanliness was not matched by any visible creative ability or artistic sensitivity. Renowned throughout the industry as very poor payers, the establishment was known as the 'Porridge Mine'. The large double entrance gates were crowned by several layers of coiled barbed wire and kept firmly closed at all times. The way in was via a miniature Checkpoint Charlie, the barrier manned by grim-looking security police, who subjected you to close and suspicious scrutiny on your way in and out each day, showing no sign of recognition even after months of the daily routine.

Each afternoon a meeting was held of all heads of departments, including the production managers from any film being made in the studio. At the conclusion of one of these meetings, the studio manager rose gravely to his feet and reported that a man had been seen the previous evening scaling the barbed wire of the main gate. He had eluded all attempts at capture, disappearing into the crowd of Borehamwood High Street. A very grave view was taken of the situation and could anybody present throw any light on the matter? 'Was it established whether he was climbing in or out?' asked a devoted member of the management. 'Do you seriously imagine that anyone would be trying to get in?' asked John Wilcox, a production manager with a wry sense of humour.

Twenty-Four Hours of a Woman's Life was directed by Victor Saville, and starred Merle Oberon and Richard Todd. With an extensive location in the South of France and Monte Carlo, it was pleasant enough to work on.

Victor Saville had made his name as a director with Gaumont British but was now settled in Hollywood. With a very realistic approach to the problems of film making, and little or no time for the ABPC hierarchy, he took no notice whatever of the daily progress reports, knowing full well that he could finish the picture easily within the schedule. Each day on location they published a list of scenes which it was considered vitally necessary to complete, usually arrived at by breaking down the script into so many pages per day to keep abreast of the schedule. This rather overlooked the fact of what happened to be written on the pages, but although a commonly accepted way of arriving at a rough estimate of the time needed, it was looked upon with Calvinist rigidity by the Lairds of Elstree. Victor devised a simple way of dealing with them. Each morning he would remove the relevant pages from the script, producing them from his pocket in a screwed-up ball when he arrived on location. As each scene was completed, he would tear up the page and throw it away, contriving with devilish ingenuity to complete the day's work by early afternoon, when he would dismiss the unit. This unorthodox approach, not to be generally commended, nevertheless quickly made his point with the producers, who from then on left him well alone.

Although not of the same calibre as a director, he shared much of Alfred Hitchcock's attitude towards movies, particularly in the way that he treated actors, with whom he had little rapport. He once told me that the most important thing to remember when producing a film was the ability to sort the grain from the chaff. 'Concentrate on the things that really matter and let the others go. You will never have time to get it all perfect, no matter how long the schedule.' This philosophy was, of course, in total opposition to that of Al Lewin, who placed equal importance on every detail, but I think it had a lot to commend it. How often have I seen directors and producers lose themselves in a morass of irrelevant detail and, like Hamlet, 'Their native hue of resolution sicklied o'er with a pale cast of thought, and enterprises of great pitch and moment, with this regard their currents turn awry, and lose the name of action.'

Merle Oberon was a 'star' of the old school, always beautifully dressed and looking every inch of what the public used to expect of their idols. At all times the gracious lady in her dealings with the crew or the press, she nevertheless concealed beneath this charming exterior a character as tough and uncompromising as any. I remember one occasion on a night exterior in a small village in the mountains above Nice when shooting was delayed because of her late arrival. An hour late, she arrived, seated in the back of the Rolls-Royce which was part of her contract. Dressed in a beautiful evening gown and crowned by a glittering tiara, she looked the quintessence of gentility. Victor immediately set about her for her late arrival, and toe-to-toe they slogged it out in front of the whole unit and a small crowd of delighted spectators in language which would have brought a blush to the weather-beaten face of any bargee. One more illusion was destroyed in my rapidly dwindling collection, fondly built up in those far-off days when I avidly read the movie magazines.

At the opposite end of the social scale came Harry Black. Harry was the chief electrician, the gaffer. Of more or less square construction and incredibly strong, Harry had the gentlest of natures coupled with a crude and graphic means of self-expression. A tower of strength to any cameraman because of his vast experience, he had one great weakness. During the course of innumerable foreign locations, Harry had developed an inordinate fondness for the Vin du Pays of whichever country he found himself in. Unable to indulge this new-found passion at home, where prices were prohibitive, he contented himself with a pint of bitter in the studio canteen. He set about rectifying this enforced sense of deprivation the moment he set foot on foreign soil, not particular about the vintage so long as it was red and strong. We were shooting in the Maritime Museum in Monte Carlo, permission being finally granted after much discussion and the signing of forms of indemnity in case of damage. Filled with huge plate glass display cabinets, the sombre interior needed a lot of artificial light to make it a photographic possibility. This took the form of large arc lamps mounted on hydraulic stands, capable of elevating to 20 feet, at which point they became very unstable to move around. We had agreed to cover the marble floor with hardboard whenever we moved any equipment, and not to touch or move in any way the hundreds of glass cases, which of course posed a terrible problem with reflections. Under the watchful eyes of the museum staff, who bore us little affection, the situation was a delicate one. It was also marked by the absence of Harry Black.

The previous evening had been a particularly heavy one and, on retiring in the early hours, he had inadvertently set his bed on fire, damaging part of his room. Unscathed, but in disgrace with the hotel management, he had taken refuge in further drinking and the morning found him unsure of his exact whereabouts but with a willingness to come to work if anyone could tell him how to get there. 'For heaven's sake stop him coming,' I pleaded, but to no avail. Unlike many people who become aggressive, alcohol kindled in Harry the desire to help. Arriving at the museum, he painstakingly, if unsteadily, weaved a tortuous path through the display cabinets to his place of duty beside the camera, beads of vin rouge visible on his troubled brow. At this very moment, I called out for one of the arc lamps to be moved to illiminate a reflection. Harry sprang to my aid and, waving all help aside, pushed the lamp straight into a large case containing the remains of a small shark. To the sound of breaking glass, and amidst the ensuing panic, he was forcibly escorted out of the building, proclaiming all the while his willingness to help in any way we saw fit.

Dear Harry. I will never forget the debt I owe him for all the help and advice so generously given to me on my first picture as lighting cameraman. A character among characters, with which the industry abounded, their contribution so large and their rewards so small compared to so many others.

* * *

Shortly afterwards, I worked on a picture called *Fire over Africa*, starring Maureen O'Hara and produced for Columbia by Mike Frankovich. Set in Africa and southern Spain, it was a story of gun-running and smuggling, with a great deal of it to be filmed aboard a boat which was described in the script as being the fastest in the Mediterranean. The reality, due to lack of organisation in the production department, turned out to be an ancient steel tug with a maximum speed of eight knots. Her bottom plates were so corroded that the maritime authorities refused to give permission for her to venture out of Malaga Harbour. Like the steamer on the Amazon, she was a managerial *fait accompli*, for at this eleventh hour there was nothing else available. The harbour was fairly large, and surrounded by cranes and moored freighters, which of course we could not show since we were meant to be in mid-ocean. To overcome this problem, everything had to be filmed looking down into the water, a quite ridiculous restriction in view of the number of scenes we had to shoot. It also uncovered a second difficulty. With the boat travelling flat out, the water gave no sense of speed and we could anyway never get a long enough run to complete a scene. In desperation we tried lashing several launches alongside, their engines at full throttle to churn up the small area of water we were able to see, which at least gave a mild sensation of speed. But since they were all on one side, it also resulted in the tug describing a circle, with the direction of the sunlight altering through 360° or more during the action. This astronomical aberration, repeated in every scene, passed unnoticed by the critics, who were more concerned with tearing apart what ended up as a very bad picture.

The location ended with several sequences to be filmed in a night club and bar. Nothing suitable could be found and, with time running out, the art department discovered a courtyard in the old part of the town, looked down on by picturesque balconies. It could easily be dressed to look like an interior and the atmosphere was marvellous. It was pointed out by the more prosaic among us that, since it was open to the sky, it would have to be shot at night and as the scenes consisted of dialogue between actors it was unlikely we would ever see high enough to take advantage of the balconies. 'We can easily cover the top with tarpaulins and keep out the daylight,' they replied, enamoured with their balconies and determined not to build a set in the studio at home. 'What about the electrical supply? There is absolutely nowhere to put a generator in the narrow streets.' 'We can arrange to get a direct supply from the town without trouble,' chimed in the production manager, suddenly allied to the art department by the prospect of avoiding another studio set. The lure of the 'invisible' balconies, coupled with a possible saving on the budget, already swollen by our slow progress on the 'fastest boat on the Mediterranean', won the day. I had little faith in the electricity supply as it was being organised by the selfsame people who had arranged the boat. My worst fears were soon to be confirmed. The supply came from the same source as that which operated the tramway system, our lamps dimming or going out completely each time a tram passed in the narrow street behind. The noise, reminiscent of Marrakesh, brought consternation to the sound department. Why had this not been foreseen when the location was first looked at? The answer was simple. The tramway network had been on strike, the problem being resolved the day before we started shooting. Lookouts were posted down the street, equipped with walkie-talkies to warn of the approaching menace, but progress was painfully slow. In mid-afternoon a tremendous storm broke, accompanied by torrential rain, filling the bulging tarpaulin with hundreds of gallons of water to the point where it burst its bonds, deluging crew and actors alike and shorting out all the lights. We were saved from several days of misery by what I felt was an intervention from above when the courtyard was abandoned in favour of a set back at Shepperton.

The author 1937.

THE DRUM

1937

ABOVE. High in the Khyber Pass with an Indian Army battalion. BELOW: The huge Technicolor camera needed a squad of sherpas to manoeuvre it into position. With three rolls of film running through the camera simultaneously it weighed over one thousand pounds.

ABOVE. En route to India in 1937 as a Technicolor technician. A journey that took some two weeks.

WORLD WINDOWS

GHT: On location in the Trans-dan desert. Director cameraman k Cardiff on left of author. The pair k as if they have been dressed by e wardrobe department.

THE END OF THE RIVER

1947

ABOVE. The Mersey Ferry that was to take the film crew up the Amazon River. BELOW LEFT. A Director of Photography at last at the age of 28. The author, Chris Challis, on right of Mitchell camera. BELOW RIGHT: Having built an airstrip, supplies had to be flown in from British Guiana to the Amazon location.

ABOVE. Amazon – Brazil. There was not much to do in the evening after shooting other than play cards with the crew. BELOW. The author with pipe and dog. His first picture as director of photography, some two thousand miles into the Amazon jungle.

RAF FILM UNIT

1941

ABOVE. Author behind Mitchell camera in rear gun turret of a Bristol Beaufort – not a good place to be when under attack. BELOW. Author behind camera, films WAAF pilot in World War II Hurricane.

Wedding day, 20th September 1941. Sylvia Marguerite (Peggy), on the author's arm at St Mary's, Harmondsworth.

TALES OF HOFFMAN

1951

Moira Shearer. 'To Chris with very best wishes and many thanks.'

SAADIA

1953

ABOVE. The author with an extra member of the camera crew – always welcome.

RIGHT. Rita Gam with the white tallion – being subdued by a nember of the property staff.

BATTLE OF THE RIVER PLATE

1956

A difficult picture photographically with much model and back projection work. The end of the picture crew photograph portrays what appears to be a happy crew. Director Michael Powell, in polo neck, behind clapperloader. The author retiring to the back row with his pipe beneath the bows of the infamous pocket battleship.

ILL MET BY MOONLIGHT

1956

RIGHT: A difficult location picture set in Crete. Director Michael Powell is in white sun hat to left of the huge Vistavision camera. The author surveys the scene from beneath a flat cap.

BELOW. Waiting for the sun, the author behind the Vistavision camera with spyglass. Michael Powell, seated centre, in shorts.

SINK THE BISMARCK

1960

ABOVE. World premiere at the Odeon, Leicester Square, 11th February 1960. The Duke of Edinburgh chatting to film technicians. *Left to right:* The author, Peter Hunt (Editor), Lt. Cdr. P. Peake (Technical Adviser), Arthur Lawson (Art Director), Richard Goodwin (Unit Manager of Model Unit), Lord Mountbatten is seen on left. BELOW. Lord Brabourne and Kenny More listen to director Lewis Gilbert. The author is more concerned about the lighting in the under-ground command post.

HMS DEFIANT

1962

Produced by John Brabourne. Directed by Lewis Gilbert.
The author at home with customary pipe in the forepeak of a square-rigger.
A keen yachtsman and accomplished sailor.

Many hours were spent on the camera raft waiting for the right wind and wave conditions for the model shooting.

THE VICTORS

1963

Eli Wallach chats with the author during a break in Carl Foreman's film.

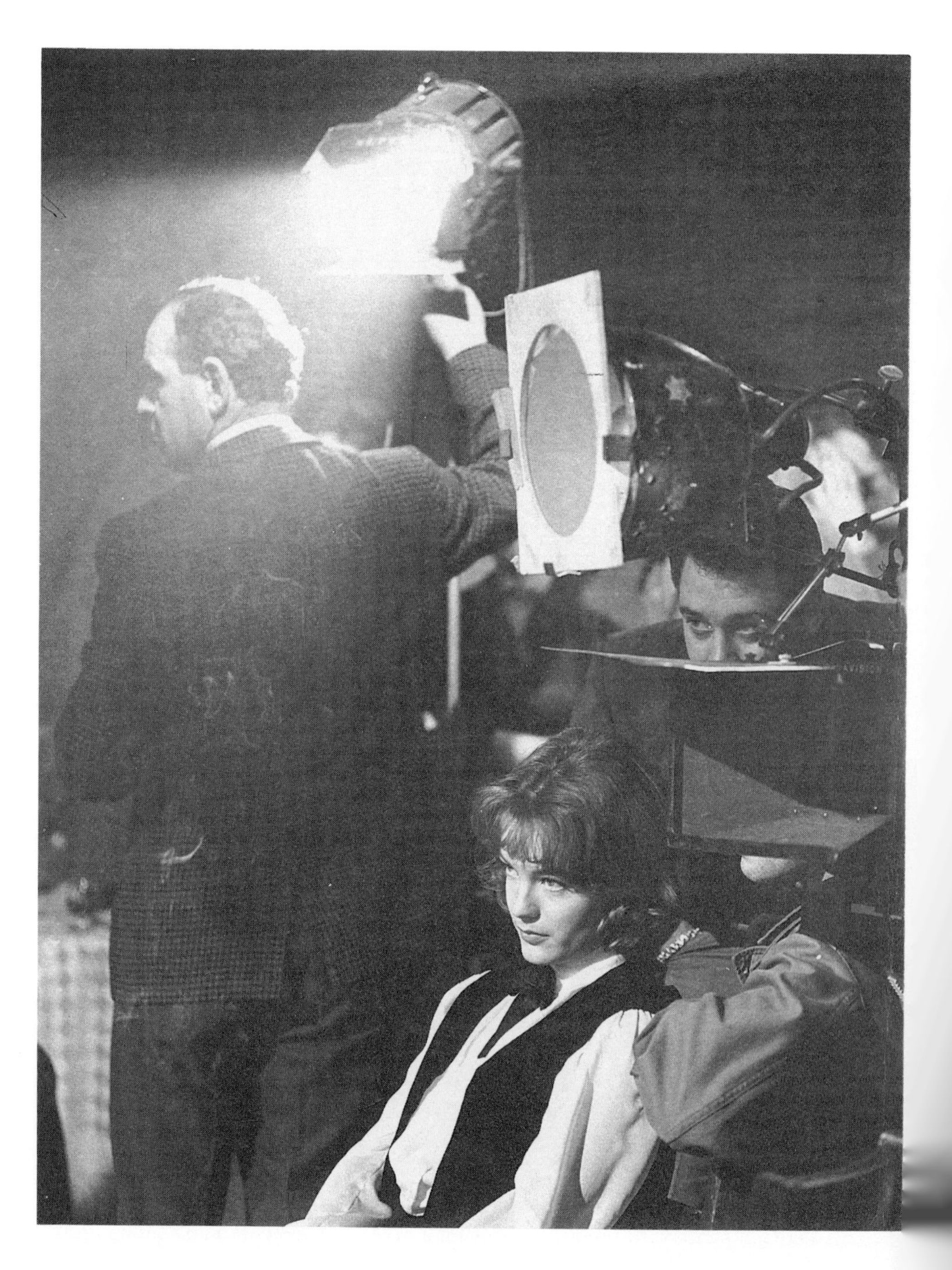

Romy Schneider looks on as Christopher Challis makes final adjustments to the lighting.

THE PRIVATE LIFE OF SHERLOCK HOLMES 1970

On the set at Pinewood Studios. *Left to right:* Billy Wilder, I.A.L. Diamond, Sydney Samuelson and the author.

LITTLE PRINCE, 1974

Director Stanley Donen *(left)*, listens to a camera department solution to the rising flood. Only the Little Prince seems to enjoy it.

'QUILP'

1974

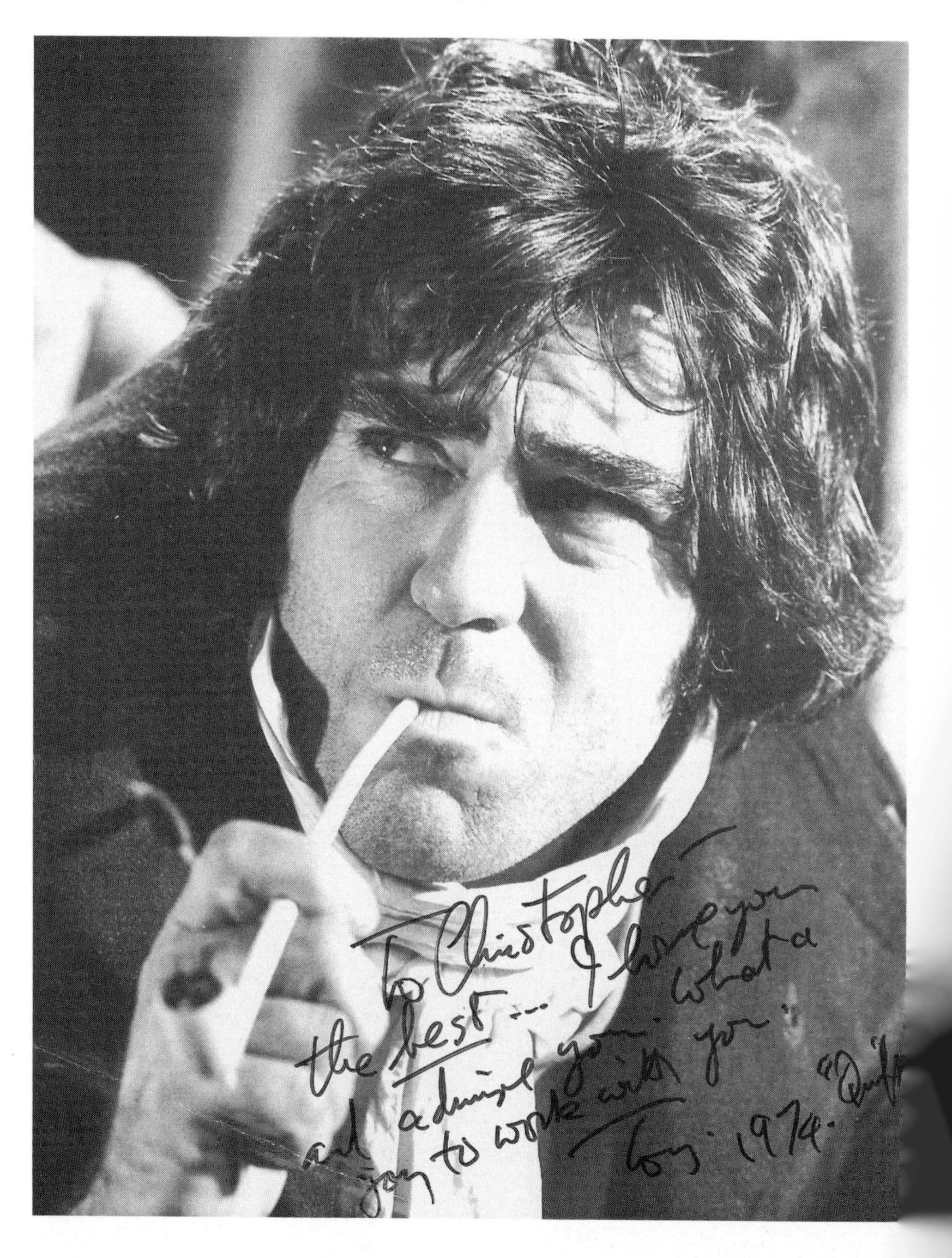

Anthony Newley, 'To Christopher, the <u>best</u> . . . I love you and admire you. What a joy to work <u>with</u> you.'

WHITE ROCK

1976

The author called into service by producer son Drummond on the official Winter Olympic film.

THE DEEP
1977

The author shares a joke with the camera crew atop a hastily built rig.

THE DEEP

Camera operator John Palmer surveying a rehearsal with the author alongside a Panavision Panaflex camera. The Panavision wide screen system of cameras and lenses was greatly favoured by the movie profession. Its reflex shutter and compact size made it very flexible.

THE RIDDLE OF THE SANDS, 1978

Produced by son Drummond. The author in his element, pipe in mouth, on the deck of a sailing boat. Director Tony Maylam in the background.

ABOVE. Michael York and Simon MacCorkindale prepare to dock Erskine Childer's fabled yacht 'Dulcibella,' BELOW. Christopher and son Drummond. A Producer/Director of Photography team that made four feature films.

THE MIRROR CRACK'D

1980

Elizabeth Taylor. 'To Chris. Thanks for shooting me through an Indian blanket'.

EVIL UNDER THE SUN

1982

Standing left to right: Peter Ustinov, Colin Blakely, Jane Birkin, Nicholas Clay, Maggie Smith, Diana Rigg, Emily More and Dennis Quilley. *Seated left to right:* Sylvia Miles and James Mason. *Foreground:* Roddy McDowell.

Christopher Challis holds court with John Brabourne and director Guy Hamilton.

TOP SECRET, 1984

Omar Sharif probably wished he never joined the cast of this disappointing spoof from the directors of Airplane, brothers David and Jerry Zucker.

19

HMS Defiant

In 1961 I spent five months in Spain, working on *HMS Defiant*, a film set in the Napoleonic wars and featuring Alec Guinness, Anthony Quayle and Dirk Bogarde. With my lifelong interest in the sea and sailing, it was for me the perfect subject to work on. With an excellent and cooperative cast, and a well-organised production department, the many difficulties which are bound to arise when working at sea were all resolved without the usual sense of panic.

Produced by John Brabourne and Richard Goodwin, *HMS Defiant* involved large-scale model shooting of the battle scenes because we had only two 'real' ships to play with. A top specialist from Hollywood, Howard Liedeker, had been engaged to supervise the model work and he expressed the firm opinion that the only way to achieve something near realism was to shoot it at sea. If we could find a protected bay somewhere, he was certain it could be achieved. We all agreed wholeheartedly with him and I left the meeting greatly encouraged. I had given the problem a great deal of thought and, after talking to various friends in the boat building industry, I was convinced that we could find stock fibreglass hulls on which we could build whatever we liked. There is a golden rule with model work. The bigger they are, the better they are, until the optimum is reached and absurdity taken to the extreme, when they are full size.

With these thoughts running through my mind, I was dismayed to get a call from Richard Goodwin to say that Leideker had carried out a grand tour of all the studios and had hit upon some old models, relics of some long-forgotten picture which, with a bit of work on them, would fit the bill and save a great deal of expense. They were being transported to a firm of model makers next day and I could go along and see them.

Needless to say, I was horrified with what I found. They had been constructed for a sequence which was shot in a studio tank, only four feet deep. They were built around an oblong, galvanised flotation tank with large pieces of iron grid battened onto the bottom to keep them upright. They had been pulled along by rails and cables on the bottom of the studio tank and looked, or could look, fine above the water, but below they were open-bottomed, not boats at all. Even with engines installed, there was no way they could be manoeuvred at sea. I forcibly expressed my feelings, and after numerous arguments with Liedeker I was told in simple terms to take care of the photography and leave the models to the experts.

Some weeks later, I was called in to see photographs and a chart of the place picked by Liedeker for the model shooting. It was on the Costa Blanca, at a little town called Villajoyosa, which boasted a large, artificial harbour with a long breakwater. The area chosen for filming was outside the breakwater, with a fairly wide arc of view of the open sea. Work was under way on building a tubular jetty for the models to be moored on the seaward side of the breakwater. I found it impossible to curb my tongue and pointed out the significance of the breakwater, which, if it followed the normal convention had to face the prevailing weather! Six weeks later, I arrived in Spain to start 16 scheduled weeks of model shooting, to be greeted by the news that a storm had demolished the tubular jetty and most of the models. 'I told you so' would not have helped but, oh, how hard it was not to say it.

A local boatbuilder was approached, a very bright and shrewd chap, who quickly understood what was needed and equally quickly appreciated that he was dealing with a wealthy film company in dire need of boats yesterday. It was obviously a heaven-sent opportunity to turn a dishonest peseta or two, and a welcome alternative to building fishing boats for hard-headed fishermen who drove a harder bargain and for whom *manana* was soon enough.

Of course what he produced was built in wood in a conventional way, but at least they floated – and the right way up, too!

Model-filming on water has its own particular problems, the chief being scale. If the model is in one-eighth scale, then the height of the camera lens above water has to be an eighth of normal. This makes the water in the foreground a matter of inches from the lens, so the waves must be reduced to ripples for it to look right.

A special raft was built for the camera, with a sunken well and glass panel extending below water level so that we could get the lens within inches of the water. Large outriggers were added, onto which were lashed empty oildrums to improve stability and an awning erected overall to keep the crew from 'frying'. Day by day more thought was given to creature comforts; an ice box, a place for swimming gear, and an outboard dinghy to maintain contact with civilization and to bring out the sustenance so essential to ward off the pangs of boredom brought on by the hours of waiting on our floating island for all the minute detail to click unwillingly into place.

Each morning at first light we would be towed out to the selected camera position, looking more and more like the crew of *Kon-Tiki* as the sun tanned our bodies and bleached our hair. We held ourselves in position by means of four anchors, one at each corner, which were dropped daily amid much shouting in both Spanish and English, all the instructions passing unheeded as each followed his individual ideas of where we should be.

Then came the rafts with the wind machines, old aero engines mounted on rusty iron frames which, too, had to be anchored, hopefully out of the lens angle. Then more rafts with smoke machines and an electric generator to power the smaller fans for breaking up the surface in the immediate foreground. The old aero engines looked suicidal to me, usually failing to start. Suddenly, with a bang and a cloud of black smoke, they would be away, often in full throttle, the raft heeling to a terrifying angle. The anchor ropes would snap taut and more often than not the whole thing would take off across the bay, dragging anchors behind it, sometimes depositing the operator in the sea. In that case we would have a rogue aero engine on our hands, trying hard to become airborne but minus the necessary appendages of an aeroplane.

Add to all this the problems of wind direction and strength, as the models were supposed to be sailing and so the sails had to be filled, and all the electrical gear on board to work the guns, to trigger the masts to come down and cause fires to start, and it becomes easy to imagine that the odds against success were stacked pretty high.

The height of absurdity was reached when, after hours of preparation, a convincing British frigate of the Napoleonic wars sailed towards camera and at the crucial moment the broadside failed to go off. All hell broke loose, with Leideker heaping American blasphemy on all and sundry. From the bowels of a hitherto 'real' ship emerged the giant, eight times normal size figure of an oily, powder-blackened cockney prop man, who more than made up for the missing broadside with a verbal equivalent tracing Leideker's ancestry in detail.

The scheduled 16 weeks were up. We were all burned to a rich mahogany, and there were still 22 model shots to go. With the arrival of the artists and the main unit, I left the model work in the capable hands of 'Sheets' Kelly, and repaired to the comparative sanity of photographing actors and real ships.

The model work turned out well, and the decision to do it at sea was right but, who knows, it might have all been easier. There is always a first time for everything, and it is easy to be wise after the event.

HMS Defiant gave me the opportunity of meeting and working with Alan Villiers, the greatest living authority on large sailing ships, who had converted the two ships he had used on the film *John Paul Jones* into Royal Navy frigates of the period. We quickly struck up a close friendship which continued until his death some years later. I believe he was relieved to find someone in the company who knew a little about the sea. For his part, being an accomplished photographer, he was well aware of our difficulties, accepting at all times the seemingly ridiculous demands we made from a purely nautical standpoint in order to get some of the scenes. So many experts, when called in to advise on a film, lose sight of the fact that it is a commercial undertaking, designed to entertain and not a training manual on the particular subject they happen to specialise in.

Lewis Gilbert, the director, left the sailing sequences very much to Alan and me. Big sailing ships are things of beauty, indeed they have been called man's most beautiful creation, not without reason, and I was determined to film everything 'for real' without recourse to process work later. The artists were willing to go aloft with the camera crew and my assistant, John Jordan, made a most ingenious camera mount in a local garage workshop which enabled us to sling the camera anywhere in the rigging, holding it steady and leaving the operator free to pan and tilt to follow the action.

Of an evening, Alan would recount past experiences on the numerous films he had worked on. His advice as to location and choice of vessel was more often than not ignored, the art department converting unsuitable old hulks complete with matchsticks for masts and 'Cape Horn' canvas, which refused to fill in the light weather conditions required for filming. Directors, he maintained, by and large, hadn't a clue. Setting up a shot, they would scream hysterically through the loud hailer for him to stop, move sideways or maybe back a few yards under the impression that he had brakes and a reverse gear.

One of the compensations of working in the industry is that from time to time it brings the opportunity of meeting outstanding people from other walks of life, brought in for their expertise and knowledge of a particular subject. Alan, an Australian by birth, first went to sea, much against his father's wishes, in the Tasman schooners. With a natural ability to write, he discovered that there was a demand for the articles he jotted down about life aboard these little vessels. The sight of the big grain-carrying barques alongside the quays in Sydney filled his imagination. Somehow, he would find a way of sailing in them, recording in articles, or perhaps even a book, the twilight of these beautiful ships and the particular breed of men who sailed them while there was yet time. This he succeeded in doing in a style particularly his own, for he had a feeling for the sea perhaps second only to Conrad.

He became convinced that life aboard these big sailing ships, full of hardships and privations beyond the imagination of the average landsman, provided the ideal way of training and developing young men. Why not film a voyage round the Horn with a cargo of grain for Europe? He managed to buy two simple clockwork-driven movie cameras, together with a meagre supply of film and, together with friend, shipped before the mast on the *Lawhill*, bound for Plymouth. Sadly, his friend was killed only a few days out when he fell from the upper topsail yard in heavy weather, playing his full part as a crew member while at the same time trying to film the frightening process of taking in sail in gale force winds. Alan continued alone, filming unique sequences of life on board a big sailing ship which, together with later material he shot when part owner of the *Parma*, constitutes the only record of a way of life that has passed away.

During the course of many visits, he ran all this material for me at his house in Oxford, stopping frequently to expand on something with a wealth of anecdotes. Much of the material he used in later years to illustrate his lectures and television programmes, but much remains unseen, safely deposited with the National Maritime Museum, together with his unfinished manuscripts and huge collection of books and articles on the subject which dominated his life – 'Men, Ships and the Sea'. His talents as a writer and lecturer, with the occasional foray into the hysterical world of films, were devoted to the support of his delightful wife and family and to an almost single-handed attempt to convince the authorities world-wide (but, perhaps, particularly those in Britain which, almost alone among maritime nations, had abandoned the idea) that training in sail was still the best way to prepare young men for a life at sea. He personally financed the last circumnavigation of the world in a fully rigged ship, crewing her with young men from both sides of the Atlantic. The small, ex-Danish schoolship which he purchased for the great adventure, renamed inevitably the *Conrad*, now lies preserved at the maritime museum in Mystic, Connecticut.

He sailed with the Arabs in their huge dhows, unchanged for centuries, from the Persian gulf to Zanzibar, in the process temporarily losing his sight, which was miraculously restored by bathing his eyes in human milk. Then there were the Portuguese Grand Banks schooners, followed by the *Mayflower* project. He masterminded the construction of this exact replica, sailing her to America in the face of much criticism and accompanied by prophecies of doom and disaster. His final wish was to repeat the performance, this time by building *Endeavour*, Captain Cook's Whitby collier, and taking her round the Horn to Australia in the footsteps of the greatest navigator of all time. Would I go with him and join in filming every detail of the building of the ship, followed by the voyage? There is no need for me to record my answer. He felt that it had to be done before his 70th birthday or he would be too old for the arduous journey. Problems of finance and time conspired to make this impossible, losing to posterity the story of a great adventure.

20

The Victors

I FELT THE need of a break after the long Spanish location, perhaps a family holiday in Cornwall and the chance of some sailing. 'Would you get in touch with Carl Foreman as soon as possible?' was the message that awaited me. He was planning to produce *The Victors,* his personal definitive statement on war and all its attendant evils. He had decided to direct it himself, feeling that his very deep convictions about the subject could not be trusted to someone else. An accomplished writer and producer, he knew little or nothing of directing, or in fact how a picture was put together during the shooting stage. He was very frank about this, making it clear that he wanted people around him willing to help turn the script and his strong ideas into camera angles, choice of lenses, etc, breaking down a scene into a form in which it could be filmed and finally cut together, to make most effectively all the dramatic points it contained. These shortcomings in a director, for shortcomings they must be, need not be disastrous providing that the help given does not turn into dictatorship or the direction fall into the hands of a 'committee'. It was a situation unique only in the sense that Carl admitted it from the first, gaining complete support from everyone, yet retaining full control in every respect to tell the story 'his way'. I make the point of it being unique because I have worked with many other directors who shared the same shortcomings, often to a greater degree, yet without the humility ever to admit to them.

'I don't want to discuss any form of detail. Go away and read the script as soon as you can, today if possible,' he said, passing me from a drawer in his desk the largest volume to be designated 'script' I had set eyes on. 'If you like it and are prepared to accept the situation I have outlined, then you have a deal. Ring me back as soon as you have finished, with an honest opinion and as much criticism as you like.' Reading it in what was left of the day was a physical impossibility, so I telephoned him the following afternoon to say I would like to do it. 'Come up tomorrow and we can discuss the details.' 'When do you want me to start, Carl? I have planned a short holiday starting next week.' 'Right away,' he replied. It was September, with the proposed start date not until March, so surely a couple of weeks would make little difference? 'I want you right now. Geoff Drake, the art director, is already with me and I need the two of you to be in on every detail of the pre-production planning. Now is the time to sort out all the problems, not when we get down to shooting.' It was a sentiment with which I found it hard to disagree and so, my ever-elusive holiday once more postponed, I was on the payroll that very afternoon.

Geoff Drake and I had a short meeting with Carl during which he was called to take an urgent call from the States. He did not reappear in our lives again for upwards of two months, apart from the odd telephone conversation from Hollywood, where he was busy casting and arguing finance. He did, however, leave behind one insoluble problem. Somewhere he had read the account of an unfortunate GI who was executed by firing squad for cowardice in the face of the enemy. Many of course were convicted of the same offence, but this was the only case where the supreme penalty was carried out. The execution took place in the courtyard of a Belgian chateau in midwinter, the ground covered with snow to complete the futile misery of the scene. Carl had written the sequence into the script with the idea of using the voice of Bing Crosby singing *White Christmas* as a background, to underline his feelings about the morality of war. Owing to problems with artists' contracts and the schedule, the sequence could not be filmed before the middle of April. Geoff and I were dispatched to the Continent to find a suitable chateau situated in a place with the guarantee of snow at that time of the year. Naturally enough, it did not exist, a fact which we telephoned back to the office in London. 'Stay where you are while we let Carl know,' was the response. Two days later came the reply. 'Carl says why don't you try up in the mountains? The snow stays there until May at least. He knows, because he's been there at that time on holiday.' What he did not know was that it is not the habit to build chateaux in these situations. We did, however, find a number of large houses which might have well passed for what he had in mind, which we photographed from every angle, while Geoff made sketches of each proposed shot in the sequence.

All this material was rushed back to London, to be forwarded to Carl in Hollywood for approval. 'Stay where you are. We'll call and let you know what he thinks.' So once again we waited. But, this time, events overtook our endeavours. Due to whatever deals Carl was making in Los Angeles, the schedule had to be readjusted and the execution sequence put back until May. 'Look higher up the mountains where the snow stays longer,' was the helpful advice from LA, via London. The whole exercise was repeated, including yet another change of schedule, putting the sequence back until the end of May. Only two alternatives were left to us, the summits of the Matterhorn or Mont Blanc, neither of which had as yet been developed for housing. Back to London we went, admitting complete defeat. 'We have to get the sequence, no matter what. Think of somewhere else,' decreed the cable from Carl. 'Why can't we shoot it next winter after the main filming is over?' 'Because Carl is directing his first picture and he wants to shoot in sequence.'

Next day, in desperation, I walked into the Swedish Embassy and asked to speak with the Press Officer. 'What do you want to see him about?' they asked. I dared not tell them, in case they had me forcibly ejected as a person of unsound mind, so I concocted a plausible story which gained me entry to his office.

Once in, I bared my soul to him while he sat, unflinching, at the opposite side of his desk. My incoherent story finished, he looked at me in silence for a few moments, then with a smile said, 'Leave it with me for a day or so. I'll be in touch as soon as I have anything to tell you.' Next afternoon came a call from him. 'Come over and I'll show you what I've got.' What he had 'got' was a reproduction French chateau built by an eccentric industrialist at a place called Ostersund, just north of the Arctic Circle. 'It's so cold up there that the lake stays frozen over until June, with the ice thick enough to run the railway across it. They re-lay the tracks each winter to save the long detour round the shores.' So Ostersund it was, with a unit of over a hundred, the execution finally taking place on the vast frozen lake with the house in the background which, Carl rightly felt, was more dramatic than the original courtyard. If there is an award for sheer persistence, then Carl wins it hands down!

Carl was one of a number of Americans with left-wing leanings who came to England during the McCarthy purge in Hollywood. Just how far these leanings went, I would not care to hazard a guess, but they certainly did not extend to distributing his wealth among his less fortunate brothers. Being politically naive, I have always thought wealthy socialists an anachronism, with millionaires of this persuasion an even greater one. For some reason our industry has more than its share of them. Carl, who was by nature, I think, a generous man, was in day-to-day affairs incredibly mean, concerning himself with salary details of the very lowest member of the crew. An untidy dresser, usually in jeans and sneakers, which were perhaps worn as an outward manifestation of his dislike for the establishment, he punctiliously insisted on being accorded all the 'perks' of a big producer. The best suite in the best hotel and the biggest available car were not part of his social conscience. We all took a mischievous delight, when out for a meal with him, in ordering the most expensive items on the menu, irrespective of what we really wanted to eat, just to witness the pain on his face as he checked the price of each dish, even though good old 'Columbia' were paying.

A very clever man and an excellent script writer, he was a slow thinker without any visual imagination whatever. Everything had to be thrashed out to the smallest detail and gone over a dozen times until it was absolutely clear in his mind. For this reason, he wanted every sequence fully 'story-boarded'. This meant sketches of every shot of every sequence with a background of the chosen location or set. 'There aren't enough sketch artists available, Carl. Most of them are already working on other pictures,' pleaded Geoff. 'You have to get them, Geoff. Offer them more money to come over to us if you have to,' replied Carl, temporarily abandoning his sense of economy.

After Sweden, our first location was a farm, meant to be in Germany. The scene was a group of GIs lining up for 'chow'. In the queue was a young boy, a sort of company mascot, adopted by the troops. An orphan of war, he was dressed in a German uniform many sizes too large, probably taken from a dead soldier. The search for a suitable farmhouse and buildings containing all the essentials called for in the script followed roughly the pattern of the chateau quest. Carl had once again disappeared to 'the coast', taken up with casting and contracts, to be contacted only by cable or telephone in case of extreme emergency. The starting date drew relentlessly closer with the location, as yet, unseen by Carl. He wanted to check all the uniforms and 'props' himself and some of the smaller parts were still not cast; as a good case of 'extreme emergency' as one could wish for. In the midst of chaos came 'the word'. 'Carl flies back tonight. He wants everyone in his office first thing tomorrow, all the sketches, the clothes, everything.'

Nearly four months had passed since he first needed me so desperately and this was our third meeting, apart from Sweden. Slowly he went through the pile of sketches which represented about two minutes' screen time in the final picture, studying each one with care. 'Tell me, Geoff, how old do you see the boy on these drawings?' asked Carl. 'I don't really know, Carl. About fifteen, I suppose,' replied the puzzled Geoff. 'No, no, he can't be so old. If you read the script you will see that to behave the way he does he can only be ten or eleven at the most. Get them to do it over with a younger boy.' 'But Carl, what about the location, the farm and the surroundings?' 'I can't judge any of it until you get the boy right, Geoff,' was his farewell as he left to take another call from LA.

Armed with the massive script and a huge international cast including George Peppard, Melina Mercouri, Jeanne Moreau, Elke Sommer, Rosanna Schiaffino, Eli Wallach, Albert Finney, George Hamilton and Robert Mitchum Junior, we laboured painstakingly to give Carl what he wanted. The schedule stretched into eternity, with Carl giving everything he had to a subject in which I am sure he believed implicitly. Many of the sequences I found very moving, with Carl getting excellent performances from the actors, something which did not come easily to him as he was not the best of communicators. He did not share a great affinity with them, yet managed to assert his personality from the start, an absolute essential with a cast of that size. So what was he like as a director? Very much better than average, for he knew and believed in his subject. The picture was too long, much of it falling below the standards set by what was best in the script. Perhaps he was too close to it to be able to judge, for the end result was not successful, and some of the critics were particularly harsh.

Before I leave *The Victors*, just one more anecdote. We were in Italy looking for a location, the sequence being broadly based on the Salerno landings. As is so often the case, the script had been written about imaginary places, full of detail, all vital to the story. The problem was to find reality which matched the writer's ideas. Why, oh why, don't they write about real places in the first place? I am sure the answers are there, thick on the ground, but it does at times appear a little illogical. During the agony of scheduling and budgeting, when ex-thousand dollars have to be cut in some way, the search for economies grows hourly more frantic and unrealistic.

Can we beat the clapper boy down by two pounds a week, do without a 50-mm lens or take one less electrician on location, where a bit of extra manpower is vital? What about the scene on top of the Empire State Building with just two lines of dialogue which could just as effectively be played in an underground lavatory? This question, which is, of course, apocryphal, I ask to illustrate the fact that a writer's whim is rarely questioned. In most cases, when they realised the financial and technical implications of a few simple words, they would be more than willing to compromise, I am sure.

But to return to the search for the Italian location. A group of us were gathered in Carl's apartment which, true to form, was the largest in the hotel. Sicily had been suggested as a likely place – but where to begin? A great believer in maps if you know how to read them, I suggested we obtained some large scale ones of the area, complete with contour lines, which give a clear idea of the terrain. 'A good idea,' said Carl, to whom contours, I felt, were a comparatively new discovery. He rang for the concierge, who was dispatched with a list of our requirements which he seemed to understand. While waiting for his return, a call came through from Carl's wife in Los Angeles, in the middle of which the concierge returned triumphant with all that we had asked for. Leaving his wife on the line, Carl came over to see if we had got what we wanted. 'Yes, they are fine. With a couple of hours' work we can narrow the field down to just two or three alternatives,' we chorused. 'How much do I owe you?' asked Carl, turning to the concierge. The answer, a matter of a few pounds, proved totally unacceptable to Carl's idea of what maps should cost, based upon the purchase of the odd road atlas, or maybe even the ones given free at filling stations. A heated argument followed with the concierge who, firmly standing his ground, refused to do any sort of deal. The maps were folded up and returned to him. 'Take them back to the store. I'm not paying that sort of money for something I only want to look at a couple of times.' During the 10 minutes or so occupied by this altercation, Carl's patient wife had been hanging on to the phone, clocking up a bill many times the cost of the maps.

Apart from the endless 'story board' sketches, Carl also asked for models of all the sets, including scale figures of the actors. He spent his evenings at home, pushing them around like figures in a toy theatre, working out how he intended to play the scene. In this way he came up with many good ideas, some of which proved intractable when translated into flesh and blood. The main street of a small Italian town proved the most traumatic. With several weeks of work in it, both by day and night, it was decided to build a studio set for the night scenes, which included interiors of houses, while shooting the day scenes on location. Geoff designed a huge street set based on photographs of a likely little town chosen by an Italian art director, who was helping us to find suitable locations. When we finally met up with the real place it did not, of course, exactly match up with the model set on which Carl had worked out all his scenes.

All the problems were small ones, easily resolved by changing the odd camera angle, or cutting in a different way, but to Carl it was total disaster. I remember him sitting at the roadside, head in his hands, refusing to speak to anyone for an hour or more, while we walked around with a view finder, looking for ways to make it work. 'I think it's a disaster, but show me how you all think we can shoot here,' he finally said, relinquishing his position of tragedy on the kerbstone. Shot by shot we went through it all, Carl pushing us around in place of the model figures. I would explain an angle and then, while he looked through the viewfinder, I would run in and play the part of Rosanna Schiaffino or Eli Wallach, with Geoff and the others doing the same. So the day passed and darkness fell, but still we were not through. With a torch to read the script, we stumbled around in the dimly-lit street until every shot was clear in Carl's mind and he grudgingly admitted it would work.

I don't want to leave *The Victors*, every painstaking 62 weeks of it, with the impression that I did not care for Carl. On the contrary, I had the greatest respect for him as a committed film-maker. He was just Carl, that's all!

21

The Vikings

I HAVE TWICE ventured into Yugoslavia in the course of film-making, on the second occasion with considerable reluctance as I had the experience of the first to call upon. Many years separated the two visits, but in terms of my story it seems best to group them together.

Yugoslavia was becoming popular with producers as a venue for film-making for a number of reasons. A beautiful country, it offered a wide variety of scenery and the nucleus of a film industry. But, above all, it was cheap. In simple terms, you provided the dollars and most of the equipment and they provided the facilities. The spoils, if any, were divided by various obscure means involving currency exchange rates, frozen assets and possibly even frozen goulash! It sounded dishonest, and probably was, but anyway it was no concern of mine. The first picture was *The Long Ships*, a sequel to *The Vikings*. The director was to be Jack Cardiff, who had forsaken the camera which he used so brilliantly for the director's 'baton' which, sad to say, he did not. Belgrade in January was to be our base; no more miserable city on earth in which to be away from home.

The Metropole Hotel rose high above its dreary surroundings, at that time the only modern hotel in the city. A sort of grade eight Hilton, it existed specially for the use of foreign visitors, sporting an air conditioning system which did not work, together with other minor concessions to the Western way of life.

Among these was a sophisticated group of elevators of Swiss manufacture, supposedly giving access to the 30 or so storeys. Automatic in operation when buttons were pressed on various floors, the computer worked out the most efficient order for the elevator to proceed. Due to total lack of skilled maintenance, its progress was unpredictable to the point of exasperation. If you were waiting to get in, it would fail to stop, or, if it did stop, the doors would open and close so quickly that you could get neither in nor out. Once in, you could well be treated to numerous journeys up and down the building, wildly pressing each and every button in the vain hope of release. The red emergency button had the disconcerting habit of putting the lights out, without in any way preventing the erratic progress, apart from occasionally stopping between floors. The sight of a desperate passenger, overcome by claustrophobia, flinging himself out through the momentary gap in the fast-moving doors, to land in a heap on the floor, brought not a single raised eyebrow from among the more hardened inmates.

The rooms had no windows, perhaps considered unnecessary in view of the air conditioning, but instead, two large glass doors, an inner and an outer, so designed that if they were opened to gain air, the handle on the inner door broke the glass on the outer door which crashed down into the street below. As a matter of course, the nights were broken by the sound of breaking glass at frequent intervals as new residents sought means of ventilation. The hotel always put the cost of a new window on the bill, resulting each day in long queues of irate guests flatly refusing to pay.

The first location was the Viking village, built on the shores of a fjord in the north of the country, near the town of Pula. The picture had been on and off several times over the previous year as money ran out or faith in the script evaporated to the point of no return. The village and the two long ships had been built during this period of changing ownership so that they were now a bonus or a liability, depending on how you looked at it.

The scene was a race between the King's boat and one belonging to the village headman. Magnificently manned by the village lads and captained by Richard Widmark, the latter inflicts humiliating defeat on the royal vessel, ending up with a flourish of oars alongside the platform where the King and the Elders are assembled. The longships had been built on an island some 30 miles away, and for six months the crews had been training hard to reach perfection in their handling. A visit to inspect them convinced us all that they had indeed done a fine job. Just one unforeseen snag remained. There was not enough water in the fjord for them to get within 100 yards of the shore! Unlike a conventional film set, built of plywood flats and plaster, with the buildings only complete on the side that faced the camera, the Yugoslav 'Viking' village was massively constructed of huge pine logs, complete in every detail and ready to live in. There was no question of being able to move it to another site where the water was deeper. The scene was filmed up to the point when the longship ran aground. The cameras were cut and the crew taken off, together with any other pieces of gear which might save weight and reduce draught.

By stages the boats were dragged in towards the jetty, the crew and actors joining in, aided by an ancient tractor and several apathetic horses. At various points during this last desperate 100 yards, the crew were put back aboard, together with their gear, to enable us to shoot a short flash of them rowing furiously while hard aground in two feet of water. Their sail, with its proud emblem, draped limp and bedraggled despite attempts by the prop department to pull it out into shape with lengths of fine nylon line. With the cheering crowd surrounding the King in the foreground, it was hoped to distract attention from the fact that the longship was stationary. This laborious routine was repeated four or five times, with the intention of using just a few feet of each shot in the final cutting, interspersed with close-ups of sweating oarsmen, Richard Widmark, the King and the elated villagers. Such is the 'magic' of the movies that the deception passed unnoticed among the many other incidents in the completed film, which aroused the scorn of the London critics.

Due to fickle weather conditions, which alternated between sunshine and snow showers, progress was slow. Once committed to sunshine for the sequence, we had to wait for the next burst, frantically sweeping the snow off the boats, the actors' clothes and those portions of the landscape that featured in the shot, by which time the sun had disappeared and it was snowing again. A further complication was the 'siting of the village', situated at the foot of a large hill behind which the sun set at around three in the afternoon. It had been chosen almost two years earlier by an anonymous art director, long since departed from the pay roll, who, much impressed by the Nordic character of the landscape, had neglected to take count of the inexorable movement of the heavenly body.

The female members of the cast had a problem of their own. Clad in Hollywood's ideas of what a well-dressed Viking girl would be wearing, which was a minimal garment of animal skin, the large areas of exposed flesh, traditionally meant to allure, turned a mottled blue, with a generous complement of goose pimples added for good measure. A fairly simple sequence, scheduled for half a day, had taken nearly a week. Never mind. The village was inherited from an earlier would-be producer at a knock-down price and, anyway, things were cheap in Yugoslavia.

There still remained the departure of our Viking crew. A night scene with a background of the sacked and burning village, it would have to be shot at 'magic hour'. This is a term used to describe the last half an hour or so before dark, when there remains just enough light to get a minimal exposure over the whole area. Flames and burning torches show up brightly, with actors and selected areas being picked out with artificial light, giving the overall effect of night. The timing is critical photographically, necessitating many rehearsals coupled with a high degree of organisation if there is to be any chance of getting such a complicated scene in the limited time available. Organisation not being one of our strong points, doubts grew in my mind as the daylight started to fade.

It had been planned to put the main camera in the longship with the oarsmen in the foreground. Richard Widmark, fighting a valiant rearguard action, would jump aboard just as we started to move, and end in a large close-up, urging his men on, his face lit by the flames of the burning village. Another script writer's dream, of course, because the longship was hard aground. 'Why not build a large flat-bottomed punt? We can rig up pieces of the real boat in the foreground and seat a few Vikings in the picture to complete the illusion.' This, we were assured, would be better than the real thing. The punt would float easily in the shallow water, being pulled away by a cable attached to the ancient tractor whose owner-driver came from a nearby smallholding. 'Where do we get the punt?' I asked. 'The art department will build it,' replied the producer, Irving Allen, whose faith in their ability as naval architects was far greater than mine.

They worked all night on their creation, which was launched next afternoon and immediately started to sink. 'Don't worry, the timbers will soon start to take up. By tomorrow it will be fine. To be on the safe side we'll get a small petrol pump.' Tomorrow came all too soon, together with the need for the aforementioned organisation. Cues were worked out for the special effects to set the village alight, for the different sections of the crowd to engage in mortal combat and for Widmark to commence his fighting retreat to the already-moving ship.

The hours passed, then the minutes. It was time to go! 'Light the fires!' shouted the assistants. Unlike a normal set, which goes up like a Guy Fawkes bonfire, the village was made of sterner stuff and refused to burn. Blackened special effects men threw on more petrol gel and kerosene, their hair and clothes singed and in some cases burning to greater effect than the village. 'Let's go, let's go!' shouted Irving, 'There's enough flame to get by with. Throw on more kerosene.' The crowd started to slay each other with a fervour engendered by the thought of home and an evening meal. Widmark started his action, felling the invaders by the dozen as he retreated towards the ship. All was now up to the bemused farmer on the tractor. 'Watch Mr. Widmark carefully,' he had been told, 'and just before he reaches the jetty, start to move gently away.'

Richard arrived on the jetty, killing his final stunt man on the way, stepped aboard the raft, ending up in perfect close-up, but we did not move. The farmer, carried away by this insight into Nordic war, had forgotten his cue. He awoke from his reverie to the screams of the Yugoslav assistants, topped by the stentorian voice of Irving Allen, his American vernacular clear above the chaos. We leaped away from the jetty like a BMW jumping the traffic lights, proceeding in a series of wild jerks towards our destination – 'Africa and the golden bell'. As darkness overtook us, the fires flickered and died, leaving the village unscathed while the pump laboured in vain to stem the rising water in the punt. Beached in the nick of time, it was decided that we had the shot in the bag. Far removed from its original conception, with the addition of a few judicious close-ups to be shot in the comparative calm of the studio, it would get by. The decision was Irving's, to whom the thought of doing it again was infinitely worse than any artistic compromise that may have to be made.

Hotels seem to feature largely in what is supposed to be a book about films, but since they are so much a part of one's life on location, I feel they constitute a justified digression. The one at Pula, a vast rococo building and relic of the old Austro-Hungarian Empire, when it was rumoured to have been a once-proud officers' mess, stood crumpled and forlorn amid derelict land overlooking the docks. The crumbling façade, broken by rows of tall grimy windows, curtainless, the glass cracked or missing, was capped by legless and armless cherubs, the missing members often laying unclaimed in the street below. This unwelcoming exterior hid an even grimmer interior. A vast dusty hall was flagged with black and white checked marble, the surface in places worn away by the tread of countless spurred jackboots but now long since abandoned as an object worthy of cleaning or polishing. At the far end were four ancient lifts, padlocked and unused for many years, the wall between them dominated by a large and extremely bad portrait of Tito, draped in dusty red velvet. Beneath stood an ornate table, a relic of better times, in the centre of which drooped a plastic bowl of artificial flowers, faded and overawed by the once-majestic surroundings. Near the entrance was a small desk behind which sat the concierge, sole representative of the hotel staff. Dressed in a faded grey alpaca jacket, with greying hair and complexion to match, he seemed to me to personify all that was hopeless about the regime, and for that matter, the hotel. He showed no interest whatever in the guests, conversation being limited to one word, 'passport', of which article he was at pains to relieve you in order to present it to the police. The decadent convention of room keys had long since been abandoned in favour of a small scrap of paper torn from a ruled exercise book, on which was scrawled in pencil the number of your abode. 'Don't be put off by your first impression,' encouraged the Yugoslav assistant. 'This hotel is a staff training centre for the state-run hotel system, the food is good and the service excellent!'

Ascending from the hall was a beautiful, curving, marble staircase, flanked by an ornate bronze balustrade. The wide, sweeping steps, once carpeted in darkest crimson, now had a narrow strip of threadbare haircord in lonely isolation down the middle. Large holes in the marble at the edges of the steps betrayed where the stair rods had once been fixed, to be ruthlessly prised out as a gesture of newly found freedom from the old Monarchy. We quickly learned that the haircord strip was to be avoided at all costs, particularly if taken at speed, when the stair rods had the habit of falling out, resulting in a miniature 'Niagara' composed of haircord, dust and guests. This frequent occurrence brought no reaction from the concierge, who, like the artificial flowers below the portrait of Tito, had given up any attempt at authenticity.

The rooms were large and bare, with plumbing a vanished art. Each equipped with a hand basin, the taps produced a far-away gurgle accompanied by a puff of brownish dust. Doors were numbered with plywood cut-outs resembling the efforts of a child with his first fretwork set, pinned into place with a sense of careless abandon. Many of the pins had broken or rusted away, the numbers turning sideways or upside-down, which added to the conundrum of finding one's room, particularly after a few drinks in the evening. As doors could not be locked, stories abounded which gave a certain substance to popular belief concerning the loose morals in the world of entertainment.

We were still left with the good food to sustain us, and very good it proved to be if you could master the art of getting it. The dining room was vast and decoratively in keeping with the exterior façade. Plush and peeling gilt, it was furnished with plastic-topped metal tables and chairs, among which a host of young egg-stained trainees moved at the double, accompanied by the sound of breaking china and glass. There were no menus, it being their proud boast that you could order whatever you wished and they could produce it. This claim proved to be largely true, but was seriously marred by the fact that the slightly hysterical young waiters, confused by language and variety of orders, could rarely remember who had ordered what! The more travel-wise among us discovered that the best system was to get a table near the double swing doors which gave access to the kitchen, keeping a careful watch on what emerged. As soon as a likely dish appeared, we would signal the waiter over and stake a claim, he being only too willing to find it a caring home.

The village sequences behind us, there remained all the scenes aboard the longship before we settled in Belgrade for the studio work. Due to the size of the camera it was not possible to be in the longship with the actors for most of the scenes, a situation which it was proposed should be overcome with yet another raft. Once again designed by the art department, whose nautical prowess appeared to decline with experience, it took the form of a welded steel pontoon some sixty feet square, decked over with massive timbers resembling railway sleepers. It would be large and buoyant enough to take the generator, make-up and hairdressing caravans, another caravan for the artists to rest in, and even a mobile toilet with facilities for both sexes. The longship would be lashed on one or other side, depending on the direction of travel, with the Viking oarsmen on the far side able to have their blades in the water while those unfortunates on the pontoon side would make do with sawn off versions attached to elastic strops to give them something to pull against.

There remained only the crew to accommodate. All anxious to get to sea, it proved difficult to reduce the numbers, everyone having a good case for being present, reinforced by a keen sense of adventure. Whittled down to a mere 60 or so, plus Viking crew, we set sail on the first morning, towed by two launches with conflicting ideas about the direction we wished to travel. Apart from the few actively engaged in the shooting, the crew sat around in the warm early morning sun, stripping off shirts and anointing themselves with sun-oil. The artists lolled in their production chairs, sun glasses destroying the illusion created by their costumes of animal skin. Everyone got in the way of everyone else as we set up the camera and lights for the first shot.

Slowly, in a series of erratic curves, we gained sea-room. The holiday atmosphere was rudely broken by the assistant directors shouting, 'All Vikings into the longship for scene 36. Take off your sun glasses and wrist watches and get ready to rehearse.' The rowing was ragged, with the actors clearly outclassed by the trained crew who had practised all winter, those on the inside making heavy weather of their elastic bands. Instructions were shouted to the men in the launches to turn us so that the background was clear of land. They proved to be individualistic chaps, pursuing opposite courses as more and more people shouted instructions. At last, amid an atmosphere of mounting hysteria, we had a clear horizon, which coincided with the sun disappearing behind a large black cloud. 'Hold everything where it is while we wait for the light,' shouted the hopeful director. As the sun emerged, we slowly twisted back to face the land and the whole operation started over again. The gentle swell of the open sea started to lift our maritime indiscretion, the movement bringing groans of protest from the longship, tethered firmly alongside and unable to rise and fall of its own volition. A faithful copy of an original, the planking and timbers were lashed together by leather thongs, the painstaking Yugoslavs who had built her not deigning to use modern fastenings which might have stood up better to the unseamanlike demands of film-making.

One by one the thongs slipped or broke, the longship slowly falling apart beneath the feet of the intrepid, Africa-bound crew. 'Everybody onto the raft!' came the frantic call of the assistant, already anticipated by the Vikings, who were mostly engaged in abandoning their vessel anyway. With the wind and sea slowly rising, we retraced our corkscrew course to the safety of the harbour, water lapping over the deck and soaking the confusion of equipment and personal belongings that littered the pontoon. 'Women and children into the caravans and toilet!' shouted a wag among the crew, anxious that the traditions of the sea should be preserved, even in this hour of our undoing.

22

The Vanquished

WITH THE PONTOON abandoned, we took to the sea again in the more conventional method of a separate camera boat, able to manoeuvre at will around the repaired longship. This brought with it the added advantage of shedding the hangers-on for whom there was no room, they being free to enjoy the pleasures of the beach, complete with chairs and 'overnight bags'.

* * *

This seems a good moment as any for me to record my hatred for production chairs and the 'overnight' bags carried by non-combatant members of the unit, whether on location or in the studio. Usually containing sun glasses, reading matter, sun tan oil, Kleenex, artificial sweeteners, bikinis, small towel, personal make-up, an apple or orange and possibly even a small transistor radio, they are scattered at will around the set. Once a claim has been staked to a particular site, it is abandoned with great reluctance and then only under extreme pressure, to give way to a camera or a lamp. I have to admit to a degree of sadistic pleasure when the opportunity is afforded to kick these symbols of my distaste out of the way or when they are crushed beneath the wheels of a hurriedly moved rostrum. On location, the sudden arrival of an unheralded deluge brings equal delight to my heart, twisted as it is by years of battling with this unnecessary litter.

* * *

With the sailing sequences completed, it was back to Belgrade for the studio work, with ten weeks in the Metropole accompanied by the nightly sound of breaking glass.

The object of the Vikings' voyage to Africa was the search for a giant golden bell. Standing some ten feet high, it had been planned to construct it in fibreglass, gilding it by a special process developed at Pinewood Studios. The Yugoslavs' national pride and jealousy of their technical ability prompted them to insist that they could easily make it in their workshops. Detailed drawings were handed over by the art department, who anxiously waited for news of its completion. Each day committee meetings were held with the studio management and representatives of the government ministry, when every single request, no matter how trivial, was discussed at length through interpreters, whose linguistic and technical knowledge left much to be desired. Quite often it would dawn on us that we were in fact discussing two completely unrelated subjects, with good humour and perseverance shown by both sides. The object of these meetings was to monitor progress or more often than not the total lack of it. Construction of the sets was going well, including the Moorish City on the studio lot. Standards of workmanship, though primitive, were extremely high. The largest studio stage was not sound-proofed and had an earth floor. Above hung the most precarious spot rails for the lights, suspended on old and rusty wire cables, dangerous enough to warrant immediate closure of the studio by any factory inspector in England.

From me, they required drawings of all the sets, with details of every lamp, its size and exact position. I explained that the lamps would be constantly moved and anyway, at this juncture, I had no such exact idea of our requirements. 'We must have it,' they insisted. 'The ministry must approve everything. Just make something up, anything, and we can submit it to the authorities.' Beaten by bureaucracy, I spent two evenings drawing little lamps on blue prints of all the sets, making as near a guess as I could as to what we needed. Two weeks later a long report came back, translated into excruciating English, the gist of which was that they didn't have the lamps anyway, or, in the cases where they did have them, they had no bulbs. Each day the subject of the bell was raised, only to receive a stock answer that all was in order. With the day fast approaching when it would be needed for the first time, our art director made a firmer request. 'If it isn't ready, at least I must go and see it to satisfy myself that it is what we want.' 'That is not possible,' replied the interpreter, after a lengthy discussion in Serbo-Croat, 'perhaps tomorrow or the day after.' Tomorrow and the day after came and went, together with several other days, after which, one morning, the question unasked, the interpreter, her face wreathed in smiles, volunteered triumphantly, 'Tomorrow I take you to see your bell.'

As an interested party, concerned as to how the gold finish would photograph, I joined up with the party next morning, setting off in two large cars. After two hours or so we stopped outside a long forbidding wall, too high for us to see what was on the other side. Crowned by barbed wire and fearsome-looking spikes, its façade was broken by just a single door, guarded by two heavily armed soldiers. 'Film crew arrested in Yugoslavia. Denied access to British consul.' The headlines sprang readily to mind. 'Come, we get down,' smiled our guide. 'What about the bell?' persisted John. 'Come, follow me, I show you very soon.' Down long, echoing corridors we trudged, each corner heavily guarded, eventually stopping before a door with a soldier either side.

A sharp knock by our interpreter and we were all inside, facing a well turned out, high ranking officer. 'This the prison commandant,' was her far from reassuring introduction. As we stood in momentary silence, the sound of approaching footsteps could be heard in the corridor, followed by a knock on the door. Into the room stepped a tall, gentle-looking man in late middle age, dressed in prison garb. The commandant rose, offering us each in turn his hand in friendship, while he delivered himself of a short speech. 'He is saying,' translated our guide, 'this is Professor Petravich. He is leading authority on plastics in Yugoslavia. He is serving 20 years sentence for killing wife. He is making your bell here in prison. We go now and see it.' Bidding a relieved farewell to the commandant, we were escorted to where the bell was being made in the prison a perfect, if unorthodox, job.

* * *

Some years ago an acquaintance of mine, a canon in a well known cathedral, volunteered the opinion that the hierarchy with which he had to contend must have been conceived by the Devil himself, so riddled was it with petty jealousies and frustrated ambitions. Human nature being what it is, this accusation could, I am sure, be levelled against any organisation where small groups of people live and work closely together.

A film unit on location is perhaps the classic example of this phenomenon. Living together in a hotel or maybe a specially constructed camp, with more than its fair share of extroverts, some better actors off the screen than on, a destructive delight seems to be taken in other people's failures. There is no better subject for conversation among directors and actors than someone else's bad review. Little enclaves quickly develop with this or that actor as patron, evening conversation fuelled by anecdotes of how someone looked or played in yesterday's rushes. Nobody likes the production manager or the accountant, whose aims in life are economy, and very few like the director who, like the captain of a ship, steers a lonely course amid the surrounding intrigue. Not necessarily of a truly vindictive nature, the gossip makes a not unpleasant alternative to long hours spent waiting in the cold or heat during the day. There is also the question of protocol – who has the larger suite, the bigger bedroom, the more luxurious caravan to while away the tedious hours between shots. At the other end of the spectrum, it is a question of who gets a room with a bath or maybe who is called upon to share. As the location drags on, particularly in the case of a dull or dreary subject or an even duller and drearier director, the various factions become united in a common wish: to get home.

The Long Ships was no exception to this rule. A poor story with a bad script, from the word go it had no chance of being a worthy successor to *The Vikings*. Jack Cardiff, a man full of creative ideas, was for some reason unable to develop them into ways of shooting a scene. Heading the cast were Richard Widmark and Sidney Poitier, both of them wonderful actors and directors in their own right. Convinced, probably quite rightly, that they could make a better job of it, they seized upon this fundamental weakness, playing hell with every rehearsal. News spreads, with the result that the rest of the cast and crew soon shared these feelings although not manifesting them in such an open manner.

A director without contact with his actors, be it on a friendly basis or enforced by strength of character and reputation, is surely a man clutching at straws. I felt sorry for Jack, a friend of many years, who day after day put up with humiliation in front of all the crew.

Even the gentlest of creatures finally turns, this moment coming for Jack after a flaming row with Widmark over a point of direction which I have long since forgotten. Jack took the ultimate action which a director or an actor can take. He walked off the set. Unfortunately, the set he chose to do it on was the largest in the picture, in fact the Moorish City built on the studio 'lot'. Long before his receding figure had passed from view, Widmark and Poitier had taken over, a God-sent opportunity grasped with both hands. Jack retired to the office to speak to his agent in London, a feat in itself with the Yugoslav telephone system. As we continued to shoot with our new directors, rumour spread that he had gone home, in fact was even now at the airport. What transpired, I do not know, but I would guess that he was advised that he was in breach of contract and had better return. His final humiliation was the long walk back, his return heralded by spies from the office who had alerted the whole unit. Somehow he found the courage to go through with it, working his way up via the third and second cameras until he reached the main unit. The incident was never mentioned again but, with little support from the producer, the atmosphere on the picture was never a happy one, the unit being split irrevocably into various factions.

This situation happens all too often for various reasons during the making of a film, reinforcing my belief, mentioned earlier, that a crew's loyalty should be entirely with the director, whose sole responsibility it is to tell the story with the rest of us his willing, if critical, instruments. If a producer is unhappy at the way things are going, unless of course it is a technical criticism, he should settle his differences with the director and not try to solicit support for his point of view from various members of the crew and artists. The next ten weeks of studio shooting passed like an eternity, with endless meetings and the filling-in of forms, most of the requests becoming confused in the process of translation.

When we arrived, the drab city was under a carpet of snow, the sidewalks cleared spasmodically by sad groups of shawl-clad women, who shovelled it into horse-drawn cars. Now it was summer, with unbearable heat, particularly in the studio. The stages had no ventilation, never having been designed for the high levels of light required for colour photography. Food in the canteen was uneatable. Like an army, a film unit's stomach is a matter of prime importance, particularly in times of widespread dejection. It was rumoured that the same caterers were coming with us to Budva and Sveti Stefan, our final locations with the firm intention of ruining what appeared to be a delightful area.

We in the camera department were fortunate, for we had our own transport, including a large truck. Why not do our own catering? We engaged the services of a cook, an elderly and none-too-clean individual who had seen service with the Americans during the war, consequently speaking a better brand of English than any of the interpreters although his culinary ability was an unknown quantity. After a somewhat tenuous beginning, our catering department scaled ever greater heights of gastronomic ingenuity, in the process investing in more and more equipment, including folding tables and chairs and a specially made awning which attached to the side of the camera truck. Each morning the camera car could be seen parked in the open air market, busy about the day's shopping which assumed ever greater importance as the menus became more elaborate. Every item of camera gear not considered vital was dispensed with to make room for our expanding 'kitchen', until it reached the point where our photographic activities were in danger of becoming curtailed. There was nothing for it but to hire another van given over entirely to this new and unexpected side to camera work. The envy of all, vast numbers of dinars were offered for inclusion in our closely-knit little group, all such offers being disdainfully refused.

The studio and all it represented became such an object of hate that my camera operator and I, who travelled together, always took a devious and much longer way to work through a large park, which afforded a brief moment of rural tranquillity and delayed the inevitable start of another unwelcome day with its 'good mornings' in Serbo-Croat, handshakes all round, and even a kiss on both cheeks for good measure. What an admission to make, when most of them were very nice people, trying hard to be friendly. Such are the effects of melancholia and frustration on a normally cheerful nature. Lest the reader might think that this was a situation confined to Yugoslavia, I must hasten to add that I have experienced the same feeling of dejection at the start of a new day when working in the studios in England. With a certain degree of shame, I must admit to taking any measure on arrival to avoid the inevitable 'good-mornings' to people I had no wish to meet, let alone exchange conventional pleasantries with.

23

Yugoslavia revisited

My second venture to Yugoslavia came about 15 years later on a picture called *Force Ten from Navarone*. Like *The Long Ships*, it was a sequel to an earlier and very successful film, in this case *The Guns of Navarone*. The story and script were poor successors to the former picture and several abortive attempts had been made by various people to get it off the ground. Based largely on location, its main requirements were a dam and a bridge across a mountain gorge. It also needed cooperation from the local army, who would be dressed as partisans and members of the German army. We also needed tanks and other military equipment of the Second World War period, all to be painted and marked in German camouflage. Finance played a major part in the decision of where we should go, for once again a complex deal was needed to get the picture started.

Pakistan at that time was anxious to attract international film production, and the government offered everything in the way of facilities, in terms of army and tanks. The mountainous country to the north abounded in bridges and dams, most of them virtually inaccessible, without communications or accommodation for the crew and artists. Logistically the whole thing was ridiculous, but the financial attractions were irresistible to the producers, who brushed all technical considerations aside, to the intense dejection of all those who would have to make it work. This location was only finally abandoned when someone pointed out that Pakistanis didn't look much like Serbo-Croats, and the prospect of making up hundreds of soldiers and partisans each day proved too daunting for our eager, if unrealistic, producers.

So it was to be Yugoslavia once again. A studio in Zagreb offered the usual good deal. Yes, they could supply anything we wanted in the way of lights and generators. Via the ministry, they would get the complete cooperation of the army, who had all the tanks and other equipment we needed of the right period. They had found a bridge and dam in Montenegro, pictures enclosed, which looked just what we wanted. Yugoslavia had changed a great deal since my last visit, with well-stocked shops, cars on the streets, and hotels that worked, at least in Zagreb, but the endless production meetings were the same. In the light of past experience, I had insisted on taking the chief electrician on the reconnaissance with me. The arc lamps were without carbons, the incandescent lamps without bulbs, and the generator, which was not sound-proofed, would only deliver half its rated output. Never mind, as long as we knew, we would bring everything with us, an inevitable decision which brought pain to the producers' faces.

After three days of talking it seemed that we had reached a fair level of mutual understanding. 'Is there anything else needed?' the interpreter asked. 'Yes. Would it be possible to obtain two army searchlights for the night sequence in the dam? It is a huge area to light and they might give a very dramatic effect, sweeping the vast concrete face.' 'How many would you like? They are easy to get, would you like six?' 'No, just two,' I hopefully replied. To end the meeting, discussion then turned to the question of accommodation. The small town of Durmitor was to be our base, several hours' drive from Titograd up a winding mountain road. 'It is being developed as a winter sports centre with a brand new hotel where you can all stay,' was the encouraging response. Lured into a false sense of security, we returned home, all arrangements satisfactorily concluded.

Two months later, after a delayed and very uncomfortable charter flight, we arrived in the gathering dusk in Dubrovnik, there being no night landing facilities at Titograd, our original destination before the delays. 'Too late for travel on the mountain roads,' they said, 'tomorrow we leave early in the morning. All luggage must remain on the plane as it is not arranged for it to land here.' After a pyjama-less and toothbrush-less night, we set out the following morning under lowering skies and in pouring rain on the six-hour drive to our mountain Mecca.

At first sight, Durmitor gave the impression of a First World War photograph of Passchendaele or Ypres. The streets were ankle-deep in mud and slush, the unmade-up surface broken by large water-filled craters tentatively fenced off by odd lengths of wire and rope attached to drunken posts as a doubtful safeguard to unwary pedestrians. The buildings were equally dilapidated, many of them half-finished and showing little sign of any will to complete them. The seediest of all was a large chalet-type building, its entrance approached by a duckboard 'gangway' spanning a huge hole filled with water and accumulated rubbish. Conviction rushed upon me that this was the hotel, an assumption arrived at with bitter experience to draw upon. 'What about the new "resort" hotel?' asked our production manager. 'There have been delays,' was the all-encompassing reply, delivered in a tone which brooked no further questioning. A later inspection of the site revealed that they would be lucky indeed if it were finished within two years!

As a member of the technical hierarchy, I rated a room with a shower and a toilet. The room was devoid of furniture apart from a bed and one chair, no wardrobe or hooks of any sort, the bedding in need of a brisk spin-dry. The shower and toilet consisted of a small bricked-off corner, unpainted, with the walls extending to only half room height. The shower was a wall-mounted electric hot water cylinder, its wiring hanging in dangerous profusion across the room. From the bottom of the cylinder came a short, flexible pipe with a hand spray, the length of which dictated that one had to crouch beneath the low-mounted cylinder, the water alternating between stone cold and boiling hot. The floor of the cubicle sloped casually towards the drain, which was situated in the bedroom, resulting in the worn and dirty carpet becoming increasingly saturated. This unorthodox arrangement was probably devised to encourage strict economy in the use of water, a commodity so abundant in the streets outside. The toilet was of conventional if ancient design, its only shortcoming being that the water tank fell on my unsuspecting head the first time I pulled the handle-less chain. There it hung, on its piece of tired lead pipe, during the eight weeks of our stay, despite all attempts at repair.

Unlike Pula, the rooms had keys, kept in a reception cubicle in the hall, which was presided over by a lady sporting a single tooth and the most overpowering body odour yet encountered by any member of the company.

After several days' experience and careful analysis of the situation it was found that a normal, healthy person could take a deep breath before entering, obtain the room key and get safely out of range before drawing the next breath. However, any delay was fatal, necessitating careful survey of the approaches before taking the plunge. The food I will not dwell on, except to say that it matched the total lack of heating, curtains, or indeed glass in many of the windows. The guardian of the keys, who appeared to keep a 24-hour vigil, albeit in a semi-comatose state, was nicknamed Bella Lugosi, an apt description which stuck for the rest of the location.

The production manager, who had also experienced Yugoslavav catering on a previous occasion, had the great foresight to bring caterers with us from England, descendants in fact of the Hobbs brothers who had done us so well many years before on *Gone to Earth*. They found fresh food in short supply, but armed with a truck full of tinned sausages, bacon and ham, they produced wonderful breakfasts out on the location each morning. Six a.m. calls are never a popular start to the day, yet, such was the loathing for the hotel, that each morning found the crew outside in the cold and dark at least 20 minutes early, waiting for transport and Phil Hobbs' breakfast.

The bridge was some 20 miles away in the mountains. The army were there as promised, the tanks and trucks already in their German markings, the troops camped in a nearby valley out of sight. The searchlights were there too, although I did not want them until the dam sequence, which was to be filmed near Mostar, over 100 miles away. 'We thought it would be safer to have them with us,' they explained. 'Since we have them here, I would like to have a test one evening after dark,' I suggested. 'Unfortunately it is not possible, as the generators are not with them. They have gone direct to Mostar and, anyway, we do not have the experts to work them.'

Two days were spent working out all the scenes, the wardrobe department handing out the German uniforms while other soldiers were designated as partisans and issued with suitable clothing and arms. All seemed set for a perfect start the next morning. The colonel in command thought it all good fun, as did the troops who were being paid as film 'extras'. He threw a party for us that evening in a large tent and everyone had a bit too much slivovitz, helping to lull us into a false sense of security.

The first day's shooting dawned cold and clear. As we stood around the catering truck in the bitter wind eating our breakfast, the tanks and trucks were already lining up according to plan, the exhausts rising like a mist in the first rays of the sun. 'We must get this big master shot of them driving across the bridge while the light is low,' said Guy Hamilton, the director. With cameras in position came the magic word 'Action!' With a shattering roar of revving engines, the long column started to move, the colonel, dressed as a

Wehrmacht General standing in the hatchway of the leading tank. As it made its turn to move onto the bridge, a small figure clad in long raincoat and trilby hat emerged from the trees, ran to the centre of the road with hands held high, and signalled the column to stop. To the accompaniment of frenzied shouting, everything ground to a halt. The figure was surrounded by the Yugoslav assistant directors, interpreters and finally, by the colonel. A protracted and heated argument followed, voices rising in anger and frustration, yet, confronted as he was by the might of the Wehrmacht, our little friend held his ground. 'What the hell's going on?' shouted Guy, who had joined the fray. 'He is the chief engineer for the district. The bridge is his responsibility and his permission has not been asked. Anyway, even if it had been, he could not have given it as it would have to be referred to the Ministry in Belgrade. The bridge was blown up during the war and the plans and details of the repair are lost. He has no idea of the structural strength.'

Three days of argument followed, with numerous abortive phone calls to the Ministry and the manager of the Zagreb studio going in person to seek a solution. In the meantime, we amused ourselves filming odd shots of partisans firing from behind rocks, indeed anything we could get on with which did not involve the bridge. The Belgrade party returned, accompanied by another little man in a long raincoat and trilby hat, a senior engineer from the Ministry, who also did not have the plans of the bridge. He was equally adamant that our armoured column could not drive across. Since this action was the sole reason for our being there, the situation could safely be called an impasse. 'A compromise must be found,' pleaded our desperate producer. 'We can't contemplate looking for an alternative location at this stage.'

Next day, the two engineers convened a meeting outside the catering van to deliver their first and final proposal. We could take one tank at a time onto the bridge, up to a maximum of four, each one to be stationed over one of the supporting pillars, filling in with foot soldiers and trucks once they were in position. A poor alternative to what we had intended, it was a repetition of the *Long Ships* situation, to be overcome by lots of quick cuts to try and give the impression of a moving column.

As the first tank rumbled into position, the whole structure swayed visibly beneath our feet and I was converted wholeheartedly to the little man's point of view.

The next six weeks passed in more or less abject misery, our party variously taking refuge in gambling and drink during the evenings. The boredom was relieved on one occasion by a shooting in the bar, the result of a family feud among the intensely independent locals, whose frustrations appeared to be greater than ours. At last came the move to Mostar and the dam.

A lovely little town of Turkish origin, the hotel overlooked the river which was the main deposit for refuse and sewage, precluding the opening of windows although the temperature was now in the eighties. At least there were some telephones, a matter of some importance to me as my wife was leaving for America at the end of the week. Each day when I came in I booked a call without success until, with Friday my last chance, I placed the call before going out in the morning. 'No trouble,' I was assured, 'as soon as you come in, tell us and all will be arranged.' That evening, I duly reported to the desk, where I was greeted with smiling confidence. 'The call is booked for six, it is not five-fifty. Wait in your room, please, and we will call.' Hopefully I sat by the silent phone as the minutes ticked away, six, six-fifteen, six-thirty, then seven. With the passage of time, my scrutiny of the phone became more detailed. My gaze wandered to the cable beneath the table, where the ends hung disconnected and forlorn. In a paroxysm of rage, I seized the instrument, ran down to the reception, and threw it onto the counter. 'We have been trying to call you,' they said with mild reproval. 'You did not answer and now the call is lost. It is no use you bringing the phone down here, it will not work in the reception area.'

My first concern was with the searchlights on which the success of the night sequence at the dam depended. 'Could I see a demonstration after filming tomorrow?' 'If you come just before it gets dark, all will be ready.' There they were, this time complete with the generators, but, alas, a test was not possible. 'All is complete but we have no fuel. The generators run on petrol and we have only diesel. Tomorrow a supply will be available.' The next two evenings followed the same pattern, only this time they had not been able to get the army operator to run them. On the fourth evening the problem was different. The operator had been found but the generators would not start. In desperation, I asked our maintenance engineer to have a look. He discovered that the searchlights were empty shells, completely devoid of any mechanisms. 'The mechanisms must have been stolen on the way from Durmitor. We sent them by train,' was the unlikely excuse. I finally discovered that they were not army property at all, the Ministry having refused to cooperate in a matter concerning such advanced pieces of technology. They had been unearthed on a dump of old wartime equipment and never checked in any way. With great ingenuity, our chief electrician managed to fit the works from two studio arc-lamps into the cases, resulting in about half the light output I had bargained on, but enough to get by – just.

Our final destination was Rijeka, for the partisan camp sequences. Situated in hills some 20 miles from the town, the approach was by a single track dirt road, not the most accessible place to reach with all our heavy trucks and caravans. Before embarking on this, we had a week of night shooting among the sheds and railway yards of the dock area. As usual, all had been arranged apart from the fact that customs decreed that everything had to be checked against the import lists before we could gain entry, a process which took nearly three hours. 'Yes, it will all have to be unloaded and checked again on the way out.' It was pointed out that we would be working in the dock area for a week, so perhaps we could leave everything inside. 'It is forbidden. We have checked with the Ministry and it is necessary to enter and leave each night.'

With a rare flash of sanity, the producers decided to shift the whole sequence to England. There only remained the partisan camp, where we struggled with rapidly deteriorating weather for three weeks. With two days' shooting left, we woke up to deep snow. On reaching the beginning of the single track road, we were stopped by a distraught Yugoslav assistant who told us that all the heavy trucks, the generators, caravans, catering, and even the honey wagon (film jargon for toilet truck) were stuck in varying degrees of distress, unable to move backwards or forwards and equally unable to turn. 'Nothing can get through,' he said, 'there is even no room to get a tractor past to help pull them out. It may take days. It is best you return to the hotel.'

Sound advice, I thought, which we took with great alacrity. Sitting in the car on the way back to Rijeka, it occurred to me that in all probability this might be the film industry's equivalent to Napoleon's retreat from Moscow. The same thought must have passed through the mind of Guy Hamilton, for he decided to call it a day and return home on the first available flight from Trieste, kindly demanding that I should travel with him.

* * *

This unforeseen retreat brought with it one remaining problem. We had a schedule of just three weeks back home, dictated by various tax problems involving Guy Hamilton, who resided abroad. With the incompleted scenes from Yugoslavia still to be done, it was impossible in the time. There was one extensive night sequence on an airfield involving two Lancaster bombers, in which the partisans and a group of American and British agents were to be flown into Yugoslavia. We would have to find a location outside the tax net, and Jersey in the Channel Islands was the choice. This was not because it had an airfield or any Lancaster bombers, but because it was near, in the sterling area, yet outside UK income tax jurisdiction.

Off we went again on the night ferry from Portsmouth, the car deck packed with resurrected Jeeps, German staff cars and anything else of the period that could be found. Since the scene took place at night, any flat ground would do for the airfield. The Lancasters were to be plywood cut-outs, the rest being up to providence. The only available site was the racecourse, perched near the cliff edge and open to all the winds of heaven. It was January and, sure enough, the winds blew, force seven or eight every night, accompanied by torrential rain. The paint washed off the cut-out aircraft, which, anchored as they were to the ground by various guy wires (all of which showed up in the arc lamps), often blew away during the course of a scene, providing a most unorthodox take-off in the background.

These moments of intense misery are so often relieved by the cockney humour of British crews, ours being no exception. I remember one night standing huddled in the pouring rain while they struggled to replace one of our 'Lancasters'. Our producer, a short, rotund man of indeterminate European origin, stood huddled in many layers of clothing surmounted by a large fur coat, his feet encased in a pair of enormous 'moon boots'. 'Look at 'im, Guv,' observed Pat, our camera grip. 'I reckon 'e 'as to go down to the bloody junction to turn round in that lot.'

24

Stanley Donen

LIKE CARL FOREMAN, Stanley Donen made his home in England for a number of years, though for very different reasons. A close associate of Gene Kelly, he directed his first picture at an incredibly early age, most of his work being in the realm of musicals. He directed or collaborated on a string of successes including *Singing in the Rain* and *Seven Brides for Seven Brothers*, the latter being among the great musicals of all time. Equipped with a highly original mind, coupled with an iron determination, he was dedicated to the making of films with a difference. This ambition, shared by a number of other producer-directors, contains within its philosophy many pitfalls and difficulties. It is never easy to raise money or secure distribution for anything that savours of the unconventional for, in general, the Moguls who control these matters do not number among the most gifted or intellectual members of society. Their minds are firmly fixed on box office statistics which, in fairness, they have to be, together with an obsession for violence and sex which to them are essential ingredients for success.

For many years the 'star' system held sway, statistics theoretically proving that if you had Elizabeth Taylor, etc, in the cast it automatically guaranteed X-million dollars worldwide, irrespective of the script or the quality of the picture. This belief placed unlimited power in the hands of the artists and their agents, who were able to demand astronomical rewards and exercise powers of veto over nearly every aspect of the script, the director and the crew. For a director or producer to hold out against this system, and insist on retaining full control over the picture, required great strength of will and tenacity of purpose. It also brought problems for the cameraman, for as the 'stars' grew older so the diffusion on the lenses grew heavier, the make-up more complex and the wardrobe less revealing. Fortunately this system, a hang-over from the past, has now largely been broken, thanks to a number of really creative people who were willing to risk all in order to get their sort of pictures onto the screen.

Public taste changes overnight, one successful film in no way guaranteeing that a second in the same vein will enjoy the same acclaim. Every picture is a prototype, standing on its two feet artistically, but is judged by the box office returns since, in the final analysis, feature films are commercial undertakings. This harsh judgement is often unfair and wrong in the long term, often aided and abetted by the critics, who may have an axe to grind because of an earlier unfortunate encounter with the director, producer or one of the artists. Be that as it may, the bankers cannot wait for posterity to get their money back, so a flop is a flop. This simplified explanation of the pitfalls has always held good over the years. Experiment always brings with it the risk of failure, a fact that is particularly true of movie making, with inflation driving the cost of a box office flop ever higher. I suppose it could be argued that the ratio of failures among this experimental group was higher than among the more prosaic manufacturers of entertainment, but if one casts one's mind back to what remains of the past, it is names like Frank Capra, John Huston, Billy Wilder, Orson Welles, Powell and Pressburger, etc. who, with their films, remain worth remembering. I would place Stanley Donen firmly among them, and of course there are many others with whom I have not had the good fortune to work.

Stanley's reputation, like Richard Brooks', preceded him to these shores. With boundless energy and a short temper, he was not given to suffering fools, even lightly. His voice, bordering on the strident, was often raised in acute displeasure. He either liked you or he did not, there was no in-between. If you fell in the latter category, you might as well die. Our first meeting was in 1959, when he offered me *Surprise Package*, with Mitzi Gaynor, Yul Brynner and Noel Coward. His manner was direct, the interview over in a matter of minutes. He had seen my work and liked it, the location was on the island of Rhodes, the photography was to be in black and white because he thought it suited the subject best, and my salary would be so much a week. If I didn't like it, I might as well say so now, as he was not in the business of bargaining. If interested, would I go off and read the script, which was not good but he felt could be greatly improved in the making (a fatal supposition, I think, for the end result is usually worse), and call him back. If he hadn't heard within two days he would assume that I did not want to do it. The chance to work with him could not be missed, so of course, with a certain degree of apprehension, I said yes. Reading the script was a mere formality on my part; what mattered to me was the chance to work with someone I had long admired.

So what of the *Surprise Package*? My memories in this case are concise, being limited to three things. The first was my relationship with Stanley. The first week or so was rather like being in the ring with an opponent of greater weight and a longer reach, about whom you knew very little. A great deal of circling around took place, with the occasional jab to the jaw or solar plexus, but never below the belt. I quickly discovered that, like Michael Powell, Stanley thrived on constructive criticism, never holding a grudge because of an opposite opinion to his own. His rages were really expressions of complete exasperation, sparked off by laziness, stupidity and hidebound old theory held by some members of the unit about how things must be done. I felt that in most cases his feelings, if at times forcibly expressed, were fully justified. These first weeks marked the beginning of an association and friendship which lasts to this day, although we have not worked together for some years.

My second memory is of Yul Brynner, not a lovable character, at least in the context in which I knew him. I can see now his vast array of matching black leather luggage, in some strange way as sinister as his bald head, so extensive that two apartments in the small hotel on Rhodes had to be knocked together to accommodate it. His *ménage*, including particularly the luggage, was looked after by an obsequious young man of easily forgettable appearance, who bore the full brunt of his master's displeasure, be it over the luggage or any other shortcoming in the daily routine of living. This displeasure often manifested itself in minor forms of physical violence, borne by the recipient with old-world stoicism befitting a menial in the employ of an ex-King of Siam. On numerous occasions the whole unit witnessed him being booted unceremoniously up the backside, a fitting reward for some minor indiscretion in that far-off kingdom, reigned over so briefly by Mr Brynner in the realms of fiction.

My third and final recollection is the location of the king's palace. A large circular building of red stone, set on the cliff edge overlooking the sparkling blue sea, it was of single-storey construction. The setting was all that mattered, for the interiors would be built back in the studio. The other floors would be added by painted mattes, which would transform the single storey into an imposing building fit for royalty. What this cinematic subterfuge did not reveal was that the palace was in fact situated over a spring, whose waters held magical properties in relation to the movement of the bowels. Here, together with visiting tourists who perhaps suffered from over-indulgence in the gastronomic sense, or maybe even over-exposure to the remains of past Grecian glories, the constipated masses of Rhodes came for gentle relief to their ailment. The efficacy of the treatment was amply illustrated by the fact that the interior consisted of row upon row of toilets, happily disgorging their contents straight into the sea, whose waters lay in wait for the unsuspecting bather from Wolverhampton seeking refuge from the English winter.

I earlier said that I had only three memories, but now I must add a fourth, simply, the sheer pleasure of working with Mitzi Gaynor and Noel Coward. In the case of the latter, I feel it was a perfect example of the fact that when one is privileged to work with outstanding talent, it is invariably accompanied by charm and humility, qualities sorely lacking among many stars set in the cinematic firmament.

Stanley Donen had in many ways become an Anglophile, although he may be reluctant to admit it, fitting in well with the more relaxed relationship between director and crew which has always been a feature in this country. Equipped with a marvellous sense of humour, he was readily accepted by most people, the exception being those who did not come up to his exacting standards of enthusiasm and innovation. He relied exclusively on his initial summing-up of people, those who did not meet with approval being at once cast into limbo, never to find redemption.

His next production was to be *The Grass is Greener*, adapted from the highly successful stage play, the setting a stately home in the English countryside. To be filmed almost entirely in the studio, the co-producer and star was to be Cary Grant, with whom Donen jointly owned Grandon Productions. The cast included Deborah Kerr, Jean Simmons, Robert Mitchum and a host of other excellent artists. The sets were magnificent, based on Syon House and Osterley Park, together with other outstanding examples of English domestic architecture. Most of them were standing ready for shooting to begin, dressed lavishly with genuine antique furniture, tapestries and paintings. Cary Grant had yet to arrive, but his reputation as a consummate actor, past master of comedy, with an uncanny sense of timing in delivery of lines was well known by all. Stanley warned me that there was more than a streak of vanity in his personality. He was greatly concerned over his appearance and the perpetuity of his seemingly eternal youth. This was where I came in, for he had decided ideas about how he should be photographed, most of them based on misconceptions but nevertheless enforceable because of his position. I would have to watch my step and at least make a show of going along with it all. Stanley would give me every support but it would be a tricky situation. Extensive tests were planned, aimed at setting Cary at his ease over how he would look in my hands, and once he was reassured some of the pressure would be off.

The day after his arrival was spent on a tour of all the sets, to put him, as it were, in the picture. Immediately a problem arose. The drawing room where much of the action took place was, he felt, too large. 'But it is faithfully reproduced from Syon House,' explained the art director. 'The whole point of the story is to place the impoverished nobility, living from hand to mouth, against as rich and incongruous a background as possible.' The argument, conducted with calm and dignity, contained a steely inflexibility beneath the affable exterior. It slowly became clear that the objections were not based on a disagreement over the artistic concept of the design but were founded in a more personal concern. He actually thought that the size of the room would deflect people's attention from himself. Of course this was never said in so many words, but it was nevertheless abundantly clear. The problem unresolved, we went our various ways, leaving the matter to be sorted out between Stanley and Cary on a man-to-man basis. Next morning Stanley broke the news that the set had to be reduced in size by at least a third. No mean protagonist in an argument, Stanley had lost hands down. 'We shall have to drag each of the walls in by at least ten feet,' he said. 'But what about the height?' pleaded the art director. 'The set is built of stock flats which cannot be reduced, short of starting again from scratch. The whole proportion of the room will be ruined, changing it from early Adam to late Grant.' 'The lamps will all be at least ten feet too high, the worst possible situation when struggling with an ageing face,' I chimed in. 'I know, I know,' replied Stanley, adding with grim irony, 'it's your problem now. That's why I pay you all that money.'

The next obstacles on the slippery road to destruction were the tests. Cary held a firm conviction that a deeply suntanned face did wonders to remove the traces of approaching age. To this end he sat for several hours a day under a sun lamp, which resulted in a sickly yellow complexion which would not photograph to either his or my advantage. 'Why can't we use make-up to achieve the effect he wants?' I asked. 'Because he doesn't like wearing it,' was the answer, 'in the same way he doesn't like back light.' 'It's going to be a disaster if we don't, Stanley.' 'You talk to him then,' was the sardonic retort.

The film was being made in Technirama, a special wide film process necessitating the use of an optical printer for the 'rushes'. This printer had broken down, so the tests were printed on a standby machine which suffered from an inherent defect. It produced a large yellow circle in the centre of the screen which exactly coincided with Cary's already yellow face. No amount of explanation improved the situation, for Cary's long experience of films did not extend to matters technical. The results of days of tests did little to enhance either his looks or my reputation. Salvation came on the last day when, with the printer repaired, he assumed a more conventional appearance.

The question of backlight, so necessary to obtain separation between artist and background, soon dominated the situation. He could not abide it at any price, holding a firmly entrenched theory that if he turned his head and the light caught his nose it detracted greatly from his appearance. 'But I would never have a lamp in that position,' I assured him, to no avail. His first action, on walking onto the set when ready to shoot, was to look carefully around for the presence of the offending lights, a situation I overcame by having them all put on a separate switch which was turned on as the camera rolled, to be turned off again at the end of the take before he had time to turn around. 'There is only one way I look good and that is in flat front light with a low lamp giving a short nose shadow,' he would explain, somewhat ironically I felt, since he had been instrumental in raising all the lights by ten feet when the set was altered. He also could not abide being in shadow, insisting that, when standing with his back to a window, his face should be lit from the opposite direction to that which nature intended. I would squirm in my seat at rushes when such a shot appeared on the screen, confounding the basic law that light travels in straight lines. I suppose he was right, his large international following preferring to see him clearly lit by a low flat light rather than as part of an artistic effect.

Then there was the story of the green velvet smoking jacket. Some weeks previously we had filmed a long sequence between Cary and Robert Mitchum in the billiard room. Cary wore a green velvet jacket which everyone thought most becoming, or at least those who bothered to think about it at all.

A new scene was upon us where once again he had to wear the jacket. It was part of the plot, having been firmly established in the dialogue, and could not be changed, not that it had occurred to anyone to do so. Arriving on the set he beckoned me over for a quiet chat. 'I don't know whether you are aware of it, but back home in the States I have several times been voted the best dressed man in America.' Rather taken aback, I confessed that I had not been aware of this important news flash, hastily making amends by offering suitable congratulations. 'They have a different attitude towards these things over there,' he continued, 'they will automatically identify me as a "queen". We have to do something about it. Is there any sort of filter you can put over the lens to turn it black or any other colour?' It was on the tip of my tongue to answer that I had nothing in my box that could achieve this unique request without turning him and everything else black or varicoloured at the same time. I wisely resisted the temptation, endeavouring to explain the problem to a very untechnical mind. Convinced, I am sure, of my unwillingness to help, he then approached Stanley with the idea of reshooting the previous sequence, a small matter of some four days' work, but on this occasion Stanley emerged triumphant, his argument based firmly on the bedrock of stern reality.

On another day we were filming an intimate scene between Cary and Deborah, who were seated side by side on a settee. Stanley had chosen a wide-angle lens and a low camera position in order to make the most of the painted ceiling behind them, a situation not much to Cary's liking as it was not favourable to the disguise of any tendency towards multiple chins. Stanley was insistent, and we embarked on the first take. On the word 'action', Cary leant forward, draping his hands over his knees right in the foreground, a position which made them look enormous and out of proportion because of the lens we were using. I cut the camera and asked him if he could put his hands somewhere else. 'What's wrong with my hands?' he asked. 'Nothing at all, Cary. It is just that in that position they will look very big.' I could have added that owing to the effect of the sun-lamp, whose rays did not encompass his hands, they were an odd colour compared to his face. 'What do you want me to do with them then?' he asked. 'Anything you like, anything at all as long as they are not right up close to the lens.' He tried them in his pockets, tucked into his jacket, sitting on them, behind his head, his actions rapidly assuming those of a contortionist. Then he forgot his lines. Take after take, the words or the hands were wrong until, in desperation, the scene was abandoned for the day. I resolved never to mention hands again, even should they assume the proportions of Popeye or indeed any other part of his anatomy.

In the story, Cary and Deborah play the Lord and Lady of the manor, striving to keep things together by showing around visitors, she growing mushrooms in the cellars to augment their income. Temporarily tiring of the humdrum life, she decides to run off for a weekend in London with a visiting American millionaire, while her friend, played by Jean Simmons, moves in with his Lordship. Stanley had the amusing idea of a deceitful telephone conversation between the two couples to be filmed as a split screen shot. In one half would be Deborah and Robert in their London hotel, in the other Cary and Jean back in the drawing room. Each would go through more or less the same actions as they talked, explaining how they were alone and missing each other. Stanley had the clever idea of building the two small sets facing each other so that the two halves could be shot simultaneously, with each pair able to watch and copy the other's action. Deborah, who had gone through the whole production wearing a shabby tweed skirt, twin set and pearls, as befitted her reduced circumstances, thought her promiscuous weekend in London was an opportunity to dress up for once, so she appeared on the set in a smart cocktail dress with diamond necklace and matching earrings.

Rehearsals were a problem from the word go. Cary raised every possible objection to everything that was suggested and also forgot his lines, take after take ending in disaster. So the morning passed in failure as we broke for lunch.

Stanley announced that the scene was being abandoned for the day as there were script problems. Slowly, during the afternoon, the truth leaked out. Cary objected to the diamond necklace, the sparkle attracting attention from the half of the screen occupied by himself and Jean. Deborah refused point blank to take it off, so it was a stalemate. Negotiations continued throughout the afternoon and late into the evening, when Deborah was forced to capitulate.

Next morning she appeared ready to shoot, dressed as before but with the diamond necklace replaced by one made of mushrooms! This delightful sense of humour brought the house down, bringing a whimsical smile to Cary's tanned features. He bore no malice whatever, having won the day.

I do not want to leave the impression that Cary was in any way unpleasant, for this would be very far from the truth. A consummate artist in his own field, he just happened to be the biggest 'old woman' I have ever worked with. He was totally dedicated to the preservation of his own image at all costs, which I suppose is an understandable preoccupation for one in his position, and one certainly shared by many of his contemporaries – often in a far more unpleasant manner.

The other artists were all easy. Bob Mitchum couldn't care less how he looked, never went to rushes and always knew his lines, his main concern being to get on with the job and leave himself free to pursue his other interests in life, whose nature I will leave to conjecture.

* * *

Deborah and Jean were both charming and very professional. Deborah had quite a fund of stories to tell, the two I remember best both concerning Gabriel Pascal. This grotesque eccentric haunted the corridors of Denham Studios during and after the war, claiming Hungarian parentage, which no doubt endeared him to the Kordas, together with a background in the Hungarian Cavalry in whose service he had performed many deeds of heroism, the accounts of which varied considerably with each telling. In moments of grave doubt about the veracity of a given situation, he was much given to calling on his honour as an ex-cavalry officer, which did little to reassure those who knew him well. Addicted to rich living, affordable through the spoils of the numerous expensive and largely unsuccessful pictures over which he had presided, his habit was to lunch in the suite of dressing rooms kept for his use on a large hamper bought from Fortnums each day.

On this occasion he was sprawled as usual on the large couch, surrounded by a meal sufficient for three, his shirt partly unbuttoned to allow room for his generous stomach to spill over the front of his trousers. Usually unshaven, his breath as foul as his language which he delivered in excruciating English, he was not a lovely sight. A number of singers were to be auditioned for a small part in his current production. The first frightened creature was ushered into the room, where he stood without recognition for several minutes while Pascal continued eating. Without looking up he demanded, 'Vy do you not sing to me?' 'Would it be possible for me to have a piano, Mr Pascal?' asked the unfortunate victim. 'Vy do you vant a piano, do you sing or do you play? I vant a singer, if you sing then sing to me now.' Faced with this uncompromising approach, the shivering wretch embarked on a few tentative and quavering bars while Pascal consumed a large leg of chicken. Suddenly halting the recital with a wave of the chicken bone, he turned to his assistant and said, 'Take 'im away, 'e is 'orrible.' What happened to the other aspirants queuing in the corridor is not recorded.

The second anecdote, this time first hand, concerned a tea party Deborah was attending at a friend's smart London house. In the midst of the genteel proceedings, Pascal strode into the room in his usual dishevelled state, helping himself to a large slice of walnut cake on the way to greet his hostess. 'Just vat I vant, just vat I vant, I am dying for a cup of tea,' he greeted her. The small daughter of the house ran crying to the protection of her mother's arms, sobbing, 'Please don't give him any, Mummy! Let him die!'

25

Pasta and Chianti

SOME YEARS AFTER we had finished *The Grass is Greener*, I had a call from Stanley, who asked me to go down and see him at his country house in Berkshire. For reasons which I never fully understood, he was committed to making *Arabesque*. The script had proved a problem, several re-writes failing to overcome its inherent weaknesses. Sophia Loren and Gregory Peck were contracted to do it, so the show had to go on. 'Our only hope is to make it so visually exciting the audience will never have time to work out what the hell is going on,' was Stanley's opening gambit. 'Go away and read it. See what you can come up with. I want every shot to be different.' The time coincided with the perfection of Panavision zoom lenses, reflex cameras, and various advances in lighting equipment which opened up a whole new range of photographic possibilities.

Stanley was in his element, his quick and creative mind full of ideas about reflections. It seemed at times that the whole picture was to be seen in the backs of teaspoons, car mirrors or through tanks of fish. More often than not, the camera was pointing away from the actors, apparently dwelling in close-up on the polished back of a car licence holder in which the scene was mirrored. This unorthodox approach imposed severe restrictions on the artists, who had to hit very exact marks. Sophia found no difficulty at all in grasping what we were trying to do. She always took a look through the camera with her stand-in on her marks so that she knew exactly what the shot was and how big she would appear on screen, while at the same time making certain that the lighting was to her best advantage. An extremely intelligent woman, speaking several languages fluently, she was a cameraman's dream, cooperating to the full in everything because she understood perfectly the sort of lighting that made her look at her best. I had no worries whatever, for she looked wonderful, her only weakness being a rather large nose, which if caught in profile could prove a minor imperfection. She, of coure, was aware of this more than anybody, taking care never to be caught in that position. A professional to her fingertips, she was always on the studio floor, dressed and made-up, at least a quarter of an hour before her call, and there she stayed all day, watching and waiting, the scene gone over a dozen times, the dialogue perfectly memorised.

Possessed of a lovely sense of humour, she was a thoroughly nice person, mixing with and talking to everyone on the floor. In no time at all she knew everyone's name, whether they were married, what children they had, never failing to enquire should anyone be ill. Wisely shunning studio food, she or her secretary cooked lunch in her dressing room, invariably asking one or two of us to join her over delicious pasta with a glass of Chianti. If this sounds rather like a eulogy, then I have succeeded in my intent. Of course one can only form opinions within the context of one's own experience, which for me was limited to this one picture, but it was certainly an opinion shared by all the crew, or at least all the male members of it. Who knows? Perhaps we were all in love with her!

Gregory Peck, the same quiet, gentlemanly self off the screen as on, did not find the going so easy. At times I am sure he thought us all mad, with our strange camera angles and effects, but he bore it all with dignity and patience.

* * *

There existed a convention as old as movies themselves that if you were filming a dialogue scene in a car then the camera must appear to be inside with the actors. It would be illogical to shoot through the windscreen or the windows, for how could you possibly hear what they were saying inside? As there was rarely room for the camera in the vehicle, the windscreen glass was removed and the windows taken out, yet still there were problems with the body-work which gave the game away. Special mock-ups built to get the desired angle, usually filmed against a back projection screen. 'Why can't we shoot through the windscreen?' asked Stanley. 'I like all the reflections passing across the faces. I don't even mind if they blot the actors out from time to time.' I could not have agreed more with these heretical words, fiercely resisted by the people in special effects who had been doing it their way since the beginning of time. 'I like the idea, Stanley, but we are in a studio. We can't reflect the roof and all the lamps. A windscreen is curved and the area reflected is enormous, and anyway, the car isn't moving.' 'We will have to go out and shoot a lot more moving plates from the right angles, then we can set up back-projection screens all round and above the car to cover the reflections,' answered Stanley, quite undaunted by the prospect of a delay now that he had been smitten with the idea. After a lot of tests we achieved very good results, particularly with the night sequences, for which I rigged up dozens of small coloured lights on a giant sort of Catherine wheel to add to the effects already on the background plate. I have gone to the length of describing what may seem a rather dreary episode to those readers anxious for scandal, because I believe it to have been the first time anyone tried it. Now, as witnessed everyday on television, it has become accepted practice.

* * *

Seated side by side on the roof of a stable block, part of a large estate in the Midlands, Stanley and I gazed down on the vast array of cars, trucks, generators, caravans, and the 200 or so people who made up our unit. It was cold and it was raining. Once more we were waiting for just a glimpse of the sun to complete the last shots of *Arabesque*. The crowd around the catering truck grew as tea time approached, only a small proportion of it concerned with the delay. 'Look at them all,' complained Stanley, 'we don't need half of them anyway. Just a lot of hangers-on who couldn't care a damn about the picture or what we are trying to do. I am going to let you into a secret, Chris. My next picture is about just two people making the same journey across France by car at three different periods in their married life. All we need are the two actors and the three cars. We will take the smallest possible crew, just you and me with an Arriflex hand camera. We will cross France in our own time, filming as we go, stopping when we see locations that look good.'

Stanley had been much impressed by a number of low budget pictures he had seen of late, made very much in this manner, and he felt that this was the opportunity to rid himself of the encumbrances of an unwieldy film unit. This was, I am sure, the expression of a deep-seated yearning, shared by most directors at one time or another, to rid themselves of the unwanted hordes thrust upon them by unions, management, and the artists themselves, who insisted on caravans, personal transport, preferably in the Cadillac or Rolls-Royce bracket, accompanied by their own wardrobe, make-up and hairdressing people, who form part of a close-knit entourage. This dream of unencumbered freedom can of course be realised, but the story has to be right, with the artists young, unestablished and willing to look on the screen more or less as they do in real life, thereby doing away with the need for lights and generators. Unknown actors are never a favourite with distributors or the people who put up the money, and even the name of a successful director is rarely enough to swing the balance.

'It sounds a wonderful idea,' I replied, my imagination immediately conjuring up visions of three months' gentle driving through the Loire Valley, Burgundy and the Auvergne, digressing from the direct route in search of food and wine, with the occasional halt to film the perfect location in order to justify our existence on the progress reports, and so to St Tropez, our final destination with a few days' welcome rest on the beach. 'Who will you have in the picture?' I asked. 'Audrey Hepburn and Albert Finney . . . Eleanor Bron, together with a lot of smaller parts, some of which we may cast locally,' was the reply. After a period of reflection, I replied, 'I'll tell you what, Stanley. I'll have a little wager with you that the unit will number at least 150.' 'No, it won't, I just won't let it happen to me this time,' he almost pleaded, with perhaps the faintest trace of doubt in his voice. I hasten to make it clear that my opinion was not formed because I foresaw problems with Audrey Hepburn or Albert Finney, two of the nicest people one could wish to work with, but because I knew that this sort of cheap picture, cutting every corner because of expense, was certainly not Stanley's cup of tea.

* * *

Four months later, Stanley and I sat side by side on a camera box, a groundsheet wrapped around us to ward off the rain. We were in the middle of a field of rape on the outskirts of Paris, the straight road behind us jammed with our 'caravan' of trucks, generators, catering, honey wagons, etc. The unit numbered 182, and we were filming *Two for the Road*.

'What about our bet?' I asked, to relieve the air of general depression. His reply was a wan smile, and I never did get the money. The idea of driving across France had been abandoned as totally impractical, thank God. Instead we would work on a daily basis from Paris, moving to St Tropez for the second half. A six o'clock call each morning, then a battle with the rush hour traffic to the location, different almost every day, ended in another traffic saga on the way back, followed by rushes in a cinema in the Champs Elysées. It would be a lucky day if we were back in our accommodation by ten, so, you see, movie making isn't all that it might be imagined. This was of course for six days a week, or even seven when we got behind, which was always. For the artists it was worse, for they mostly had an hour or so in make-up and hairdressing before we even started.

With literally hundreds of shots of the two of them driving in the three cars, it had been decided to develop the technique we had worked out on *Arabesque*. As no suitable back-projection equipment existed in France, the whole lot was to come from England, a whole trainload of it, in fact, complete with its 'minders', the dreaded process department whom Stanley heartily loathed. Once again waiting in the rain, our thoughts turned to their impending arrival. I broke our dejected reverie with, 'Stanley, I've been thinking. Why don't I shoot a test on the real car? We could fix a camera on the bonnet together with two or three battery-operated quartz lamps and see what it looks like.'

In no time at all the bonnet was off, replaced by a sheet of plywood onto which was screwed the camera and lights. With the tape recorder and all the batteries in the boot, we were ready. Of course there was no way to know what we were shooting, or how the much-admired reflections would work out until we saw the scene next day. 'I think it's a great idea, do you really think it can work?' asked Stanley, already caught up with enthusiasm and spurred on by the thought of getting rid of the process department. 'As long as you don't mind waiting until the following day to know what we have shot, yes, I am sure it will. We are bound to get some failures, but I am certain we can do it.' Never a man to hesitate over a decision, Stanley straight away sent off a cable cancelling the projection equipment and, with a sense of relief coupled with a feeling of careless abandon, the die was cast.

The test proved a great success, so we set to work making all kinds of brackets and platforms to fit to the three cars in order to fix cameras and lights in almost any position. It was all very rough and ready, planks of wood, boxes, wedges, fixed to the cars with clamps and rope lashings. When ready for a take, the car presented an extraordinary appearance. As nobody could travel with them, Albert Finney had to switch on the camera, then the lights, followed by the tape recorder, put in the dash board, announce the scene number, get everything out of sight, then set off down the road and start to act! It was all rather a laugh to watch, Albert adding caustic comment of his own on the sound track before the scene started, which was of course heard by everyone next evening. This usually took the form of, 'That bum director is never here when we shoot. I have to do the lot – direct, act, light and photograph, as well as record the sound – and they'll get all the credit.' I came in for the same sort of comment, as did the sound recordist. As we progressed and became more adventurous, so did the fittings on the cars multiply, the weight increasing until they were well down on their springs.

Whenever possible, Stanley and I would attempt to watch as much of the scene as possible through the field glasses or run beside the car, usually falling over each other and landing in the first ditch. Whenever the car took a bend which would bring us into the shot, we would dodge behind a tree or go flat on our faces in the mud, shouting at passing motorists not to look at the camera, our hysterical voices unheard but giving a fair impression of two escaped lunatics to any unsuspecting onlooker who might be around. Albert and Audrey took everything in good part, the end result being very successful. I think it would be fair to say that it marked a turning point in photographing things for 'real', at last getting away from the artificial look of most process work. We could never have done it without their cooperation, leaving me with the fondest memories of them both.

I particularly admire Albert, for with the world at his feet as a young actor, he chose to reject vast financial rewards in favour of doing the things he wanted to do, returning to lowly-paid work in the theatre when he believed it was really worthwhile. Most of the car 'shots' had to be repeated three times, once in each of the three cars which were identified with three different periods of their lives. The first scene completed, all our Heath Robinson equipment had to be transferred to the next car and the wardrobe and make-up changed, so progress was slow. Rushes were always an exciting revelation, as we could never look through the camera during a take; a big risk, you might think, but the sort of challenge that was the spice of life to Stanley.

Working with an all-French crew was a great experience, and posed little difficulty for me as I happen to be half French, at least as far as communication went. Stanley, too, liked working in France but there were certain aspects of the native working habits which drove him mad. As far as the unions were concerned, you could start early and finish late and even work seven days a week. It was just a question of money for, like the Americans, they all went into 'golden hours' and were willing to sacrifice sleep, home life, indeed all social contact for the sake of art, and money. However, being more civilized than ourselves, lunch was sacrosanct. It had to be an hour from the time they sat down, to be provided by the company, and not an affair of greasy pies and chips and soggy rice pudding. Each day a suitable site would be found by the caterers where tables were set under umbrellas or trees, when available, complete with white cloths. The meal would always be of several courses with wine *ad lib*, all followed by proper coffee.

The moment we broke, Stanley would jump into his waiting car, dragging me after him. The first to arrive at the 'picnic', he would grab some cheese and a bunch of grapes, saying he wasn't really hungry, and daring me to feel otherwise. We were already back in the car and on our way to the shooting site as the first members of the crew made their leisurely and individual way to the feast. All I had to remember lunch by was the delicious aromas which we took back with us, trapped in the interior of the car. Leaping out as he bolted the last of the grapes, Stanley would look at his watch and pace up and down like a caged lion for the next hour and a half, voicing his discontent with this criminal waste of time, his displeasure growing as the minutes passed until it encompassed the Republic in all its aspects, particularly the bit about 'Egalité'. Vainly did I reason with him, but he was not to be denied his daily *tour de force*. I, meanwhile, grew wiser, and arranged for a meal to be brought by sleight of hand, to be consumed surreptitiously, like an old lag in the army smoking on parade.

At last the 'around Paris' locations were completed and there remained the glittering prize of the sequences in St Tropez. It would be warm, with little or no travelling, and maybe even a chance to sit down in a restaurant for lunch. Well, it rained and blew a gale for two days, the charming little streets running in water and rubbish, the gay awnings on the harbourside cafés torn and flapping in the wind. The rich had repaired to their villas and yachts, the Mediterranean magic had evaporated and the town looked like Wolverhampton on a wet Sunday in November.

Stanley, no newcomer to these situations, combed the script for a sequence, scheduled for the studio, that we could do inside somewhere. 'There's this short scene where Albert and Audrey are in bed in this tiny hotel somewhere on their way across France. We should be able to find someone willing to rent us an apartment.' The art department, accompanied by a harassed production manager, set out on their quest and settled on a flat on the sixth floor of a modern block at the back of town. 'All wrong for period,' said the art director, 'but we can scout around for bits of furniture, curtains, etc, and redress the whole thing.' In a matter of hours everything had been found, all from private homes and much of it, I suspect, at gunpoint or by bribery. As if by magic, the rather nasty bedroom was transformed into a little corner of the 'Midi'. The owner's furniture was all out in the corridor but the location, being six floors up, was virtually impossible to reach. Lamps were lugged up, followed by the camera gear and sound equipment, until we had created a little studio.

One problem remained. The script described the scene in great detail. As they lay in bed, the light from passing cars filtered through the net curtains, passing over their faces. To get the lamps far enough back to shine through the window meant building a tubular tower six storeys high, and the whole platform thus created would have to be covered with a blackout to shut off all daylight. 'No problem, guv', said our cockney rigger, 'we can work-on tonight and it will be ready first thing'. The production manager winced at the thought of the overtime which was no doubt behind the riggers' compliance, but he kept his own counsel. 'Why don't we shoot it at night?' suggested someone. 'Because the whole silly bloody idea is to have something to do during the day,' hissed the production manager, who had visions of the whole crew on double time, with a rest day before and another afterwards.

The morning dawned, or rather it failed to do so, for the rain still fell and the wind howled, but the tower was up and we could shoot.

Bit by bit, we removed the art department's cherished period furniture as we struggled to get the essential camera gear and lights into the room, until eventually we were left with little else but the huge Provençal bed. 'I must have a high camera for the main dialogue. It's an awful angle if we shoot up their noses on what is meant to be an intimate love scene,' said Stanley, and of course he was absolutely right. The problem was that there was no way of getting the camera into the confined space. With only room for three or four people in the room at a time, Stanley went and sat on the floor in the corridor as we tried one permutation after another. Bit by bit we dismantled the bed, and suddenly the solution was revealed to me. If we stood the bed on end and took the feet off, the artists could stand and we could hold the bedclothes in place with nylon thread and adhesive tape. I went outside and broke the news to Stanley, who was squatting with head in hands, amid the debris of plastic cups and half-eaten cheese rolls. 'OK, I guess it's the only way', was the resigned reply. We were interrupted by the assistant director, out of breath after six flights of stone steps. 'Just to let you know, Mr Donen,' he said in his brightest voice, 'the weather's completely cleared up.' With dark murder in his soul, Stanley answered very simply, 'Thank you.'

With the die cast, we struggled through the scene, the temperature in the room reaching into the hundreds, desperately covering the gaps in the blackout through which the sun now streamed, as Audrey and Albert gamely stood in bed and murmured sweet nothings to each other, the car headlights caressing their faces as the sweating electrician out on the platform swung his lamp to my cue.

26

Back in Paris

BACK TOGETHER AGAIN in Paris a couple of years later, this time for *Staircase*, adapted from the successful West End play by Charles Dyer, which had starred Paul Scofield, we were to have Richard Burton and Rex Harrison. Set in the East End of London, the story centred on two homosexual barbers. Ideally suited to be shot on location in the real place, it might occur to you that Paris was an unlikely venue and, in so thinking, you would be right. The reasons for this strange decision were numerous and complicated, taken in the rarefied atmosphere in which financiers and distributors dwell, their reasoning often totally unrelated to the reality of shooting the picture. Since I was not a party to such high level discussions, I have no clear idea of what happened, but certainly the fact that Richard Burton refused to make the picture in England was an overriding factor. At the time he was heavily involved with one of his marriages to Elizabeth Taylor, who was also making a film in Paris, a fact which even to my uncomplicated mind savoured of more than a mere coincidence.

A large London street complex was built on a disused building site, complete with a church, shops, pubs, even a public lavatory, with the barber's shop in pride of place. Everything had to come from England; cars, trucks, buses, every single piece of dressing. The French art director was immensely proud of his creation, faithful in every detail down to the red post boxes with already a population of stray dogs and cats in residence. All was perfect apart from one limitation. We had to exercise care not to pan the camera too high, or into the background would come an elevated section of the Metro together with a distant view of the Eiffel Tower.

We were scheduled to work what are euphemistically known as 'French hours', which entailed starting at midday and working straight through until eight at night without a break. With the introduction of a five-day week, this system had been further modified, the starting time being brought forward to eleven a.m. I had to be in the studio at least an hour before the start, which meant an unbroken day of nine hours, with rushes to view at the end.

By the time we had worked out a scene and rehearsed it, I and my crew were always left with the lighting to do, during what would have been lunch time in a sane world. Everyone else seemed to get away, including most of the electricians, who split forces at this critical time. The restaurant was always full of people who were not so indispensable, it seemed, as they would have you believe when negotiating their contracts. The artists, of course, could always have food served in their dressing rooms or during make-up, which in the case of Richard Burton was a minor misfortune as it usually took a liquid rather than solid form. He had problems with drink as he had with marriage and they seemed to manifest themselves at more or less the same frequency, resulting in afternoons of relative incoherence just when we were supposed to be working at maximum efficiency. This was the second occasion that I had worked with Richard, both of them during the latter part of his career. I felt deeply sorry for him, for I admired him greatly as an actor with that wonderful voice and unique ability to deliver lines. He seemed to have prostituted these great natural gifts for the sake of huge financial rewards, marching slowly but inexorably towards a tragic end. He had little contact with the crew, rarely pausing to exchange the briefest of pleasantries.

On *Staircase*, his *bête noire* was a pair of felt carpet slippers which he had to wear in many of the scenes. For some reason he took great exception to them, going to any lengths to avoid wearing them. First thing in the morning, usually half an hour late, he would walk onto the set dressed in a three-quarter length mink jacket, a present from Elizabeth, still rubbing sleep from his eyes. 'Freddie,' he would call across to the camera operator, busy lining up the first shot, which in his absence we were rehearsing with the stand-in, 'are my feet in?' This appeared to be his main concern, the question his only contact with us for days. Freddie, with his ready wit, quickly learned to have his answer ready before the question was asked. As soon as Richard appeared he would call across the stage, 'Good morning, Richard. Your feet are in.'

Surrounded by a large retinue of hangers-on, including a huge black man who we assumed to be a bodyguard, his Welshness seemed to increase in importance to him as his way of life cut him off both spiritually and physically from the land of his birth. Being a free agent, he could have returned to it at any time had his expressed longings been genuine enough to overcome his love of wealth and all that it could buy. Perhaps, unless one has been subjected to the same temptations, it is unfair to comment, but I find the urge irresistible. The saddest manifestation of this pride in his origins was his large, black Rolls-Royce, a red dragon emblazoned on each of the front doors, with the chauffeur dressed in a dark blue blazer, on the breast pocket of which was embroidered yet another dragon, occupying every inch of available space. A small man of swarthy appearance, the final irony for me was that being, I believe, a Basque, his English was minimal and his Welsh not at all.

I had always rather envied the French their National Film School, offering degree courses in almost every aspect of film making – that is, until I met up with the end product at first hand. We had four or five of them allocated to our production in various capacities, their day usually spent in discussing the early French and Russian cinema, or the finer cinematic points of *The Battleship Potemkin*, usually in front of the camera when we were trying to light, and always in the way. One of them was the third camera assistant, whose duties would have been to load the magazines, had he been able to. This lowly task, fundamental to the success of photography, apparently did not feature on the syllabus of the Academy. Neither did the gentle art of learning to be first in the tea queue, a basic requirement of every aspirant to the title of Director of Photography in the more practical world in which I grew up. One day, under pressure, with a difficult scene to light, the non-existent lunch hour was upon us. Our group of graduates all managed to find the time to get over to the restaurant, so Freddie asked Michael if he would mind bringing us some sandwiches and a couple of bottles of beer. 'No, I cannot. I am a technician, not a waiter,' was his reply. This debatable fact ceased to hold true as far as our picture was concerned from eight o'clock that evening, the only occasion in my whole career when I have felt truly justified in getting rid of anybody.

Elizabeth Taylor's film was based at the nearby Billancourt Studios, where a suite of dressing rooms had been knocked together to house her retinue, considerably larger in size than Burton's. They were both much given to entertaining the higher echelons of society, throwing elaborate luncheon parties which were not catered for in the schedules of either picture. On one very special day they were to entertain the Duke and Duchess of Windsor, together with Maria Callas. Stanley Donen and Rex Harrison were of course invited, while we were left to set up and light the next scene in readiness for their return. This would ensure that time was not wasted during their absence, while we would be gainfully employed during the non-existent lunch break. By a strange quirk of fate, the scene happened to be one with Richard and Rex in bed together, a situation which Rex found very distasteful. He fought hard to get it taken out of the script, unsuccessfully as it turned out because it was fundamental to the story. After much discussion, Stanley devised a complicated way of shooting it which would overcome some of the more obvious objections. To get the shot, we built a bridge across the bed consisting of a plank of wood supported at either end by a pile of boxes. A miniature railway was then added, consisting of a small platform for the camera, running on furniture castors so that the lens could be kept as low as possible. This makeshift arrangement took two or three hours to complete, while all the time I expected them to return, only to find us still fiddling about.

At last all was ready, so we tried a couple of rehearsals, the camera tracking across the bed with Freddie, the camera operator, sitting on another little platform also running on castors, so that he could look through the camera. It all worked perfectly in spite of its ludicrous appearance. Still we had no director or actors. The minutes ticked away as the pangs of hunger increased, yet we dare not slip away in case they made a sudden, unheralded appearance.

Four o'clock came with the sound of animated conversation, accompanied by high-pitched laughter. Onto the floor stepped a very unsteady Richard Burton, who had drunk a rather better lunch than the others, followed by a rebellious Rex. To everyone's consternation, Stanley ushered in the Duke and Duchess followed by Maria Callas and Elizabeth Taylor. They had all decided it would be fun to come over and watch us at work! Chairs were hurriedly found for them in the hastily arranged 'stalls' as they settled down to watch the professionals at work. Richard had meanwhile climbed into bed, unabashed, probably feeling there was no better place in his condition. For Rex it was utter humiliation. His least favourite scene was to be enacted before the eyes of the most famous uncrowned heads in Europe.

After a few pleading words with Stanley, he too got into bed, keeping as much space as possible between himself and his now dozing bedfellow. 'We won't rehearse, we'll shoot right away,' said Stanley, in slightly muffled tones, hoping to get the exercise over as soon as possible. 'Turn over and . . . action!' The camera started on its track, but Richard, by now possibly asleep, forgot his lines. These were to be the cue for the camera grip pulling the camera, who was left nonplussed. Freddie hissed a new instruction to him, hoping to save the day, but in his moment of confused uncertainty he kicked the boxes at one end of the plank, bringing the ingenious little 'via bed' down in ruins, with Freddie and the camera thrown in between the actors. Rex jumped out of bed and swept off the floor in high dudgeon, presented with the perfect excuse for seeking the seclusion of his dressing room and avoiding further humiliation. The irrepressible Freddie, from his position beside the unruffled form of Richard, turned quick as a flash towards the startled Duke, reassuring him with a broad smile, 'Don't worry, your Grace, we'll get it!'

One morning we arrived at the studio to be greeted by a worried production manager. Richard Burton could not be found, nor indeed any of his entourage. The cars had called for them but they were not in the hotel. Then came an agitated call from Billancourt. Did we know what had happened to Elizabeth? She was missing with her minions and perhaps she might be with us? As the day wore on, the story slowly pieced itself together. A relative of Elizabeth's was ill in America. The Burtons had one and all folded their 'tents' and, like the Arabs before them, stolen off into the night, their departure in a specially chartered aircraft unheralded to either of the productions eagerly awaiting their arrival on set. A week or so elapsed before they returned, during which time we could do nothing.

Not a particularly happy picture to work on, it finally ground to a halt and was consigned to oblivion by the critics and public alike, a fate shared by so many other productions. We tried hard to make a go of it, but it lacked the vital spark which transcends problems along the way.

27

The Little Prince

MY NEXT, AND sadly last, picture with Stanley was *The Little Prince*, adapted by Alan Jay Lerner from the allegorical fairy story by Antoine de Saint-Exupéry, written for his son. It was to be shot as a musical, the lyrics and music by Lerner and Loewe. The book was based on Saint-Exupéry's experiences when he crashed his 'plane in the Sahara, suffering hallucinations caused by heat and thirst. They took the form of a visitation by a small child, a Little Prince from another planet, into whose mouth Saint-Exupéry put the wisdom of eternity. More than half the film took place around the crashed aircraft, both by day and night. The night scenes we would shoot in the studio, using the new front-projection process. This made possible the vast backgrounds, together with the ability to create the effect of moonlight, with a star-studded sky, something we could not possibly achieve on location. The day scenes would all be done in the desert.

I had numerous discussions with Stanley on the telephone in between his many trips to the States in connection with the script, but whenever I brought up the question of a contract and money, I met with a stony silence. Finally, a call came from the production manager. Could I come to Elstree the next morning at 10.30 for a meeting? I was greeted by him with the warning, 'You're going to have trouble over the money bit. He is digging his heels in with everyone. I'm afraid it's a take it or leave it situation.'

Stanley arrived just before one o'clock. 'Hi, Chris, nice of you to come. I have to rush straight back to town. Why don't you come with me and we can talk about things on the way?' I had not seen him for some months, during which time his appearance had undergone a dramatic change. He sported a long black beard, his tall figure enveloped in a black cloak which reached almost to the ground, which immediately brought to mind, or at least *my* mind, an image of 'The Wandering Jew'. Perhaps, I thought, he is already acclimatising himself for a long sojourn in the desert. Off we set in the back of his chauffeur-driven Rolls, while his conversation ranged far and wide over all his ideas for the picture with not an opportunity to bring up the sordid question of salary, so dear to my materialistic mind and the upkeep of my family. As we were approaching the West End, he suddenly turned to me and said, 'I have to stop and look at something I've ordered. Come in with me and see it.' We stopped outside a large shop specialising in architects' equipment where we were ushered into an upper floor showroom in which was displayed an elaborate drawing board capable of being angled to any position hydraulically, the very latest from Sweden, costing several thousand pounds. After a comprehensive display of all its virtues, we were back in the car once again. 'What do you think of it, isn't it great?' asked Stanley. 'I imagine it's wonderful, but what's it for?' 'It's for me,' he replied, 'I am going to use it as a desk in the study of my new house in Montpelier Square. Stanley Kubrick has one. I think it will look great in the room.' Here was my long awaited opportunity. 'I think it will too, Stanley, but I also think if you can afford to buy that to write letters on, you can afford to pay me my money.' Turning to me, with a wry grin beneath his beard, he said, 'All right, you bastard, you win. I'll drop you off at the nearest underground.' Deposited unceremoniously but victoriously outside Marble Arch, I was left with the unpleasant reality of a train journey back to Elstree to collect my car.

Several months earlier, a stills photographer had been dispatched to Algeria in a Range Rover to conduct an exhaustive search for suitable locations, returning after eight weeks or more with a wonderful collection of pictures. The rolling sand dunes looked just as I imagined they would be, with memories of my childhood and *Beau Geste*. There were several alternatives, all of them good, so the choice was not easy. Lengthy discussions went on, arguing the pros and cons from our several points of view. Suddenly all was changed; Algeria was out and, instead, we would be going to Tunisia. The political situation in Algeria was unstable to such a degree that the insurance companies were refusing to give cover to the artists and crew. Accommodation and communications were also primitive, posing problems with the large number of people who go to make up a film crew. Tozeur was to be our photographic Mecca and contained all that we wanted – a large oasis and nearby desert, with the added bonus of a modern hotel at Nefta, the next village, built on the lines of a Hilton as a tourist attraction to open up the hinterland. Complete with swimming pool and air conditioning, it was too good to be true. Stanley had recently married a very beautiful actress named Yvette Mimieux, American, but of French extraction. Because of the pressures on him during the period of intense preparation, there had been no time for any sort of honeymoon, a fact which could have tipped the balance in favour of Tozeur, as his wife was to come with us and share the joys of the location.

The heavy equipment was assembled to be shipped by sea, having driven overland across France; the generator and trucks containing the lights, a low-loader with the aircraft aboard, prop van and catering truck, construction vans, in fact the usual film caravan. In addition there was to be a helicopter with a special stabilised camera mount, which had caught Stanley's eye as it opened up the possibility of fast tracking shots across the desert, quite impossible with a normal car on the uneven surface. We followed two weeks later by air, all meeting up in Bizerta, which stands by the remains of ancient Carthage. Nine hours' drive away lay Tozeur, a hair-raising experience as the good coastal road rapidly deteriorated into a dusty track, frequently torn asunder by water courses swollen by recent rains.

Arab drivers throughout the world share a common death wish, always travelling flat out with never enough petrol to reach the next filling station and equally happy on whichever side of the road appears momentarily to be the most advantageous. Ours were no exception, so with the prospect of his marriage being terminated abruptly in the wastes of North Africa, Stanley decided that he and I would share the driving, leaving someone to share the back seat with our driver, whose heavy perfume did little to disguise the underlying smell of garlic and sweat which grew stronger with the ascent of the sun. The sensible orders were to keep together as a convoy, which of course reduced the speed of our progress, but at last, after nine hours of misery, the village of Tozeur was in sight. The dusty street was bedecked with strings of artificial flowers and electric light bulbs, strung up on makeshift poles across the road, not, it was explained, to welcome our arrival, but because President Bourgiba was arriving in two days' time on a ceremonial visit.

Slowly we drove through the village, followed by crowds of children and hordes of barking dogs. The generator, our largest vehicle, which brought up the rear, neatly removed the decorated posts as it passed on its way, for the planners had not envisaged anything of its size in their calculations. Immediately we were involved in a minor international incident, the solution to which was left in the hands of the production manager, who spoke not a word of the language. On through the gathering dusk we drove to Nefta and the comfort of the hotel, whose ugly yet familiar outlines appeared on the horizon.

The hotel's construction had been heavily subsidised, we were informed, by the Tunisian Milk Marketing Board, which seemed to me an odd alliance since the one commodity virtually unobtainable in Tunisia was milk. Yet there it was in the middle of nowhere, identical in most respects to the rash of international hotels which have sprung up all over the world, offering the same food, the same bedside chocolate to succour the weary traveller. The rooms were large and hideously furnished, with an air conditioning and heating unit built into the wall which we quickly discovered did not work. The bathroom, also spacious, was even equipped with a bidet. The plumbing, which appeared modern, did not extend below floor level, all waste matter being ejected onto the stony ground below. A Frenchman engaged on a nearby engineering project, and a resident of some months' standing, warned us to close every outlet, bath waste, handbasin, bidet, etc. before going out in the morning or the smell on our return would render the room untenable.

Apart from the large swimming pool, the hotel also sported a shop full of spurious antiquities at exorbitant prices and a hairdressing salon presided over by a tall and effeminate young man with persuasive manners. The meals, a disastrous attempt at French cuisine, were awful; dinner in the evening being enlivened by a floor show which consisted of an Arab orchestra who accompanied a female singer in endless and tuneless songs, some of them vaguely recognisable as Western hits of past decades. The highlight was a traditional belly dance followed by a form of heavily censored striptease which conjures up visions, no matter how remote, of Salome, with perhaps the head of John the Baptist to follow. The realisation dawned on us during the first performance, which was repeated nightly, that the dancer was none other than the hairdresser, either a man in drag or a male impersonator during her daytime hours cutting hair. You could take your pick.

The desert, just half an hour's drive away, was a flat, brown plain stretching unbroken to the horizon, its surface of dust and stones serrated by cracks, the result of centuries without adequate rain, with only small rocks scattered here and there to break up the utter monotony. It could not possibly have been further removed from the billowing dunes of my imagination, with perhaps the odd camel train on the skyline against the setting sun. On one side it was bounded by a range of parched hills, while on another stretched a line of telegraph poles which meant that we could virtually only shoot in one direction. With the crashed plane in position, I realised that everything was the same colour. Brown desert, khaki shirt and breeches, with brown boots on the artist and a khaki-coloured aeroplane, in fact a photographic nightmare. The only relief was the brightly coloured costume of the Little Prince. It could not have been a better job of camouflage if we had brought in the army. The plane would have to be repainted to give some sort of contrast to the background. The original colour had been carefully chosen to give the best results on the night sequences, so our choice was very limited, being reduced to making it either lighter or darker while retaining the same hue.

As we could only shoot in one direction, whenever we needed a reverse angle we had to turn the whole plane around, at the same time moving boulders and humps in the ground which would have given the game away. The fact that, as a result of this manoeuvring, the sun always shone from the same direction, was a small compromise compared to all the other problems. As there was no nearby theatre to run rushes, we had brought out with us a Moviola, a device used in the cutting rooms which gives a small picture on a ground glass screen. This was set up in Stanley's hotel apartment, where we crowded round to try and get a view of the small flickering picture, barely visible because of the low voltage. It was extremely hard to see the plane, let alone the actors or the finer points of composition. In spite of encouraging reports from the laboratories back in England, my spirits fell daily, until I reached the point where I lost all confidence in what I was doing. I had to see some of it in a cinema.

The production manager arranged to run it at the nearest one, two hours' drive away across the dirt roads. It would have to be on a Sunday and he kindly elected to come with me to bolster my fading morale. We set off early in the morning, our demented driver doing his best to emulate the closing moments of the Indianapolis 500. We twice took the wrong route, had a puncture, ran out of fuel, salvation coming in the form of a passing truck, and arrived two hours late, to find the cinema firmly bolted and barred. The exterior of the building did little to raise my hopes, the whitewash wearing thin to reveal the mud block construction. Over the door was a garland of coloured electric light bulbs swinging wildly in the dust-laden wind with, on either side, a lurid poster of the current attraction.

A village-wide search was mounted for the projectionist, who turned out to be the proprietor, manager and usherette embodied in one and the same person. Dragged unwillingly from his Sunday lunch, or its Arab equivalent, he reluctantly set about screening our film. He had no anamorphic lens, so we would have to settle for viewing it with everything looking thin and elongated. Patiently we waited, sitting on hard benches, as sounds of frustration and impatience came from behind the dirty brown curtain which masked the projector. At last there it was, flickering on the dirty brown screen even dimmer than our Moviola and upside down! The short, fat aeroplane and the tall, thin actor were barely discernible. On the wild journey back, my confidence at a new low, I decided to cast it all from my mind, placing my faith in higher regions and the twice-weekly cable from my friend back at Technicolor, the only link with sanity.

The weather was unbelievably cold, with everything frozen in the early morning, including the water in the catering truck. With our personal wardrobes, like our imaginations, based on a more conventional idea of the desert, we huddled round the plane in the biting wind wearing every article of clothing we possessed, including our pyjamas. Urgent cables were sent, pleading for supplies of thermal underwear and long johns, which due to a suspicious customs man back in Bizerta, arrived on the day of our departure.

Word had reached Alan Jay Lerner back in Hollywood that impromptu changes were being made to his script, so in righteous anger he decided to visit Tunisia to see for himself what acts of sacrilege were being perpetrated in his name. Suffering from a back complaint, he undertook the drive from Bizerta prostrate in the back of a Citroen Safari to the 'desert' location. He emerged from his mobile sick bed dressed in a lightweight black suit, white panama hat and two-tone shoes, helped from his horizontal position by his travelling companion, an attractive girl in slacks and a see-through blouse, a welcome diversion for the male members of the crew. Stanley walked over to greet him and there followed the biggest stand-up row I have ever witnessed, just out of earshot of us all huddled round the braziers we had set up in old oil drums. His points of discontent forcibly put on record, he crawled back into the ambulance, sweeping off the location in a swirl of dust, never to be seen again.

Our only other diversion was the presence of an attractive Frenchwoman and her teenage daughter, lured into spending a holiday there by some glossy travel brochure. In the afternoons when the sun warmed things up, it was their daily habit to swim and lie topless by the pool, an attraction which proved irresistible to the whole crew on their days off. Forsaking the many opportunities to visit archaeological sites or the scenes of Second World War battles, they unanimously decided that a day off by the pool was a better way of conserving energy for the following week. The Arab bartender found the situation no less attractive, forsaking his religious scruples and the world of the yashmak to remain constantly on duty during the hours of daylight, his gaze never leaving the two of them in case they should desire his services. One afternoon, carrying a large tray of aperitifs, his mind on things other than service to the Milk Marketing Board, he walked straight into the deep end of the pool, his gaze unswerving as he sank below the surface.

The oasis was our other main location. Exhausted and dying of thirst, the aviator in his delirium is led by the Little Prince to a world of sparkling water, with palm trees waving their fronds in a soft, gentle breeze against the azure sky. A lyrical sequence, accompanied by lovely music, they gambol together beneath the glittering cascades of crystal clear water, lying down to drink their full of the life-giving liquid. The palm trees were moth-eaten and dusty, many of them bereft of foliage due to the recent frosts. The water was a brown and muddy trickle at the bottom of a 50 ft ravine, its side a muddy wall reminiscent of a gravel pit and which obscured all view of the trees above. Undaunted, the art department set about building their oasis above, a faithful interpretation of the description in the script. Pools and cascades were constructed in cement, carefully disguised to look like sand and pebbles, overhung by trailing plants and vines. The worst of the palm trees were embellished with artitifical fronds to produce a paradise in the middle of nowhere.

But what about the water? That was no problem either. It would be pumped up from the stream below into a large concrete tank, filtered, then circulated by other pumps through the intricate channels of our water garden, a delusion as fevered as anything in the mind of the heat-crazed pilot. It would take three days of pumping to fill the tank from the trickle below, the process halted on the second day by another minor international incident. We were taking all the water from the irrigation system of the oasis, already in dire straits due to lack of rain. Dollars were the answer, pressed into the hands of the village elders, who probably thought it a far easier way of making money than cultivating date palms.

At last the art department's labours were crowned with success; a chain of pools sparkling in the sunshine, with cascades and little rivulets running everywhere, artistically dressed with rich tropical vegetation, some of it from the foyer of the hotel. The only trouble was that the real palm trees, now revealed in the background by the increase in altitude, looked distinctly dusty and past their best. 'I can easily supplement them with fibre glass ones, which we can make on the spot,' said the art director, and true to his word, the 'oasis' grew as if by magic overnight, to the astonishment of the oasis proprietors who had spent generations nurturing the reality.

The first day's shooting was a great success, with everything going to art department plan. The sun shone, the cascades cascaded, the water sparkled, and the palm trees, both real and phoney, nodded gently in the hot breeze. We had created a veritable 'Garden of Allah' in a stormy, dusty land. We all slept well that night, in spite of a crêpe Suzette for dinner made, I think, from some form of expanded polythene, and possibly even cooked by the hairdresser, as the floor show was not 'on' that evening. Secure in certain knowledge that we had conquered nature, we rose enthusiastically. We arrived on the location to find the oasis dry. The sparkling pools were reduced to concrete dishes; we had sprung a leak. It would take several days to repair and refill, and more greasing of Arab palms to get the water, so it was back to the crashed aeroplane and the stormy desert for more sequences until things were ready.

All the night sequences were to be shot back in the studio, using the front projection process which allowed one to have vast backgrounds. I had many discussions with Stanley about how dark it should be. 'Could we not have some sort of source light, a torch or a small lamp which might be on the plane?' 'No,' said Stanley, 'it's got to look absolutely real, we have to rely on the stars, or perhaps the moon.' 'I know what you say sounds right', I countered, 'but you know as well as I do that photographically it doesn't work.'

'Well, it's got to this time,' was the helpful reply. One evening at supper the argument started again. It became more heated under the influence of some rather nasty Tunisian wine, accompanied by the discordant and feverish strains of the hotel orchestra as the hairdresser reached the climax of his/her version of the dance of the seven veils. In exasperation I said to Stanley. 'Instead of talking about what a moonless night is like, let's step outside and take a look at the real thing.' I grabbed his arm and propelled him, complaining and unwilling, from the relative brightness of the dining room into the Stygian blackness of the desert night. A few, perhaps slightly unsteady, steps and we fell together into a large, open concrete rainwater drain which undoubtedly also carried other less mentionable things from the plumbing, or rather the lack of it, beneath the bathroom floors. No doubt a health hazard by normal standards, it had crept unnoticed past the local 'Town and Desert' planning act. 'Now what about it?' I demanded triumphantly, as we lay in a heap, uninjured and unsanitary in the bottom. 'If we cannot see to walk, how can we bloody well tell a story and see the actors?'

Returning to our dinner, he conceded with a wry grin that perhaps I had a point. Back in the studios and up to our eyes in front projection drama, he fought a valiant rearguard action over each tiny concession to visibility and we never did get the lamp, be it ever so small, yet so dear to my heart.

28

Cutting the crap

LONG LOCATIONS IN remote places always produce problems, not least of which is the inability to see on the screen next day what you are doing. You rely entirely on reports from home by garbled cables or inconclusive telephone calls. With responsibility weighing heavily upon him, the viewer back home seeks to be over-analytical, a chance remark by him, probably quite inconsequential, becoming blown up out of all proportion. A contemporary of mine, photographing his first major picture in North Africa, met with just this fate. Someone in the studio at Pinewood noticed a shot of Trevor Howard in strong backlight in which his ears appeared red. This quickly built up into an issue of major importance, distorted by communications. Could it be cured by make-up? The answer was no. They decided that the problem, which by now transcended all others, was that his ears protruded more than was acceptable in a leading actor, causing the light from behind to shine through them, creating the, by now, *catastrophic* defect. The fact that it had occurred only in one scene and was totally unimportant anyway since it had not impaired Trevor Howard's performance in countless other films, was completely overlooked. The answer cabled from the make-up department in England was to stick his ears back with double-sided adhesive tape. Due to the heat and perspiration, this stroke of genius produced the alarming effect of first one ear and then the other popping out during a scene as the tape became unstuck. The idea was abandoned, the problem quickly forgotten as it was replaced by a fresh crisis.

These sudden and total preoccupations with trivia can occur at any time, temporarily relegating all other matters to obscurity. We had embarked on two days of tests with Sally Ann Howes for her part in *Chitty Chitty Bang Bang*. There were dozens of wigs, dresses and costumes to be photographed, the concern of the moment being what she should wear for each scene, and how various hair styles would look on the screen. Midway through the afternoon of the first day, Dick Van Dyke arrived from California anxious to meet his co-star. Walking onto the test stage where we were working, he went straight over and greeted her with a kiss, turning towards the camera which was still rolling, to greet us all with a big and friendly smile. Next day at rushes the shot with Dick appeared on the screen. 'Look at the gap in the teeth,' said Cubby Broccoli, the producer. 'Whose teeth?' 'Dick Van Dyke's, he has a large gap between his front teeth.' This phenomenon had passed unnoticed by anyone else in the theatre, probably because it was the way nature had intended him, not proving until this moment any obstacle to a long and successful career. 'We have to do something about it. Is there anything you can do photographically, Chris?' he asked, turning towards me. Completely taken aback by the sudden turn of events, I had to admit that I could not think of anything I could do to help. 'If you really feel so concerned, I think you have to see a dental surgeon,' was the best suggestion I could offer. With a worried frown creasing his normally happy face, Cubby left the theatre without a word of discussion about Sally Ann Howes' appearance, which for the moment came a poor second to the subject of teeth, or rather the gaps between them.

* * *

On looking back over what I have written so far, it does seem as though I may have dwelt overlong on just a few of the pictures I have made. This is not a deliberate attempt to consign the many others to obscurity, but is just the natural outcome of the way my mind has ranged over the past. My only clear idea when starting was to avoid at all costs a long and dreary catalogue, written in eulogistic terms, about the magic world of the movies. This has been attempted so many times before by people more able than me with the pen, the pages full of famous names and illustrious anecdotes. It was far from my mind, in the comparative safety of retirement, to set out to bite the many hands that have fed me over the years. The industry has afforded me with a very good life, with travel, fun and friendship with so many amusing, talented, and interesting people along the way. I must confess that I have never been totally consumed by films, retaining friends and interests outside my work, which no doubt accounts for the fact that I have achieved retirement while keeping a certain degree of sanity. As I approach what must be the closing chapters, the names still come flooding back.

* * *

I made *The Private Life of Sherlock Holmes* for Billy Wilder in 1969. With a track record of success longer than most, his subjects were more varied than his contemporaries. Viennese by birth, he was first and foremost a writer, the written word dominating his whole approach to his pictures. The delivery of lines had to be exactly as he intended, making him at times very tough with actors. This was his first picture in England, where, in common with most Americans, he found the relationship with the crew rather different. The first few days were taken up by careful manoeuvres around each other, like two boxers meeting for the first time in the ring. He perhaps felt that we offered too many suggestions as to how scenes might be shot, while we were all in great awe of his reputation as a master film-maker. It was all very formal, Mr Wilder, Mr Challis or Mr Cooper being the form of address. Freddie Cooper, the camera operator, asked him to look through the camera and check on every move. We quickly realised that in common with many other directors he had not got a visual mind. He knew exactly what effect he wanted, describing it in detail so that it was clear in everyone's mind, but he could only judge if it was right when he saw it on the screen. On about the fourth day, Freddie called him over to check on the lens he proposed to use. 'Mr Wilder, would you like to look through the camera and see if you think the wide-angle is right for this shot?' With a broad smile, Billy replied, 'Let's cut out all this technical crap from now on, Mr Cooper. I have never been able to understand how the radio works when you shut the window.'

This marked the beginning of one of the happiest relationships I have ever had with a director. He would arrive dead-on 8.30 in the morning, followed by Izzy Diamond, his co-writer, whose function it was to sit with headphones on during a take, not watching the action but checking every word against the script to make certain that not a comma was missed. His greeting was invariably the same. 'Good morning, boys, I have to go to the can!' This necessary function completed, he would return to the set and ask for coffee. Being Viennese, he set great store by this, bringing his own supply in each day. Never in a hurry to start, the next half an hour or so would be taken up with stories which he loved to tell to the largest possible audience. By far the best actor on the set, he is also one of the world's greatest raconteurs, his fund of anecdotes inexhausible.

His favourite was about the top-level American diplomat visiting Russia. He was given the full treatment, the Kremlin, Lenin's tomb, the Bolshoi, ending with a visit to the Moscow underground railway. Slowly he was conducted through the palatial booking hall, hung with crystal chandeliers, great paintings on the walls, then down to the platform, equally magnificent, with its statuary and lighting. 'Well, what do you think of it?' asked his host. 'Rather better than the New York subway, eh?' 'In all my travels I have never seen anything to compare with it, no litter, no crowding, it really is spectacular. But tell me one thing, what about the trains?' he asked. The reply came instantly and with venom, the mood changing in a flash. 'Never mind about the trains, what about the lynchings in the South?'

The sequel was a dinner given in Hollywood to a group of visiting Russian screen writers. Billy, as president of the Screenwriters Guild was called upon to address them. He decided to tell them this story, speaking to his po-faced audience through an interpreter. As he embellished the yarn in his inimitable way, the interpreter struggled to convey the humour to the unreceptive audience, with not a glimmer of a smile to be seen among the sea of grim faces. With the sense of failure increasing with each word, he struggled to the end, the biggest lead balloon of all time, as he put it.

One day he was interviewed by an earnest young man from *Films and Filming*. 'Tell me, Mr Wilder, with all your vast experience and the many wonderful films you have made, is there a simple message you can give me for any young director who might hope to follow in your footsteps?' 'Yes,' replied Billy without hesitation, 'I think it very important that he can read.'

Carol Reed I will always remember as one of our greatest directors. My one regret is that I only worked with him once, towards the end of his life, on a picture called *Follow Me,* with Topol and Mia Farrow. It was produced in 1971 by that doyen of Hollywood producers, Hal Wallace, who was renowned for keeping a tight rein on every department, watching how every penny was spent. All directors who worked for him had a clause in their contracts giving them the right to the first 'cut', or assembly of the completed film, after which Hal Wallace could, if he so chose, re-edit the whole thing, even shooting extra scenes if he felt they were required in order that the final result was a reflection of his interpretation of the story. I was intrigued to see how he would work with Carol, whose films were highly personal in approach, for there seemed little in common between them, certainly in the artistic field. Carol was a quiet, diffident person who avoided confrontation at all costs with both artists and producers, yet he always got his way by more subtle means. Stuck with a disappointing actor, he would extract a performance line by line, in the end obtaining something that the person really was not capable of. With charm and guile he could convince the biggest of 'hams', stumbling over his few vital lines, that he was giving a performance worthy of Olivier at his greatest. With never a trace of impatience, he persisted until he had just the performance he wanted, hiding with consummate skill beneath his calm exterior the burning hatred he must have often felt for the floundering idiot who through some quirk of fate was irreplaceable at this stage in the shooting. He shot with great economy, putting his films together like a fine watchmaker. Every single foot had its place in the overall pattern which existed in his mind and nowhere else, and here lay the answer to my mental query as to how things would work out with Hal Wallace. The final picture could only be cut one way, Carol's way in fact, and of course he knew this from the start. This high degree of craftsmanship stemmed from a long apprenticeship served in the cutting rooms and on the studio floor, which enabled him to use his creative talent to full effect. This background seems to be sorely lacking in so many directors today, who through lack of experience or knowledge of how a film is put together, or both, overshoot to an unbelievable extent, covering everything from every possible angle in order to leave all the options open. This inevitably results in the picture going wildly over schedule and budget, with a near newsreel coverage to be sorted out in the cutting rooms later. With this sort of approach, Hal Wallace could make six different versions when he wanted to. However, this was not what he was getting, though Carol's subtle approach completely concealed the fact even from Hal's experienced eyes.

Though by no means a slow director, Carol evinced little outward concern for the schedule or the daily progress reports showing us a quarter or a half a day behind, matters of great concern to someone like Hal Wallace, who would be on the 'floor' sharp at 8.30 each morning to make sure we were off to a prompt start, followed by almost hourly visits throughout the day to ensure that momentum was not being lost. Far too experienced a producer to confront his director with his criticisms and concerns over what might not be to his liking whilst in the middle of shooting, these messages were conveyed by a hatchet man named Bill, whose lack of hair was matched by his lack of sensibility. Not among the most intelligent of Americans, he stood somewhat in awe of Carol Reed, torn between loyalty to his master, whom he followed like a faithful dog, and a sense of deference due, he no doubt felt, to an English knight. In common with many of his compatriots, he was highly susceptible to atmosphere, being at all times over anxious to deliver his messages of condemnation and gloom with the correct degree of respect. Unsure of the correct method of approach which etiquette demanded, he prefaced every message with 'Sir Carol', accompanied by a half salute and a strange bending of the body and knee, a compromise between a bow and a genuflextion. 'Sir Carol, Mr Wallace says that we have to be off this set by 4.30 this afternoon or it will put us a day behind.' Carol would study him in silence for a minute or so, rubbing his troubled brow the while. 'Yes, yes,' he would reply, the two words drawn out to eternity so that Bill would retire secure in the belief that he had obtained a constructive answer, while Carol continued untroubled on his way.

A gentleman in every sense of the word, Carol had a way with people, getting the very best out of them, artists and technicians alike, by the simple process of involvement. He was equipped with a great visual sense, knowing just how he wanted a scene to look in the overall pattern as well as how he wanted the actors to play it. He would never come to me and say, 'I want you to do this or that,' but instead, would take me aside, put his arm round my shoulder and say, 'Chris, I have been thinking about this scene, and I wonder if it would be possible to get a certain effect, but of course I don't know if it is possible.' Now of course he knew perfectly well that it was possible, in fact he knew from past experience just how it could be done, but he had the happy knack of making you feel it was your idea. I think he took a secret delight in baiting producers, many of whom he did not hold in very high esteem, a feeling I have to confess to sharing. It is, of course, wrong to generalise, but the temptation in this case overcomes my sense of justice. Numbered among them, naturally, are the truly great impresarios of the industry to whom we all owe a lifelong debt, but they seem to be getting thinner on the ground with the passage of time, replaced by the wheeler-dealers, expert money-raisers though they may well be, who have little or no commitment to the artistic merit or integrity of what they make. For this reason, so many top directors combine the two functions in order to retain their freedom from the baser intrigues which can become part of the making of a film.

* * *

Actors are another matter, a commodity coming in all shapes and sizes, with, like us all, widely differing personalities. Perhaps it would be true to say that they tend to be rather larger than life, some of them identifying themselves too closely with the sort of people the publicity department would like them to be. Success, not always merited in terms of their craft, brings with it enormous wealth and great pressure on what might be considered the more normal aspects of life, and it takes a strong character to survive. I often wonder why so many really funny men are in fact very sad men when off the screen, haunted by doubts about their performances and future. In this respect I think particularly of Tony Hancock and Peter Sellers, whose personal lives missed so many of the laughs they so brilliantly created for other people.

Peter Ustinov, of course, is another matter, for he would appear to be perfectly adjusted to enjoying every moment of life, remaining quite unscathed by success and the inheritance of such brilliant and diverse talent. Surely one of the world's great raconteurs, the stories and anecdotes roll from him in an endless stream, delivered in a dozen dialects and accents. Waiting for the weather, an occupational hazard in movies, is never dull if Peter is in the cast, for he keeps everyone entertained to the point where returning to work becomes a very unwelcome reality. There was a time when I felt that some of his stories might be figments of his very fertile imagination, but I have since heard him repeat them, perhaps after a gap of several years, exact in every detail, which convinces me that they are true. Anyway, who cares? They are all intensely funny.

Then there was Robert Morley, a Gilbertian figure with the power to be totally outrageous without causing offence, at least in most cases. One day while making *Those Magnificent Men in their Flying Machines*, we were shooting out at Booker Airfield. The part of the Japanese entrant in the great race was to be played by a leading young actor and pop star from Tokyo, who was due to arrive that morning. He was brought out to meet the cast and crew by the publicity department, hoving into sight surrounded by a large crowd of Japanese press, draped with Nikon cameras and every sort of tape recorder. He was introduced to Robert through an inscrutable and smiling interpreter, bowing politely before him. Robert gazed for some moments on the busily snapping throng, then turning to the interpreter he asked, 'Now tell me, have you brought your Emperor with you?' Translated into Japanese it somehow lost its humour, or maybe they didn't share our ideas of what was funny, for, while retaining their fixed smiles all round, they retired from the scene, deeply offended so we were told, threatening to board the next flight home. After lengthy and laborious explanations, again via the smiling interpreter, they were convinced that what we thought funny was as odd as the things we ate, so averting the threat of a second Pearl Harbor.

On the same film we had a particularly obnoxious shop steward whose waking hours were exclusively devoted to stirring up trouble wherever the opportunity presented itself. These activities of course took place in the background, while openly he went to great lengths to ingratiate himself with actors and producers alike. Robert Morley, being a keen follower of the horse racing scene, had a clause in his contract which gave him two days off during Ascot week which, when the time came, caused a number of problems with the schedule so that most people were aware of where he was going. The first person to greet him on his return to work was the shop steward, who ran over in front of everyone to shake him warmly by the hand and enquire, 'Did you have a nice time at Ascot, Mr Morley?' 'Yes, as a matter of fact I did,' replied Robert, 'it is one of the few occasions left which afford me the opportunity of mixing with people of my own class.' A retort worthy of Oscar Wilde at his best, it brought the house down. Our activist friend, to whom the very word Ascot must have been anathema, appeared quite unaware of the irony behind the disarming smile.

Noel Coward's wit and charm touched all who ever worked with him, his talent to amuse dominating most of what he said and did both on and off the stage. His many witticisms are well recorded, yet I venture to add just one more to the list, told to me by a friend in Bermuda. During the period when he had a house there, he was entertaining a group of friends to tea on the lawn, among whom was a small girl aged four or five. At the far end of the garden two dogs appeared engaged in copulation. 'Uncle Noel, what are they doing?' demanded the small child, running over to his side. 'Well, my dear, the one in front is blind and the other one is kindly pushing her home.'

29

The corset

INCONGRUOUS SITUATIONS SEEM to be part of making films. With little or no relationship with the sane world outside, they just happen. A sequence of events is set in motion by a chance decision and in no time at all you are beyond the point of no return. On location, with weather a constant hazard, 'cover' sets are a necessary standby. Suitable interior scenes are selected from the script which can be shot in houses, hotels or apartments, the art department searching for suitable nearby venues. The unsuspecting owners, more often than not flattered by the idea of giving hospitality to world-famous names, agree to make their homes available in exchange for a suitable remuneration. They probably imagine one or two interesting days with the charming director, whom they have already met, the stars who are idols of theirs anyway, a small camera with perhaps a couple of lights and a few people to work them; a fascinating chance to see how films are made in the intimacy of their own home. The reality, too awful to bear thinking of, comes when it is too late to go back. About 120 people, many of them bearing a close resemblance to displaced persons in their attire, a large and noisy generator parked on the lawn, a catering van, mobile lavatories, prop vans, construction trucks, make-up and hairdressing caravans all appear in the street outside. In a matter of minutes, friendly neighbours of many years standing have turned into bitter enemies with already the threat of legal action in the wind. By this time the director or the art director may well have taken exception to the pattern of the curtains, or perhaps the furniture. Piece by piece it is moved out into one of the waiting trucks, to be replaced by things hired or bought which are more in keeping with the period of the film or the lifestyle of the characters in the story. The horrified owners retreat, perhaps to the bathroom, which is already full of lamps and sound equipment, or more sensibly decide to forgo inside knowledge of how films are shot and spend the day out in the country, in spite of the rain which has driven the film crew in. The director's charm has evaporated overnight together with the star's glamour. The production manager who negotiated the deal with such disarming geniality has become a man of iron, reminding them that they have signed a legal contract. The company will restore everything to its original domestic harmony, leaving no trace of the invasion and making good any damage which might occur. Grasping this one small thread of hope, they pick their way over the cables and mounds of equipment, jostled by the crowds of shouting electricians fighting their way up the stairs. Outside the windows are already being covered with blackout material, while tubular towers are mushrooming everywhere to raise the lights to window level. Perhaps something could be redeemed if they could just say 'hallo' to Elizabeth Taylor. 'Sorry,' says the assistant director, 'she's not here yet, and anyway she will be too busy in make-up when she does arrive.' The company, each morning faced with an ambiguous weather report, is in a fever of indecision. Should they go in or out? Once the die is cast, with the whole circus set in motion, it is too late to change. Many is the day I have spent sweltering in a claustrophobic interior while the sun shone outside, the outcome of just one more pessimistic weather forecast.

With the development of small cameras, fast film and lightweight miniaturised lamps, and with sound recorded on tape and radio microphones, a new freedom has come to feature production. No longer do we need studios; everything can be shot in the real locations. It does have certain drawbacks, both artistically and photographically, but these are outweighed in the producer's mind by the carrot of cheapness which, in the final analysis, is very different from economy. When a 'long shot' is required in the studio, one or two walls of the set would be 'floated' to enable the camera to get back far enough. Working in a 'real' room, with one's back literally against the wall, and often metaphorically, resort is made to the ultra-wide angle lens which distorts perspective, making anything near the camera larger than life and diminishing the background. This has unfortunate consequences if the near object happens to be an actor's face. Then again, lights cannot be fixed in the most advantageous position to hide double chins, wrinkles, bags under the eyes and the physical shortcomings which at one time the idols of the cinemagoing public were not supposed to be heir to.

Times have changed however, and a new sense of realism is upon us. People, it would seem, do not want escapism, with glimpses into a world of beautiful beings basking in the sort of luxury few achieve. The call is for the sordid and seamy side of life. A reflection, perhaps, of the sort of life most of us have to lead. Whether this is entertainment is a point which can be argued. Obviously there is room for both approaches, and in spite of an apparent obsession with sex and violence among the young, old movies, as they are apt to be called, still command a vast audience on television. I have philosophised briefly because my thoughts lead naturally to another short chapter of my life.

* * *

Suffering the often recurring pains of unemployment, a necessary part of a freelance existence, and with school bills looming large on the horizon, I was called out of the blue by a production manager friend of mine. 'Chris, what are you up to?' 'Nothing,' had to be the honest reply. 'I am going to do a film for American television, all to be shot in Ireland. A full-length feature, it has a four-week schedule and a tight budget,' – a phrase which always sounded to me reminiscent of a too small corset restricting painfully the lifestyle of a woman over-anxious about her fading vital statistics. 'If you are interested,' he continued, 'we are going over to Dublin on Friday for a couple of days, where we will meet up with the director and producer to look at suggested locations. I have to know before we go if you want to do it.' Bearing in mind my current finances, I at once made up my mind to bury my higher artistic ideals and grasp the hand that base materialism was offering me. 'Be at Heathrow at 8.30. I will bring a script which you can read on the flight.'

Always, after agreeing a deal, I have awful second thoughts, for one has signed away a portion of one's life, to be released only by death or summary dismissal. On this occasion the pangs were greater than usual, the only mitigating fact being that it could only last for four weeks due to the financial 'corset'. I felt that as long as I could prise sufficient remuneration for my agony from this limiting factor, a point that could only be resolved when I met the producer face to face, perhaps I had made the right decision. The script, glanced quickly through on the short Dublin flight, was surprisingly good. But, oh, there was an awful lot of it for four weeks. *War of*

Children was set in Northern Ireland, the usual story of Protestant/ Catholic vendetta which all too sadly involved the young, who are in no way responsible. With a very good cast, headed by Jenny Agutter and including some wonderful Irish actors, with which the country abounds, it all began to appear more hopeful.

That evening over dinner we met the director, George Schaeffer, and the producer. George, with a long list of Emmy awards to his credit, was a small, genial man of mildly rotund proportions who gazed out on the world in a seemingly benign manner through thick-lensed spectacles. Soberly dressed, and wearing a large pair of elasticated orthopaedic boots on all occasions, presumably for medical reasons, he gave the distinct impression of not being over-athletic, which hopefully meant that we could keep up with him physically during our four weeks' hard labour. As dinner progressed, he quietly dominated the conversation, outlining his thoughts. It quickly became obvious that he knew the script backwards and was sympathetic to its every emotion. So far, so good, I thought, but what about the time element? I had better be honest and express my doubts. They wanted a 'feature' cameraman and crew because they looked upon it as a feature film, as indeed it was in all aspects except for money and time. George, I am sure, had heard it all before. 'I rehearse for four weeks with the artists before we shoot,' he said, 'every aspect of the script and dialogue is worked out and finalised, and after that there will be no more discussion.' 'But how can you finalise how you will play a scene when you have no idea where and in what circumstances you will have to shoot it?' 'The mechanics do not worry me,' he replied, 'you tell me the problems, what we can and can't do, and I can adapt.'

I had heard similar promises from directors before and felt far from convinced. It would be four weeks of Hell, it must be, but the road back was closed. Drawing me aside, the producer said, 'I expect you want to discuss money.' It had crossed my mind, I must confess, and, with visions of inflated American rates, I had steeled myself to ask for a fairly substantial figure. Before I could state my case and plead mitigating circumstances, he offered me, in simple terms, a fee in excess of what I had thought a good bargaining point. The shortest deal I have ever concluded was sealed with a handshake.

The four weeks of shooting that followed were among the happiest I have experienced. Hard? Yes. But never acrimonious. The hours were long, unbelievably long, and the days stretched into nights as we laboured away in all sorts of near unworkable interiors, yet George lived up to his promise and skilfully made the most of every situation. I remember well the incongruous situation of a back street in the poorer section of Dublin, decked out with Unionist flags, patrolled by crowds dressed as British soldiers and Ulster constabulary, and complete with armoured Land Rovers and patrol vehicles. The only restriction imposed was that the arms had to be fake. The inhabitants joined in the fun, clamouring for jobs as 'extras' with no remote sense of rancour. Perhaps after all, ordinary people are ordinary all over the world, incited by the few to acts of barbarism and aggression in the name of causes they do not believe in or do not understand. The Irish crew, drawn mostly from the Dublin studios, were first rate and, at that time, unspoiled by militant trade unionism. Any excuse for a singsong or a party was grasped with alacrity and the cumbersome wheels of film production were, I suspect, liberally 'oiled' with the magic of Guinness. It all ended with a final 'do' at 1 o'clock in the morning, after night shooting. Emotion ran high; a happy ending to an unexpectedly enjoyable experience, due entirely to George Schaeffer, whose cheerful personality and complete professionalism overcame all obstacles.

The film was a great success, with more Emmy awards, and I was more than delighted to be asked a few months later to embark on a second venture with George. This time it was *This House of Brede* by Rumer Godden, a story set in a convent, with Diana Rigg, Gwen Watford and Pamela Brown in the leading roles. Because of the once-again 'tight' budget, it was decided to film the interiors in a convent in Mill Hill, London, and the exteriors at another convent at Killarney in Ireland, with four weeks in each location. The Mill Hill venue seemed an unlikely place at first sight, an ugly pile of a building with a rabbit warren of little rooms or 'cells', if you care to call them that. It did, however, have a fine chapel and dining hall and the exterior did not concern us as, with a wave of the magic wand, it would become Killarney, a lovely old building on the shore of a small lake.

Mill Hill had been an enclosed order until a few years back, its inmates abjuring all contact with the outside world. Now they venture out into that same world to teach and nurse, helping mankind when they can, returning each evening to the same sparse little rooms for devotion and peace. I think they all rather enjoyed having us there, in spite of the chaos which is inseparable from filming. If nothing else, I feel certain that their vocabularies were considerably extended in the realm of basic English as spoken by the 'sparks' in times of duress.

I got to know the nun in charge of the library, a dear old lady of well over 80 who had entered the order at the age of 16. For over 60 years she had no contact with the outside world, apart from what she knew through her books and certain selected newspapers. Now that the restrictions had disappeared she had no desire, she told me, to venture outside. Her complete fulfilment lay between these walls and her world of books. It transpired that she was something of a theatre and cinema buff, in spite of never having visited one, and she was well acquainted with the careers of all our artists.

Mill Hill was a four-week slog, 8 a.m until nine or ten every night, six days a week. It would have been 7 a.m., but we were saved by being on 'hallowed' ground. Killarney was the carrot to spur us on; four weeks in the country and a chance to collect together our Irish friends from *War of Children*. We had already been there on a flying recce, so we knew what to expect. The Mother Superior had asked us, a party of seven males, to lunch. It was an invitation we could hardly refuse in the circumstances, although we had all cherished visions of a pleasant hour or so in an Irish pub.

The lunch turned out to be beyond our wildest dreams. The Mother Superior demurely explained that, since we were all males, she and her sisters would not dine with us but she hoped we would enjoy what had been prepared. Having said grace on our behalf, she retired and left the serving of a superb meal, accompanied by a choice of wines, in the hands of a small army of sisters who joined in our conversation as only the Irish can, while they busied themselves tending our needs.

The four weeks we spent there taxed George's good humour and our ingenuity to the full, for it rained every day, and almost all day. Since we were there for the exteriors and the story was set in high summer, this, by film convention, meant sunshine. We grabbed what we could in moments of watery and fleeting sun, the leaves dripping and the grass sodden under foot. The hours passed in damp misery. The tight budget was squeezed even tighter as the days came and went. What looked like disaster was averted by George inserting random lines in the script referring to the vagaries of the Irish climate, which skilfully excused us shooting in mist and rain. It conferred a sense of beauty and atmosphere more typical of where we were, though this might not be agreed by the Irish Tourist

Board. Anyway, it didn't really matter because the script and story were good and the artists excellent. Once again, George had pulled it off. More awards and critical acclaim, and all in eight weeks – just!

With these two happy experiences behind me, I was delighted to learn that a third was in the offing. It began to look like a job for life with a sense of almost Civil Service security about it, yet without the necessity of working with all the dreary people. This time George would not be with us, due to other commitments. The story was the sinking of the *Titanic*, already the subject of an excellent black and white film, *A Night to Remember*, made in 1958. It struck me immediately that this was a somewhat ambitious project for eight weeks, the previous film having taken eight months, but maybe a magic formula had been devised to make the dollars go further or the *Titanic* sink faster. I soon made myself unpopular by asking what I thought were pertinent questions about how they proposed to do things.

Some of the answers made sense. The interiors on the large transatlantic ships of those days were made to look as much like palatial hotels as possible, so we should be able to find the right places in London without trouble, assuming of course that the proprietors had no objection to removing their normal clientele and submerging everything in water. Our producer, ever an optimist, could see no difficulty with this. 'Just a matter of getting them interested in the story, and we'll promise them a screen credit'! The question of tilting everything proved more intractable, unless of course we could find a hotel which shared the same architect as the Tower of Pisa. Tilting the camera wouldn't do because then the actors would be tilted too.

I thought that perhaps a way had been found in the script to overcome some of these obvious difficulties; a more intimate approach with close ups of terrified faces, say, in place of long shots of a giant ship hitting an iceberg. But no, for upon reading it, the script bore a remarkable resemblance to the earlier film. 'If you make a movie about the *Titanic* sinking with 2000 people on board, you've gotta see it, kid,' said the producer, but he omitted to explain how. Of course he was right, but I thought it only served to emphasise the point I was trying to make about it not being a suitable subject for the sort of money and schedule we had. 'We've got more dough this time and another WEEK on the schedule, so why do we have a problem? We can buy some of the model shots from the other movie and have them coloured. It was night anyway, so they only need to look a bit blue.' This, I supposed, could equally apply to any faces that might appear, for presumably they would be feeling the cold!

'We plan to build one small set in the studio tank which can be tilted and submerged,' it was explained, and the art department drawings made very clear what was meant by small. The adjective 'tight' which was always linked to any mention of the budget could equally, I thought, apply to this small portion of the great stricken liner. Perhaps we could make the cloak of darkness cover our inadequacies, although American producers in general like their night fairly revealing in film terms if they have a lot of expensive artists to show off.

'For all the day scenes prior to the accident, we are going to have to find a ship of some sort that will be more or less correct for the period. We realise it must appear to be on the scale of the *Titanic*, but if we are careful about angles it could work. Then there is the *Queen Mary*, safely tied up in Palm Beach. Once again, she's not right for period, but at least we have the scale. We can 'tart up' shots for period and it will all work fine.'

It began to dawn on me that George had known a thing or two when he got himself committed to other things.

As I raised question after question, it occurred to me forcibly that I was saying goodbye to my 'Civil Service' future, but it all had to be said now, and not in the form of excuses later when all turned to seaweed.

Billy Hale, the director, was far removed from George in character. Of great charm, he tended to live in a dream world of his own, relaxed in the belief that all would be well on the night, icebergs and all. So the hunt was on for suitable hotels with accommodating owners, the model shots were being dyed blue, the set in the tank taking shape, but the quest for a suitable ship drew blank after blank, as I knew it must. Even had one existed, it was unlikely that it could have been hired for the sort of money we had. A cold, wet evening in November found a small group of us huddled in a hotel bedroom in Liverpool, a process of elimination having suggested that the Isle of Man ferry was our only hope. Ludicrously small compared to what she was meant to portray, she was more or less right for period, being due to retire from service any day, if she didn't founder before. All they could offer was the turn-around period of one day, when she was tied up alongside the quay in

Douglas. If we didn't get through, she would have to sail and we would have to wait for her next trip.

Next morning we went down to the docks to take a look, and what we saw was not exciting. There were odd corners on deck with wooden lifeboats in the background, a companionway and a small open deck aft. If we were very careful about angles, with period set dressing and, of course, the costumes to help, perhaps we could do something with it. 'It's great, and we always have the *Queen Mary* for any long shots,' said our cheerful producer, with an eye to a cheap charter. Billy Hale gazed dreamily over the side at the dirty water in the Liverpool docks, his mind on other more edifying matters.

So the *Manxman* it had to be, the day on Sunday some three weeks hence. We worked on the Saturday until the last possible moment in order to sink our submersible piece of the *Titanic* in the studio tank. Everyone, actors and crew, was cold and wet after innumerable duckings in the tank's grimy depths, whose waters were considerably less hygienic than those of the North Atlantic. As the last vestige of set finally sank below the surface, the assistant director was already shouting, 'Come on, boys, we've got to make the last flight to Douglas. No time to eat now, we can clean up and feed when we get there.'

I woke on the fateful day to the sound of rain drumming on the hotel window. It was blowing a force nine gale! Down at the quay, the ferry was pinned to the dockside, leaning at an angle by the force of the wind and unable to move an inch. It was impossible to find a single angle with sea in the background; just cranes, buildings, and other ships. Script changes could not possibly explain these away, so all we could do was endeavour to fill the background with ship. The weather continued unabated, the ladies' veils blew out horizontally as they sat in deck chairs, the hot Bovril whipped from the cups and over the stewards' starched white jackets. The dialogue was snatched away by the howling wind and impossible to record; costumes, wigs and make-up were all ruined in minutes in spite of heroic efforts by the wardrobe department to keep the artists undercover until the last minute. A long, dreary day dragged to a close, with a few painful shots accomplished and everyone cold, wet and hungry. Collision with an iceberg seemed infinitely preferable, when a smiling representative from the owners appeared clad in streaming oilskins and told us that the forecast was for more of the same tomorrow. The ferry could not sail, so we could have her for another day! This proved to be just an extension of the general misery as scene after scene had to be abandoned, relegated to that unknown quantity, the *Queen Mary*, which had now become essential.

With the rest of the shooting nearly completed, an extra set had to be built in the studio or we could not finish the picture. The schedule and the budget grew and burst their seams. The producer made a hurried trip back to the coast and returned with more dollars, having convinced someone that it was all a great idea. A section of the steerage was built for a sequence with the Irish emigrants, poor peasants escaping from penury and starvation to the hope of the New World. Billy was captivated by this idea. He inserted scenes of dancing and music, with that marvellous Irish group 'The Chieftains', and a host of Irish actors who joined in the fun. He wildly overshot the sequence, out of which he made something charming, lyrical and totally out of place, but it certainly helped to take care of the extra dollars and showed all too clearly what he could do with a good subject. Perhaps it may even have brought comfort to the producer, who could visualise a musical as an alternative to a sinking.

At last it was over. I had cherished hopes that I would not be needed in Los Angeles. 'You have lots of marvellous crews out there and, anyway, the unions are tough about cameramen coming in to work,' I hopefully suggested. It was not to be, however. For some reason, in spite of all the problems and differences of opinion, and the fact that many of my gloomy prophecies had come true, they still wanted me to go. My good friend, the production manager, had put up a more convincing case and was excused, which left just myself and my camera operator, who shared my forebodings, to be joined by a Hollywood crew on arrival.

We were met at the airport by the new production manager, looking much like Buffalo Bill in full western attire, lacking only a pair of pearl-handled Colts. 'Everything's great. We are living on the ship, which is now a hotel, so you won't have any travelling!'

The ship was more or less embedded in concrete, alongside a specially constructed quay on which there were traditional red British telephone kiosks and post boxes. A 'changing of the guard' ceremony was mounted twice a day to the strains of recorded music. The troops were out-of-work film extras in guards' uniforms, complete with bearskins, the marching guaranteed to give any sergeant major apoplexy. A constant stream of sightseers, mostly parties of blue-haired American widows, thronged the decks from dawn to dusk. Seeking a little old world culture, they were ushered around by Beefeaters in full dress.

In every direction there were splendid views of Palm Beach and the odd oil rig, once again difficult to equate with the mid-Atlantic and icebergs. Never mind, we would have to avoid the water once again. At least we had space and the feel of a huge ship. In fact many times too huge this time, and wrong for period. Clever angles and a bit of set dressing would take care of that. 'Up on the sun deck we have a great background of the huge funnels. If we shoot from a low angle, we won't need the sea,' said our ever-hopeful producer. 'But the funnels are painted in Cunard colours and the *Titanic* was White Star Line,' ventured a nautically minded member of the art department. 'Paint them right,' said the producer, 'and while you are about it, get permission to put smoke pots in them. It will add a bit of reality.' The cost, however, was enormous, for when we had finished they would have to be restored. The argument waxed and waned over several days, during which time I felt we had become an integral part of the circus; another quaint English act to be gazed at in curiosity. Finally it was agreed to paint one side only, which was all the straining budget could take, and this in cheap water colour which would wash off if it rained. It didn't, or I might still be there.

Shot by shot we got our sequences in between the parties of sightseers, for the deal was that we did not in anyway interfere with the routine of the 'ship', a special cut-price deal negotiated by our cowboy. The main thing lacking was all the scenes on the bridge. Of course the *Queen Mary*'s bridge was about four times the size of the *Titanic*'s and equipped with modern navigational instruments, which all had to be covered and disguised. Through the windows, once again, lay Palm Springs. 'We'll re-write most of it for night,' was the solution, but then we had a myriad lights which gave the impression of navigating down Fifth Avenue. So, once again, it was a low angle, with the camera literally on the floor and feet featuring rather more than faces.

At last it was over, the budget run dry, the future of it all in the hands of the editor. Billy Hale remained cheerful to the end and went on to greater things, while I returned home, not to be asked again by the company, if indeed they made any other films. It was a clear case of third time unlucky.

30

Under contract

All my life I had worked as a freelance, preferring constant insecurity to a position of being allocated to a production with which I was totally out of sympathy. At least I had a measure of choice, limited only by the grim reality of earning a living. I had discovered through bitter experience that the films one eventually did usually came out of the blue. More often than not, at the end of a successful association, culminating in the inevitable end-of-picture party, a sentimental and sometimes tearful producer or director would vow his eternal allegiance and unqualified admiration for my work. Surely, I would think, I can count on being offered his next production, if and when it happens. I quickly learned that life is not like that, and never to feel disappointed or bitter on learning, by chance usually, that someone else had been engaged for the job that I had felt certain I would get.

After a period which brought me to Pinewood Studios on several independent productions, in 1956 I was asked by John Bryan, a wonderful art director turned producer, to photograph *The Spanish Gardener.* A charming story by A. J. Cronin, adapted by Lesley Storm, it was to be shot largely on location in Spain on the Costa Brava, fortunately out of season! One story illustrates how, in film making, a series of incidents so often leads to a ludicrous decision. In the story, the Spanish gardener, played by Dirk Bogarde, takes the over-cosseted little son of the British Ambassador on a trout-fishing expedition, a venture strictly taboo for the child. The scene was described in the script as a romantic old water mill with a limpid and now disused mill pool, stocked with fine trout. The search was on, led by the location manager and the art department, for a suitable location. With success apparently crowning their endeavours, an expedition was mounted on Sunday, our only day off, to drive out and look at it. It would make a pleasant day in the country and lunch had been arranged in a famous little restaurant in a nearby village.

Immediately after breakfast, we all piled into a coach and were driven with abandon by a Spanish driver for what seemed hours along roads which gradually became narrower and more precipitous. Already lunch had assumed a greater importance than the quest for the mill, when at last we drew off onto the stony verge. 'I'm afraid it's on foot from now on, only about ten minutes away. I'll lead the way,' said the location manager. Down the hillside we stumbled to a narrow rocky valley, with, at the bottom, a small stream. 'There will be more water when we get a drop of rain,' he said. 'But what about the mill?' we chorused. 'We are going to build that, we only need one side and we can design just what we need for the scene.' The answer to why we were here in this barren valley, far removed from our base in San Felieu, was simple if you follow the train of thought. They had approached the local angling society for information about the best place to catch trout in the area and this particular place was the unanimous advice. 'Surely it would make more sense to find a mill somewhere near San Felieu? The trout we can always get. After all, it isn't a documentary on trout fishing. We only need a couple of shots of fish being whipped out of the water on the end of a line.' Crestfallen, the art department retired to the sidelines. 'We don't even need live fish. Just get a dozen frozen ones and keep them in the hotel deep freeze until they're wanted. You will never know the difference when they are flashed across the screen.' This suggestion was rubbing salt into the wound, the prospect of designing and building a mill, after all an artistic challenge, destroyed in favour of two or three pounds of frozen fish.

Logic won the day. A suitable old mill was found only four miles from our hotel and the trout were safely in the freezer. The day came for us to shoot the scene, which we worked out carefully shot by shot, rehearsing Dirk and the boy, Jon Whiteley. 'Slip back and get the fish now,' said Phil Leacock, our director, and after an inordinately long wait the 'prop' man returned, sweating, his face lined with the agony of apprehension. 'They've gone, guv. The bloody hotel served them for someone's breakfast.' No more trout were available at short notice, so he was dispatched to the local fishmarket to bring back a selection of anything that might pass muster in a crowd. So what might have been an angling *tour de force* was reduced to the flash of an undistinguished stand-in being whisked from the water on the end of a line, cutting quickly to a close-up of a real trout landing at the boy's feet – shot some weeks hence, back in the studio.

The film turned out a charming success and John Bryan, who I liked and admired immensely, asked me to sign a three-year contract with the studio. I quickly raised all my apprehensions. The golden days of Independent and Two Cities had gone, together with Powell and Pressburger, David Lean, Launder and Gilliat, to be replaced by a team of more-than-mediocre producers totally under the sway of the accountants, who now ruled all things both financial and artistic. John was the only one with any real ability, and they held him in a certain degree of awe. 'I promise you will only work with me. I've told them how you feel, and they have agreed.'

I signed and went on to make one more film with him, *Windom's Way,* with Peter Finch and Mary Ure. All seemed set for a happy and secure life when, as is usual, disaster struck. John had a row with the management and resigned. I remained. I had two and a half years hard labour before me.

There followed a succession of bad-to-awful experiences, among the worst a picture called *Floods of Fear.* A phone call late one evening from the studio manager informed me that I was to fly to Ireland in the morning with the director. He would bring a script which I could read on the way over. I would not be working on the film, which was allocated to someone else who was temporarily unavailable, but they needed a cameraman to go and help look for a location. I breathed an audible sigh of relief as I knew a little about the story, which had been the subject of ribald comment in the camera department over the past few weeks. Two escaped convicts, freed by the mighty Mississippi River in flood, rescue a suitably scantily-clad girl and embark on a series of adventures, floating down river on dismembered houses and barns. Next day, on the way over in the plane, the director explained that it was hoped to use parts of the River Shannon for some of the exteriors; the rest would be shot in the studio tank. 'Anyway,' he said, 'skip through the script. It will tell you more quickly than I can what we are about.' This it certainly did not do, for I could see no possible way of filming what read as a large-scale American adventure story, set against a huge panorama of raging torrent, in a very British studio tank 50 or so feet square. 'Well,' he said, as we stepped from the plane, 'what do you think?' I had to be honest and told him, adding, perhaps unadvisedly, that I was very glad I was not on it. The Shannon proved tranquil and fairly useless, short of a second 'flood'.

Two weeks after returning home, I was allocated to the picture. The very worst aspect of being under contract had me firmly in its grasp. The director, Charles Crichton, maker of a number of wonderful Ealing comedies, never held what I had said against me and we soldiered on, making the best of a near impossible job. The main actors, Cyril Cusack and Howard Keel, were heroes, day after day in the dirty waters of the tank at Pinewood, churned to angry foam by the wave machines and frantic prop men with paddles. It occurred to my patently frivolous mind that it might have helped had they given Howard Keel something to sing. The girl, who happened to be the producer's wife, hung dutifully in a clinging negligee to balks of timber or one of the actors and cried and screamed her way through 12 weeks of immersion, mercifully remaining free from any serious infection.

I tried on numerous occasions to get my release, all to no avail. I was a possession; not, I am sure, particularly wanted but the loss of which perhaps involved a certain loss of face somewhere down the line.

At about this time, the Rank Organisation held an elaborate birthday party; a champagne lunch in marquees on the studio lawn, beautifully embossed leather diaries given to all the tame producers and the film press assembled to hear John Davies announce a spectacular programme of forthcoming productions. Just a few weeks later, all had turned to dust. The productions had vanished into thin air and there was a redundancy in all departments. I eagerly volunteered to sacrifice myself for the good of the company, but it was not to be.

The unions were rightly upset by the sudden turn of events and asked for a meeting with the management. This was agreed and I, not a very active member, was asked if I would agree to being co-opted with several others to stiffen the ranks. It was, I felt, a chance to see the fun, and I readily agreed.

We were arranged formally around the mile-long table in the boardroom, a fresh notepad, pen and glass of water before each place. We lesser mortals sat in our allocated seats, humbly awaiting the entrance of the great man flanked by his 'yes' men. After a suitable period of nervous waiting, they made a triumphant entry, ushered to reserved seats which dominated the meeting. Straightaway, John Davies went on the attack. A long and carefully prepared set of statistics showed how the cinema box office was declining by the hour. In the last year more people had stayed away than continued to go. It had been unpredictable and chaotic, action had to be taken. The figures were accurate and common knowledge, and the way he delivered them made it clear that they were not open for discussion. His forceful speech completed, he sat down, no doubt considering the meeting closed, when a timid, bespectacled young man from the cutting rooms got nervously to his feet. 'Do you think, sir,' he quavered, 'that perhaps we are not making the right sort of films? Perhaps people don't want commercials and long breaks for the sale of confectionery and drinks. Should we not try and make quality pictures which are not to be seen on television?'

He was cut short just as he was gaining confidence by a scarlet-faced John Davies leaping to his feet. 'Do you think we don't know what we are doing?' he thundered, as the little editor shrank back into his seat, and hopefully from view. 'We conduct questionnaires at the box office almost daily, to be sure what our audiences like and want.'

The devil in me surfaced and I asked politely, 'Might it not be an idea to ask the ones who no longer go, since they outnumber the ones who do?' Next morning, I was called into the studio manager, who informed me that I was being released from my contract. In fact they would waive the month's notice, pay the money, and I could go at once.

31

Under water

Being a freelance has its compensations, for it gives the opportunity to choose which pictures to do and who you work with, but in practice this freedom becomes severely curtailed by the sheer necessity of earning a living. The longed-for ending of a hard and perhaps tedious picture, 16 or more six- or seven-day weeks, holds the prospect of some time at home with one's family, the chance to indulge some of one's interests, with perhaps even a holiday, although of course it is usually in the middle of winter. The first few days of freedom soon become marred by gnawing anxiety about the next job. Perhaps, after all, it would be silly to spend money on a holiday, or indeed anything else, in case the industry is in for one of its longer periods of depression. Soon you are waiting anxiously for the phone to ring, with illogical thoughts already gaining credence in your subconscious that you are unwanted and your career is over. The call, when it does come, may well be the offer of a ghastly picture with even ghastlier people, so what do you decide? You don't want the picture but you need their money. To accept such an offer would be sheer prostitution, you might say, but even that can be justified when times are hard enough.

It often surprised me how I could convince myself, against all common sense, that a thoroughly unpalatable offer was really a challenge, the chance to make a silk purse from the proverbial sow's ear. This period of self-engendered enthusiasm could no doubt be explained by the need to justify to oneself the taking of the fatal decision, quickly to be overtaken on roughly the second day of shooting by a feeling of intense gloom as the prospect of the next few weeks became a reality.

It was on an occasion such as this that I got a call in 1976 from Columbia, to ask me if I would like to photograph *The Deep*. A sequel to *Jaws*, it was to be made in the Virgin Islands, followed by a long period in Bermuda. There was nothing awful about this offer, the only apparent drawback being that it would once again mean a long period away from home. This prospect has become less attractive with the passing of the years, which have brought with them a knowledge of what locations are really like. Three days later I was having dinner with the associate producer in New York, in order that he might 'fill me in' with all the details. The director was to be Peter Yates, now settled in America, with whom I had worked briefly some years back on a series of commercials. This short experience of working together had left me with the impression that he would go far, as indeed he has, and I liked him very much. The producer was Peter Guber, an executive from Columbia making his debut in this particular capacity. The cast included Robert Shaw, Jaqueline Bisset and Eli Wallach, an old friend from *The Victors*. The crew were to be largely American, but I could have my own camera crew and electricians. Yet another underwater thriller from the pen of Peter Benchley, the villain this time, in place of a shark, was a huge moray eel whose abode was in a sunken wreck which also contained treasure. For the establishing shots they had chosen the remains of a mail steamer, lost some 80 years ago on a small island some eight miles from Tortola in the British Virgin Islands. In a good state of preservation, it looked perfect for the purpose, judging from the excellent photographs they had of it. The 'interiors', if one can use that term to describe the inside of a sunken wreck, were to be filmed in Bermuda, where it was proposed to excavate a huge tank in the coral which forms the substance of the island. In this big 'hole' the interior 'set' of the wreck would be built. The walls of the excavation were to be coated with a plastic material which could be painted to give the illusion of infinity when glimpsed through gaps in the sunken ship. When filled with water pumped up from the sea, it would be submerged to a depth of about 30 feet. A marine biologist would be in charge of populating the tank with hundreds of fish, including two small sharks, and already people were engaged in catching this marine menagerie, holding them in a penned-off area in a shallow bay in Bermuda. The company had already engaged two expert divers and underwater photographers who would be responsible for all the underwater filming, while I got on with the rest of the picture.

Filming was to start in the Virgin Islands, diving on the real wreck and using experienced divers as doubles for the artists. Peter

Yates and the assistant director had both been on diving courses and would be supervising the filming. At a meeting next day with Peter, he told me that he had certain reservations about the underwater crew as, although outstanding experts in their field, they were not film cameramen. He felt, quite rightly as it transpired, that shooting a fictional story underwater demanded the same knowledge of angles and lenses, coupled with general feature film know-how needed on dry land, to ensure that the material would all cut together properly. Although not actively involved in the shooting, he wanted me to be in the Virgin Islands so that I could hold a watching brief, viewing the rushes with him and offering suggestions.

My arrival on Peter Island coincided with the screening of the first week's work which, to put it mildly, was disappointing. They had been working on a night sequence, with long shots of the divers approaching the wreck, and had shot it at night with the aid of small underwater lights which were totally inadequate to light the vast area. Had the scene been on dry land, it would have been a problem which, almost certainly, I would have resolved by using the 'day for night' technique, using filters and underexposure to give the illusion of night in daylight. I could not see why this approach would not work equally well below the water but, of course, I had no experience to go on. 'Would you be prepared to have a crash diving course?' asked Peter. 'I feel it is essential that you come down and see how things are for yourself.' First thing next morning I was in the hotel swimming pool, complete with flippers, face mask and air bottle, my waist encircled with a weight belt of such magnitude that, in spite of the instructor's assurances to the contrary, I was convinced it would consign me permanently to the ocean bed. My temporary consolation was the fact that in the safety of the pool, if my worst fears were realised, I could always stand up. So the first morning passed, consuming vast quantities of air and not a little highly chlorinated water as I went through the routine safety training.

My companions on the course were the producer and his daughter, a particularly obnoxious American 12-year-old. As is the custom with all film crews, I had been quickly filled in on the subject of Peter Guber, the producer. Of a species not commanding universal affection in the film world, this particular example was known to the American crew as the 'electric Jew', a name derived from his habit of accompanying all speech with violent staccato movements of his hands and arms and, in moments of stress, his whole body. Since he talked more or less continuously, the overall effect was of an electrically energised puppet. Next morning my sole companion in the pool was the daughter, father having temporarily abandoned the idea of diving in favour of more lucrative pursuits. Having studied me for some minutes in silence she asked, 'What's your name?' 'Chris Challis,' I answered. 'I don't like you,' she volunteered. I replied that the feeling was mutual, it having by now extended to her father. This brief encounter, no doubt faithfully reported back, possibly accounted for a certain lack of warmth in my association with Peter Guber for the rest of the picture.

'You're doing fine,' said the enthusiastic instructor as we stopped for lunch. 'Meet up at two o'clock and we'll try a dive at sea.' Clad in all the gear, including the massive weight belt, I felt as though I weighed a ton. In spite of the reassuring exercises in the pool, I could see no way of such a grotesque and heavy object as myself ever regaining the surface. 'Sit on the side of the boat facing inwards, then all you have to do is roll over backwards into the water. Remember to hold your face mask on and don't forget to breathe,' were the last encouraging instructions before I committed myself to the deep. The first reaction, once in the water, was to regain the surface as quickly as possible, gulping vast quantities of air on the way. To my intense surprise, I discovered that it was very simple, for, once in the water, I was almost weightless. As I hung like a limpet to the side of the boat he said, 'Try to breathe normally, as you would do on land. Everyone uses far too much air to begin with, it's anxiety that causes it,' an explanation I readily fell in with. I was lucky, for in no time at all I felt completely at home below the surface, enchanted by the wonderful world which was revealed. After two or three more dives in company with him, he pronounced me fit to go down on the wreck next day. 'Keep a careful eye on your air. A bottle should last you about 20 minutes, but you are still using more than you need.'

The diving operation was master-minded by a professional salvage team from Miami, who kept a careful eye on novices such as myself. Their boat, the *Moby Dick*, was equipped with facilities for recharging the air bottles, an underwater communication system which enabled them to speak to us, although we could not talk to them, and a decompression tank in case of accident. I quickly found that, as I had anticipated, the photographic problems were very similar to those on land. After a number of tests, we worked out a system of filters, together with a level of underexposure which produced a very convincing night effect. I quickly became involved with all aspects of the filming, fortunately retaining a happy relationship with the underwater photographers, who did not seem to resent my encroaching on their domain. I learned a great deal from them, and I like to think that they in turn picked up a few tips from me. The essence of the job was to plan exactly what was to be shot before going down. We would attempt only one scene at a time, which was carefully worked out with drawings and sketches at a conference before each dive. Using two or even three cameras simultaneously, each angle and lens had to be decided on so that the camera operator knew precisely the size of shot he must get in order to avoid duplication, at the same time making certain that it would all cut together in the editing stages later on. The actors or their doubles had to be involved in these meetings as, once underwater, there was no means of communication apart from notes written to each other on white plastic boards with a Chinagraph pencil, a slow process when time was limited by the air supply.

After five weeks of work on the wreck, the long shots were completed and we moved to Bermuda to join the rest of the company. By now I had become so involved in the underwater work that Peter Yates asked me to continue with the shooting in the tank. This involved complicated scenes with the principal actors, who had in the meantime been taking diving instruction with varying degrees of success. In the light of my experience in the Virgin Islands, I realised that we would need an elaborate system of underwater lights if we were to achieve the effects required by the script. None of this had been foreseen by the original crew, who were relying on the small waterproof lamps they normally used for their work but which were quite unsuitable for the sort of things we had to do. In fact what we required were normal studio lamps, capable of being controlled and able to take diffusion and coloured filters. A telephone call to John Lee of Lee Electrics back in London, who were supplying all our electrical equipment, brought the assurance that they could supply and make all the things I needed. In a matter of days it all arrived by air.

The tank was full of water, the fishy population happily installed in their new environment, the huge, mechanical moray eel installed in his lair among the wreckage, ready to pounce on the unwary. A large notice forbade those entering the water from urinating while submerged, a not uncommon practice in swimming pools generally. This would disturb the ecological balance of the water, so our biologist said, and rapidly kill off the unsuspecting inhabitants, so carefully gathered over the preceding months. These fish, of all shapes and sizes, and in all colours of the rainbow, fascinated me from the start, for they showed no concern whatever for the floundering humans in their midst. The smaller ones would swim right up and gaze at you through the glass of your face mask, showing only the mildest curiosity. Unlike other members of the animal world, they had experienced so little contact with humans that they had no knowledge of man's perfidy.

They were fed twice daily on a gourmet diet, which seemed to consist mainly of smaller and weaker representatives of their own kind, thus sharing the common will to survive with the rest of the crew, whose problems were more emotional than physical. This feeding process was carried out by the same girl diver each day, who took the food down in a fine-mesh sack. On reaching the bottom she would snap her fingers, which obviously made a sound underwater, and the fish would gather in shoals around her, nibbling at her hair and arms. They were intent on enjoying this gastronomic bounty so lavishly bestowed on them by courtesy of Peter Guber, whose concern for their well-being was certainly not motivated by worries about endangered species, unless they happened to be film producers. It was rumoured, again by his fellow Americans on the crew, that he was the only person to contravene the urination ban, which he felt was his prerogative as producer.

In spite of the most careful planning and rehearsal on dry land of every shot, disaster in one form or another soon struck once we were submerged. The eel proved a problem, with its complicated electrical and hydraulic control system operated by two or three special effects men who sat on tubular scaffolding above the water, trying desperately to unravel the muffled instructions emanating from 30 feet below. On one such an occasion, the script required the eel to dart from its lair in a flurry of foam, snapping up a brightly-coloured fish which was to be swimming in large close-up just in front of the camera. The marine biologist had charge of the fish, which he was to release in exactly the right spot at the right time, with the actors involved also in their positions, ready to react in horror. It would probably occur to the average child of 12 that the chances of success were not very great, but film people have no such simplicity of reason. Take after take went by, with always something out of place. The fish, of course, had no intention of ending its life in the jaws of a mechanical eel, and was away each time before the biologist could get his hand out of the picture. With all of us floundering around trying to maintain position, the eel emerged half a minute or so late, making a concerted effort to consume the camera, the camera operator and various portions of the assembled company's anatomy, in fact anything that lay in its 'flight' path. At last, in an atmosphere of more or less total chaos, we were all running out of air, so it was back to the surface for another briefing and a rethink of what to do.

The fish expert came up with the answer. He would inject the fish with a mild tranquilliser, something we could all have done with at this juncture, then if communications could be improved with the eel operators up above, all would be well. With fresh air bottles, we assembled down below, carefully getting into our positions in order not to stir up too much silt. At last we were ready. Put the fish in position, signalled the director. The bemused and now docile victim was put in front of the camera. All was well, apart from the disconcerting fact that the fish floated upside down due to its semi-comatose state, so it was back to the surface for further discussion. Once again the fish man had the answer. He would ballast the fish with small weights, invisible to the camera, and this time it would work. By now the fish had decided that death in the jaws of the eel was preferable to further humiliation and after another ten or so attempts we got the shot. A whole day had passed, with many more like it to follow. For animal or fish lovers the world over, I must add that the fish lived to see another day, with a story larger than life to pass on to his grandchildren.

The actors responded in different ways to this frustrating underwater world, where means of self-expression were severely limited. We only used them in the close shots where they were readily recognised, all other shooting being done with professional divers. Nick Nolte took to it all like the proverbial duck to water, seemingly enjoying every moment. When not needed for a scene, he would come down anyway and help moving the lights and equipment. All union regulations went by the board, the many tasks being shared out among anyone on the unit who was willing and able to dive. How refreshing it was to work with a very small group of people all taking a close interest in all that was going on. Each day we became more adept at solving the many difficulties which inevitably arose. There was, I felt, a lesson to be learned from all this, to be applied to the more normal environment of filming where union regulations and lines of demarcation so often result in unnecessarily large crews. Perhaps we were getting back to the early days of film making, when all concerned were pioneers taking part in a great and exciting adventure.

Robert Shaw, who, in common with a number of fine actors, suffered from a severe drink problem, never cared much for the endless hours of waiting which would inevitably end with yet another sortie to the bottom of the tank. He never mastered the art of evacuating his face mask, which slowly filled with water as the minutes ticked away. Whenever we did a scene with him in close-up we had to be absolutely ready to shoot, bringing him down at the last possible moment. It was rather alarming to see the water level in his face mask slowly rising as we struggled to get the scene, until it reached the point when he was quietly drowning, yet all the time wearing an expression of slightly bemused resignation.

Peter Guber, acutely aware of Jackie Bisset's shape and good looks, was determined that these assets should be exploited to the full, even in the most dramatic situations of great danger. Although she was clad in the most revealing of swim suits, he felt that too much of her face was obscured by the mask, which he thought, in the final analysis, the cinema-going public would be more concerned with than the eel. To solve this problem, he had a special face mask designed with transparent sides and made in white rubber to further enhance the feeling of *haute couture* having entered the world of Cousteau. Now the Bisset profile would be revealed to the camera instead of being totally obscured by the more functional masks worn by ordinary mortals. The mask's arrival from Hollywood, where it was made, was eagerly awaited, as all scenes with her were deferred to a later date. When at last it came, it was demonstrated by Jackie in the make-up department, seemingly doing all that Peter Guber wanted, perhaps even heralding a new departure in scuba wear where the divers were concerned to see each other's profiles. Unfortunately, when below the surface at 30 feet, it lacked rigidity, the pressure pushing the front glass onto her nose and transforming her beauty into a close resemblance of a retired and unsuccessful boxer. The solution to this problem occupied endless modifications, accompanied by exhaustive tests, and was never found. The final decision was to revert to a conventional mask with the largest possible glass, sacrificing the profile for a normal front view.

Miss Bisset's concern about her looks, which after all were a large part of her stock-in-trade, exceeded even that of Peter Guber. Before going down for a scene, she would sit on the platform from which we entered the water, surrounded by make-up and hairdressing, checking every detail of her appearance in a large hand mirror which was her constant companion. While the rest of us waited impatiently in or under the water, her last act was to carefully comb her hair, an operation which took several minutes, the results of which were rendered totally unnecessary the moment she entered the water, as indeed was most of the painstaking make-up which was hidden by the face mask.

It may be worth mentioning at this point that she shared with a number of other ladies a habit supremely irritating to cameramen. It is the custom when lighting a big close-up to check the final adjustment of the lamps and effects with the artist in position, having done the preliminary work with a stand-in. The aim is to check the direction of each look during the scene, making certain that everything is as near perfect as possible, bearing in mind that the result on the screen will be some 60 feet wide. It was never possible to get her to look in the right place for more than a moment, as she would constantly try to look at her reflection in the front glass of the camera to make sure that all was well.

The principal 'baddie' in the story was played by Lou Gossett a huge black actor and one-time Mr Universe. His incredible muscular development and stature were more than matched by an intense dislike of the water, which reached paranoid proportions when required to venture below. It proved impossible to convince him to wear sufficient weight on his belt to make working on the bottom a practical possibility. He, like Robert Shaw, could not get rid of the water in his face mask by the simple expedient of blowing it out, so he quickly faced the possibility of drowning in front of the camera. When all was ready for a take, two divers would bring him down, his feet encased in a pair of the biggest flippers obtainable and flailing wildly in all directions. They played havoc with anything or anybody who got in the way and, in the process, stirred up clouds of silt mixed with flakes of paint from the 'set', so that visibility was quickly reduced to nil. As the two guides pushed him into position, his eyes would roll wildly, the water level rising in his mask, his sense of self-preservation overcoming all desire to become an underwater actor. Once the cameras were running, the guides were signalled to release him and get out of the shot as fast as possible, by which time he had floated up and stuck like a giant black bat on the ceiling. Here he remained, unable to move, until he was dragged down for another attempt.

After six weeks of struggle with adversity in the depths of the tank, unwittingly created for us by the imagination and able pen of Peter Benchley, at last it was all over. The newly found fascination for the underwater had grown dim with the passage of time, both aesthetically and physically, as the water became more and more murky with the build-up of silt and algae, despite heroic attempts by our biologist to filter it out with massive pumps. Even the fish population had become disenchanted with their rapidly deteriorating home, coupled with the ludicrous antics of the humans. The 'magic of the movies' seemed to have worn a bit thin for them, too, as they did their best to hide away in the deeper recesses of the set. It was only with the greatest of difficulty that we were able to drive a few of them into the background of a shot, all spare bodies being enlisted to act as underwater beaters. More than one scene was cut because we had more enthusiastic beaters in the scene than fish.

The rest of the picture, in the warm sunshine above, came as a welcome relief. Two large sail lofts in the old harbour area, dating from the Napoleonic Wars, were turned into studios and life returned to what passes for normal in the world of films. One more film completed, one more chapter of one's life passed into obscurity. The only record left was a piece of celluloid for the critics to dissect with little charity, unaware as they must be of the heartache and 'a thousand natural shocks' which were part of its making.

32

A matter of seconds

My story cannot end without touching briefly on the world of the TV commercial. With the decline in cinema-going, the consequent massive unemployment among film technicians has been eased by opportunities of work on these 30-second, or less, films in miniature. Unlike America, where all the massive product for television is made by outside companies, using people from the feature film industry, here in England television has provided little or no work as the BBC and ITV make most of their own subjects using staff under contract. The advent of Channel Four has slightly changed this position, but the commercial remains the chief hope of succour for the hard-pressed out-of-work with not a feature film in sight. Commercials have also undoubtedly given opportunities to young and inexperienced directors to make their mark, though many might appear a little too young and inexperienced to command much respect. Perhaps it does require great talent to get a good performance from a packet of cornflakes.

Before I write another word, I must be fair and admit that our commercials are by far the best in the world, some of them brilliantly conceived and shot. Much of what they have tried has now become part of the modern approach to films. Here my eulogy must end, for in spite of my admiration for a lot of what they did, I found most of the people involved unbearable, a sentiment no doubt they shared about me. With a hierarchy far more complex than on a major feature film, one had to contend with the 'client', the agency, and the producers. The client tended to manifest itself in large numbers during shooting, particularly if the subject was a member of the female sex. Refugees from highly paid jobs in luxurious offices and boardrooms, this was the opportunity of a lifetime to venture forth into the world of glamour and make-believe, their word for one brief day holding more sway than that of Cecil B. de Mille. Then came the agency, who had thought up the idea. They were usually represented by the executive who handled the account, accompanied by numerous assistants. The designer was the man who had committed the 'idea' to paper with the aid of the art director, who came armed with a portfolio of beautifully produced sketches illustrating every possible aspect of the subject. They usually had with them several experts in the arrangement of props, who came into their own when the pack shot was made, usually at the end of the day, or even more usually in the early hours of the morning. This could be anything from a packet of frozen peas to a jar of moisturising cream. Whatever it was, there were hard and fast rules to be observed. Certain things had been established from past experience, coupled with endless market research. They knew beyond doubt just how the public liked their peas to look, the exact shade of green, each one separate and shining with the correct amount of moisture. If they were to be shown cooking in a saucepan, they could never appear mushy. The best way, they had discovered, was not to cook them at all but instead to place a small piece of 'dry cold' under them, when they would steam and bubble convincingly while retaining the desired visual appeal. In one case it had been discovered that someone else's peas were more photogenic, so these were substituted for the final shot.

In another instance, the product was a well-known fruit drink. The bottle was to be photographed on a sheet of glass, surrounded by bunches of berries which went into its making. Beyond the glass was a nebulous background which would give the effect of floating in space. The berries and leaves were sprayed with castor oil to produce a luscious shine, then meticulously arranged one by one with a pair of tweezers by a gentleman from the agency. I think he must have been the art director, for with shoulder-length hair, he was attired in a leather jacket and trousers with tasselled hems, closely resembling a Sioux Indian, with knee-length boots to match. To complete the illusion his neck was adorned with several long necklaces made from coloured stones and what appeared to be teeth, perhaps trophies from past hunting trips among the caribou.

The camera was mounted on a very tall tripod as it had to shoot vertically down and, since he was a very small man, he had to mount a tier of insecure boxes each time he wanted to inspect the result of the latest adjustment. The necklaces proved an encumbrance, catching on the camera and tripod alike as the art director ascended his perch, the necklace made of teeth finally breaking and its grisly components scattered over the studio floor. From time to time a berry would be squashed by the pressure of the tweezers and his none too steady hand, which meant cleaning the whole thing off and starting again. The clients, the agency and the producers queued up to mount the boxes, in turn expressing delight at what they saw. At last everyone was happy with the composition and it was time to light. The picture had to be free of all shadows, with the shine on the berries and the bottle in exactly the right place, a requirement which entailed several dozen or more trips up and down the pile of boxes for the assembled company before at last universal approval was obtained. The best part of an afternoon had slipped away for a shot which would last two or three seconds on the screen.

Perhaps I am entirely unqualified to pass judgement on this very precious little world, for I was involved in very few of these experiences, either because I was not asked, which may well be understandable, or because I could not trust myself to go through with it and keep a straight face.

My feelings are perhaps best summed up by the saga of one very expensive cigarette commercial I was asked to do. It was to launch a new king size version of a well-known brand in the Far East, the agency contingent coming from Kuala Lumpur. It was to be used on television and in the cinema, including a Cinemascope version, which meant that everything had to be shot three times. There were in fact to be two commercials, one set in London, the other in New York. In each case the idea was to show a number of top executives relaxing on their yachts, playing polo or just sitting happily in their luxury homes, then being hastily called to an urgent board meeting where a decision of crucial importance had to be taken. Opinions differ, tempers rise, there is complete deadlock. In the ensuring dramatic silence, someone pulls out a packet of the cigarettes, lights up, and draws heavily on the cool and comforting brand. The pack is passed around with magic effect. In no time at all, nerves are calmed, reason returns, sweeping decisions are taken in moments and the impasse is instantly resolved.

The first meeting was to be shot in a large office overlooking the Thames; the second, 30 floors up in an apartment looking onto the Manhatten skyline.

Having completed the scenes showing the various directors being summoned by telephone, telegram or fast car from whatever they indulged in during their free moments, we set about the London board meeting. Scheduled for two days, midnight on the first day found us less than a quarter of the way through. There were endless discussions about the finer points of the script, the men's clothes, the furniture, make-up and hair. With a strong Oriental flavour entering into the thinking and emanating from the group from Kuala Lumpur, who really held the whip hand, the situation was further complicated by language difficulties. The production designer, whose opinion was sought on every single aspect of the job, was possessed of very definite ideas about most things, which he expressed at length but sadly not in English, for he was Chinese. The futile attempts of a not too fluent interpreter to clarify the situation served only to further confuse it, as everyone talked or even shouted at once. During a lull in the proceedings, I pointed out with a degree of temerity that we were in London, it was November and that darkness would be upon us by four o'clock, blotting out the cherished view of the river and replaced by large areas of blank plate glass, waiting to reflect us all in the shot. I was told somewhat tartly that it was not a feature film, where one could afford to be slipshod. Every detail mattered and must be resolved to general satisfaction, no matter how long it took. Sure enough, darkness, which like death has a quality of inevitability about it, descended on us as we laboured to please. Film producers in general seem to share a common ignorance about these natural phenomena, which include the rise and fall of the tide. It might be deemed to indicate that something is lacking in their grasp of general knowledge, or maybe they feel, like King Canute, that it is possible to control these matters.

* * *

Some years ago a film was made which centred on a small yacht. The producer had chosen the Channel Islands as the perfect location. With the large crew happily installed in hotels, everyone was called down to the harbour in the evening to see the yacht, which had just arrived from the Hamble, lying alongside the quay. There she was, her decks slightly above the level of the quayside, surrounded by picturesque fishing boats with the gulls wheeling overhead, a perfect setting for what had to be filmed in the coming weeks. Next morning at 8.30, when work was due to commence, she lay 40 feet down the harbour wall with only the tops of her masts visible. This alarming situation was further compounded by the fact, which was also a revelation to the producer, that it would not occur at the same time each day but had the habit of being about an hour later. Havoc was caused with the schedule as filming could only take place during the three or four hours during which the boat could be seen, unless they were willing to settle for a close-up of a weed-covered harbour wall as background to the scenes.

* * *

Having digressed momentarily, I must return to the boardroom, now enveloped by night. What were we to do? It was impossible to come back for another day as everyone was booked to fly to Spain the following morning. What remained of the scene would have to be re-orientated so that it could be filmed shooting away from the windows. 'But surely the reason we came here was the view of the river and Parliament?' I ventured to ask. 'We have to make do with what we have got,' was the logical answer. After much discussion, they were able to justify this decision to each other with the exception of the art director, who did not like the walls of the room which would now feature in the background. We must get pictures and drapes to make it more interesting, he insisted. This proved no easy matter as it was already eight o'clock, at which time all self-respecting dealers who hired out such things had gone home. After a chase around town by the property master, knocking up all his contacts, the background at last met with approval and we could complete the scene. All that remained was the 'pack' shot, or rather the three versions of it. It was to consist of a slow motion shot in extreme close-up of well-groomed fingertips flicking alight a gold cigarette lighter. We were then to follow the flame down the length of the king size cigarette to the tip and see it ignited, the first luxurious puff of smoke blotting out the picture.

This sort of shot demands extreme accuracy of movement by the actor, whose arm may well be held in some sort of clamp as an error in position of just half an inch could put it all out of focus. Believe it or not, there exists a breed of specialists known as 'pack shot artists', whose hands and nerves are steadier than their more ordinary brethren and who devote their lives to perfection in this limited field, no doubt forsaking alcohol along with other human indulgences in return for shake-free hands. It was after midnight before everyone was happy or resigned to the inevitable, depending on how one viewed these matters, when disaster struck.

They had brought the wrong cigarettes! Carton upon carton of them lay around, shipped over from Kuala Lumpur, but they were all the old model. Some small change had been made to the filter tip or the colour of the paper, I forget which, rendering them all obsolete. The cigarettes were not on sale in Europe so there was no question of slipping out to buy a pack. All seemed lost when an inspired member of the agency contingent came up with the solution. There was another well-known brand on the market and readily available, identical in every way apart from the fact that it had the manufacturer's name printed along the side of the cigarette. If we could avoid seeing this there was no reason why they could not fill a packet of their own with the other brand. Since it must be a virgin packet, great care had to be taken to make sure that it showed no trace of having been opened. We would need many packs because each time anything was out of position it meant starting all over again. We all sat around for a couple of hours, most of the crew on 'golden hours', while they set about the near impossible task, for not a crease must show in the foil wrapping or cellophane outer cover. To the already complicated movements involved in the shot, had now been added the problem that the cigarette had to come out of the packet in exactly the right way so that the name would not show, a fact that was not appreciated until after the first few abortive attempts.

Bleary-eyed, we dragged ourselves home as the city roused itself around us for another day, with just a few hours to pack and catch the flight to Spain and Switzerland, where more executives were to be summoned to the ill-fated meeting. These two locations were not devoid of drama, culminating in an early morning departure from Barcelona on a direct flight to New York. The director, who had not succeeded in endearing himself to many people during the few days we had been working together, had lost no opportunity to impress us with his extensive worldwide experience, particularly in the realm of travel know-how. Constantly critical of all the arrangements which he, at least, was convinced could have been more effectively made by himself, we were all delighted to find that he was unable to board the flight for New York because he had omitted to get an American visa.

With several days to wait in New York while he returned to England to sort things out, I was asked to pick the locations for the various sequences. The apartment overlooking the Manhattan skyline which was to be the setting for the board meeting had already been fixed, but they needed an expensive-looking house in a residential suburb for a 15–second shot of an executive being picked up by a large Cadillac, to be rushed off to the meeting. In this brief flash they explained, we had to convey wealth, success and New York. We found what appeared to be the perfect place, a grand, rather Regency-looking house with, in the near distance, the unmistakable New York skyline. Several days later, with the director returned to our midst complete with visa, we went out to shoot the scene. I showed him what we had planned, which did not appear to meet his 'visual interpretation of the scene', as he was wont to put it. With a viewfinder, which he constantly carried on a chain around his neck, he set about positioning the Cadillac in front of the house, kneeling in the road so that he had the New York number plate large in the foreground, while in the background there was nothing but the front door of the house. 'That says New York to me,' he said, rather overlooking the other requirements of wealth and success. 'If that's what you want, we could have done it in London,' exasperation drove me to answer. 'I feel sure that a New York number plate would work out considerably less expensive than the air fares.'

The crisis board meeting in the apartment turned out to be a near repetition of the one in London. This time we did have the correct cigarettes, but the owners of the block refused to allow us to use the elevators for the equipment. Since the apartment was situated on the 30th floor, this was no mean problem. The crew repaired to a nearby coffee bar while the management entered into negotiations with the owners of the block, the impasse being resolved by the handing over of what seemed a small fortune in dollars. This somehow resolved the safety requirements, which had apparently been the objection. The crew were at this stage mostly American, this interlude affording us the opportunity of exchanging experiences concerning commercials and the people who make them. It quickly transpired that their opinions exactly coincided with our own, so the disease must be international. By the time things were sorted out, it was midday and snowing hard, with little to see of the view from the large windows. In four hours it would be dark and there was no possibility of returning for a second day. It had emerged during the negotiations with the owners of the block that the person from whom they had hired the apartment was considerably in arrears with the rent, which was no doubt the underlying reason why there was a problem over the elevators.

Once again it all dragged on into the early hours of the morning. Everything was turned around to avoid the windows which we had travelled 3000 miles to look through. The same hunt for furnishings and drapes, and the same endless discussions about trivial detail, ended with the 'pack' shot, this time with an actor who had very shaky hands, matched by a complete incomprehension of what we were trying to achieve.

The final port of call was to be the Virgin Islands, where we were to film yet another 15-second flash of an executive being recalled from a holiday aboard his yacht by means of the radio telephone. 'Why the Virgin Islands?' we asked, though not averse to a few days down there in the sun. 'Because we have chartered a marvellous yacht and we have the certainty of good weather together with an exotic background,' was the answer. I had made the journey before via San Juan in Puerto Rico, and was aware that the final stage was in small De Havilland aircraft almost bereft of luggage space. 'We shall have a problem with our mountain of gear.' 'That's not your concern,' was the haughty reply from the producer. 'Do you imagine that this is the first time we have done this sort of thing?' I could barely refrain from replying that, after three weeks with them, this was precisely the impression I had got.

Twenty-four hours later we were in the Virgin Islands minus the gear and all our personal luggage, which was delivered by instalments over the next three days. The yacht charter had to be extended, putting the skipper in a strong bargaining position which he exploited to the full. Never mind, it was well worth it to get something so unique. This, in the final analysis, consisted of three shots: a long shot of the yacht under sail against a bare horizon, a close shot of the executive on the telephone down below in the cabin and, finally, a shot of the yacht berthing in the marina, which could well have been in Brighton, our man jumping ashore complete with briefcase before the yacht had been made fast, so great was the call of duty. The yacht, incidentally, was built in Southampton and to my certain knowledge there were at least six sister ships in the Solent.

I never summoned up sufficient courage to ask whether our efforts worldwide had achieved the hoped-for impact on cigarette smokers in the Far East. The opportunity to enquire never presented itself for I never saw any of them again. In all probability they were as glad to see the back of me as I certainly was of them.

33

Under no illusions

MY LAST FEW years of activity before retiring, I trust gracefully, from the scene, seem now in retrospect less clear or remarkable in my memory, although so much closer in terms of time. Perhaps the enthusiasm of youth had become tarnished and familiarity with the unusual, and often the outrageous, had bred contempt. Different people were making different films, the scene had changed dramatically and perhaps I had stood still. A conviction that I had seen the best years grew steadily in the wake of successively dull projects. The movies had lost their 'magic' for the audiences and for me too. The public had been transported to the ends of the earth on the magic celluloid carpet and had seen it all. The adventurous element seemed to have gone out of film making as the costs of production soared dramatically. Air travel, now the sole means of getting anywhere, was commonplace and dull, with less to look at than a ride across London on top of a double-decker bus. The smart new air terminals began to look tatty, dirty and overcrowded, the air hostesses uglier and more aggressive. I believe that the technical airline terminology for handling passengers is 'processing', and no word could possibly be more apt.

I was, however, fortunate enough during this period to make two pictures for John Brabourne and his partner, Richard Goodwin. Richard had entered the industry, if that is the correct term to describe the union's steadfast attempt to prevent keen, young people from making a start, by joining as a general dogsbody when we were shooting *Sink the Bismarck*. Willing to run any errand and undertake any task, no matter how menial, he quickly became indispensable, at the same time gaining a thorough working knowledge of all departments, including the art of making tea, so dear to the heart of film crews. He rose almost meteorically to be co-producer, and together he and John Brabourne made *Romeo and Juliet, Death on the Nile,* and so on.

The first picture I did with them, directed by Guy Hamilton, was the *The Mirror Crack'd,* with Elizabeth Taylor, Kim Novak, Rock Hudson, Tony Curtis, and those two nicest of artists, Edward Fox and Angela Lansbury. True to current fashion, it was to be filmed mostly on location in Kent, using a small manor house for the interiors. This presented a problem for me, for without in any way wishing to be unkind, Elizabeth was past the first flush of youth and needed careful lighting to present her in the most favourable fashion. Getting her from her hotel in London for an 8.30 call proved quite impossible. Time for Elizabeth simply did not exist, at least in terms of early morning starts. When she did arrive, she was always completely disarming, and offered no excuses, apart from being Elizabeth Taylor, who after all had never been on time. She made up for it all by being the complete professional in all other aspects. Kim Novak, on the other hand, presented me with different problems. She wore her years, whatever they may number, with almost alarming lightness. Slim, good looking as ever, she had more or less retired from acting to live with her husband, a veterinary expert, I believe, on a ranch in California where they raised llamas as domestic pets, which had apparently become the 'in' thing in Hollywood society.

In the script Kim and Elizabeth were meant to be at daggers drawn, fiendishly jealous of each other's looks and every movement, and it would be fair to say that this atmosphere of confrontation was more or less reflected in real life, at least for the period of the film. Kim had been used to her key light being carefully set for every shot and, like most artists, had learned just where it should be. In the confined circumstances of working in a real house, this system of lighting had long since gone by the board and on each set-up she searched in vain for what she had grown to expect. Slowly but surely she convinced herself that she was getting second-rate treatment and I became aware that day by day the gap between us grew ever wider, although the bone of her contention was never openly mentioned. Finally she went to John and Richard and told them she was unhappy with the way she was being photographed although, at this point, she had not seen a foot of the film. Richard, who told me what was going on, arranged next day for her to see everything we had shot. She rushed onto the set afterwards, threw her arms round my neck, apologised for everything and announced to everyone that she had never looked better. From there on we joked daily about her key light, or rather the lack of it, and she never again questioned what we were doing. This little incident is, I feel, a good example of the difficulties that beset the path of a cameraman. A good relationship with actors is essential, for with some a sense of insecurity, or a feeling that they might be getting second best, can undermine their whole performance, sensitive creatures that they are. Many directors do not allow them into rushes, nor indeed do they allow members of the make-up and hairdressing departments, for they of all people are often the catalysts of trouble, particularly if they happen to be part of a personal entourage, as they so often are.

The second picture, also directed by Guy Hamilton, was *Evil Under the Sun*. Once again they had assembled a wonderful cast; Peter Ustinov, Diana Rigg, Maggie Smith and a host of other glittering names. Extensive locations in Majorca were coupled with studio shooting back in Wembley. As usual with their productions, all the ingredients were there as before, their fourth time round with an Agatha Christie story. This time the mix did not work, at least at the box office. It is one more example of an observation I made much earlier, that every picture is a prototype. Of course there are many exceptions to this rule, like the Bond series, but even they run their course. Nevertheless a well organised and happy picture to work on, it remains firmly among my favourites. Among other attributes, it conferred on me the experience of living in the Goodwin *ménage* during the studio period.

A few years back, Richard and his wife, Christine, had purchased a derelict warehouse on the Thames at Rotherhithe, or, to be more precise, two derelict warehouses, separated by a narrow dockland road. They had connected the two at second floor level by an attractive old iron bridge and turned the whole complex into a home and a place of work. The building on the river bank was the domestic area, the one across the road being a studio and workshop where Christine could exercise her many and varied talents of film director, producer, painter, costume designer and dreamer-up of many and varied creative fantasies. Richard combined the qualities of an entrepreneur and large-budget film producer with a great practical ability to do things with his hands, coupled with a steadfast belief that he could do, or learn how to do, anything. He amassed a large collection of tools, lathes and sophisticated electronic equipment with which he turned Christine's wildest creative dreams into filmable, practical realities, mostly by trial and error. The household, if one could use such a conventional word to describe how they lived, was distinctly Bohemian and full of charm. The top floor of the 'house' was one vast room, with windows looking across the river. Along one side was a huge Aga cooker in an eating area capable of seating 20 or more people, and the rest of the area was strewn with chairs, settees and other more or less conventional articles of furniture, mixed together with Oriental screens, paintings and artistic bric-à–brac, the focal point a large, open log fire. As well as furniture, they collected people of all nationalities, often without a common language, who had particular skills which they needed for their various enterprises, and usually there were several of them, like myself, in residence.

Mealtimes were focal points for discussion, the only time when everyone met together during a day which started at 6 a.m. and continued until ten or eleven at night. Their children integrated into this way of life, seemingly finding no difficulty in relating at all to an otherwise conventional life at a day school. Meals were prepared by a local lady at midday, always in abundant quantity to cater for the unexpected guest who, it seemed, never failed to turn up. The evenings were less organised, with anyone feeling the urge to practise culinary skills more than welcome to try. In the event of failure, which was rare, there was always a drink, and the river to gaze at, the light and its moods ever changing, as it swirled and eddied below, bearing its cargo of barges, tugs, pleasure boats, flotsam and jetsam, both material and human.

I slept on the floor below, in a room which was virtually a corner of the warehouse, partitioned off in a seemingly temporary way and furnished principally with a huge bed, the structure of which was not in evidence since it was covered with a floor-hugging counterpane, heavily embroidered and overlaid with lace. Above it was a huge draped canopy, hung from the warehouse beams above by a simple undisguised arrangement of sashcord and all the work of Christine's busy hands. As I lay in bed at night, I often wondered what other job would confer with it the opportunity to be part of such bizarre surroundings. Two large old warehouses, once used to store figs, were now a rabbit warren of makeshift corridors and rooms, partitioned one from another by sections of sets from past films. Here a large workshop stacked with timber and artisans' tools, then through a bulkhead door in what was part of a steamer from *Death On the Nile* into a room peopled with costumes and animal masks form *Tales of Beatrix Potter*, hanging forlornly under plastic sheeting, waiting hopefully to be born again into another fantasy. Ducking under them, one passed through a film cutting room into a long gallery with shelves laden with perfect model period shops, each stocked with its wares in miniature, all perfectly fashioned and painted. Tiny pewter plates, meats, vegetables, clothes, all crafted and painted by hand, were waiting to be exported worldwide, just one more sideline to help fill Christine's non-existent spare time. Eccentric, even slightly mad, it brought into sharp perspective the world of the 'Slough man' so aptly described by John Betjeman, which ruled supreme outside the old walls, shored up here and there with ancient timbers.

Far removed from this artistic commune in every sense of the word, Richard's partner, Lord Brabourne, seemed at first sight an illogical choice for a film producer. Born a member of the aristocracy, he was referred to by my camera operator, Austen Dempster, albeit fondly, as the 'Arris-bloody-stocracy', a reference which never failed to cause John amusement. With a fascination for films, which I still do not completely understand, he had been given a job by Herbert Wilcox in the production office, where he first met Austen, so familiarity was based on many years' friendship. I first met John some years later when Austen suggested that he would be a marvellous choice for production manager on *The Battle of the River Plate*, which I was about to embark on for Powell and Pressburger. I, in return, suggested it to them and John was duly engaged.

An excellent organiser, with the ability to make instant decisions, he seemed to work entirely 'off the cuff', for I never saw him rushing around with notebooks and sheaves of paper, as is the habit of some who want to impress with their efficiency. Yet he seemed able to move cruisers and destroyers at will, asking the Navy to undertake what to them must have appeared ridiculous tasks at uncongenial hours, yet somehow keeping them happy and interested. No doubt it was a great help to be Earl Mountbatten's son-in-law, for Lord Louis, very film-minded anyway, had expressed great interest in the film, having read the script and commented on it in detail. I quickly learned that John was extremely shrewd and able with money, a hard man to 'con' with the souped-up time sheet or the boosted expenses voucher. The crew quickly tumbled to this fact, but it was never resented because it soon became obvious that he was always fair. I knew then that he would be a producer in his own right, for he had all the necessary attributes.

There is an old saying that if you watch the pennies the pounds take care of themselves, or that a rich man never has any ready money. These philosophies are well suited to film producers and the aristocracy alike, for I suspect it has served them well down the ages. John, I quickly came to realise, was attracted by the challenge of producing a film, raising the finance, doing deals with studios, laboratories, artists, directors, a jungle which only few have the daring to enter. He liked it all, and the prospect, if his decisions were right, of a large and quick profit was stimulating. He also cared very much, unlike some, about the sort of film he wanted to make, so it was altogether an ideal combination.

Some years later Richard joined, as I have already explained, in *Sink The Bismarck* and a very successful and original partnership was born. I had the good fortune to work on several of their pictures, and look back on them all with pleasure.

Before I leave them I must tell just one story which has nothing to do with either of them, except that it occurred on a picture called *Harry Black*, which they made in India.

The second unit were sent to a remote village to get one shot of an Indian woman looking out of a top floor window, fear and horror in her eyes as she shouts the warning, 'Tiger!' and slams the shutters. The cameraman in question, someone promoted from the ranks of operator for the day, determined to make his mark. Like all second units, they were bereft of lights and the more sophisticated articles of equipment which could never be spared. He found that, having selected an artistic angle, the room behind the woman was totally black and without light. 'See if we can take a few tiles off the roof,' he asked the assistant director, not such a difficult job as the house was of primitive construction. The woman who was playing the part also owned the house, and anyway had only a sketchy idea of what was going on, but she was shrewd enough to quickly relate the removal of part of her roof with additional rupees. An extended wrangle erupted, conducted through an interpreter, with nobody understanding what anyone else was saying, except the number of rupees. A deal was struck and the tiles removed, by which time the sun had moved round and the hole, its position carefully selected by the cameraman, was in the wrong place. 'We'll have to take off some more tiles,' was conveyed to the woman, whose face now registered not fear of the tiger but complete bewilderment with her debut in films. Another wrangle, another deal, more rupees and delay, and once again the sun had moved too far. 'Let's have another go. Try and work out where the sun will be in two hours' time, and we'll take off that section of roof.' Once again the bargaining, the exchange of extra money and the work began on what was left of the roof, now more hole than tiles. Sadly, in India as elsewhere, the sun not only moves round, it also sinks, as indeed it did behind some high trees flanking the house. So the day ended without the shot, and the woman was without a roof, but richer beyond the dreams of avarice.

34

The riddle of profits and losses

LIKE TEENAGERS WHO pass through an anti-parental, anti-establishment period, most cameramen, editors, art directors, etc, suffer similar times of frustration, convinced that they can direct or produce considerably better than many of the people they work with. This is a natural process of development, for to direct is the ultimate satisfaction and means of expression – or it certainly should be. Ask any bright-eyed graduate from a film school what his ambitions are and the answer will invariably be 'to direct'. I was passing through such a period soon after I first met John Brabourne, and he was at the time equally keen to produce his first film. I suggested to him a book which I thought would make an excellent subject and he became equally enthusiastic, making rapid progress in getting the backing of London Films. All seemed set fair apart from the proposal as far as I was concerned. In spite of a strong case on my behalf argued by John, the management would in no circumstances accept the idea of me directing it. Their choice was a director from television who had never worked on a feature film. The story involved the use of a small ship, an oil tanker, and would have been shot largely in Malta, where John had strong connections. The situation was resolved by the Suez crisis, which made the whole project impracticable. Fate decreed that the very next picture I did was with this same director, a man of great charm and little ability as far as films were concerned.

Directors and producers of films, particularly the latter, are among the world's great survivors. Throughout history artists, both great and otherwise, have endured criticism, hardships and penury, dying obscurely in some forlorn attic after a lifetime, often all too short, their value and praises to be sung by some future generation, their work changing hands for kings' ransoms to line the pockets of dealers and self-appointed connoisseurs. The same might be said with perhaps a smaller degree of truth for the film technicians who swell the ranks of the unemployed.

But not so the director or producer. Once having achieved the distinction by no matter how undistinguished and unsuccessful a means, they appear to lead a charmed life, surviving years of inactivity, yet maintaining the lifestyle to which they are accustomed. You will never meet a producer who, when asked, will reply that he is doing nothing, the rough equivalent to being out of work. Spurred on by what appears to be eternal optimism, rather like the doorstep salesman, they always have a number of mythical projects in hand which never see the light of day, yet apparently give rise to a very reasonable income. These observations, which may well appear bitter or even vindictive, are not intended to be such but made rather in a spirit of benevolent curiosity.

My second chance to become involved in something other than photography occurred many years later. Way back in the Sixties, Michael Powell gave me a book to read, called *The Riddle of the Sands* by Erskine Childers. I had in fact read it while still at school, enjoying it at face value as a good adventure story, but second time around I realised why he had become enamoured with it as the subject for a film. Written before the First World War, it describes the adventures of a lone yachtsman who, while cruising through the tumultuous and dangerous waters of the Frisian Islands, uncovers a plot by the Germans to invade England with troops towed across the North Sea in barges, landing on the east coast beaches. The book, the only one Childers wrote, became a best seller and over the years, until this day, a subject for debate and speculation in the yachting press. The accuracy of the chartwork, the description of the tides which rage around the islands, all prove that Childers, a keen amateur cruising yachtsman, had actually carried out the voyage. There grew up a school of belief that much of the story was based on fact, and the book, together with its author, executed in Ireland for being in possession of firearms, became an enigma.

Michael asked me to research and find out as much as I could, about the yacht, called *Dulcibella* in the book, as upon her exact type depended the plausibility of the story. While he searched for finance, I uncovered a veritable mine of information which eventually led me to the solution of what she in fact was. Michael, over the years, twice failed to get the project off the ground and a number of other producers also failed.

I continued my enquiries and my son, Drummond, and his partner, Tony Maylam, who jointly ran Worldmark Productions, became interested. Tony, with much experience of documentary and sports films, wanted to direct a feature film, and they somehow, with tireless energy and enthusiasm, succeeded where others had failed. The Rank Organisation grudgingly agreed to finance the picture, albeit with too little money for what was a complicated subject. W C Fields once said, 'Never take a part acting with children or animals,' and I think small boats could safely be added to the list. Within the Rank Organisation were a small faction who believed in the project, but they were up against the boys in Wardour Street, who say the final yea or nay. 'Where is the violence and the sex interest?' they demanded, doubtlessly never having read the book, or probably the script either. With no concept whatsoever of how widely known the book was worldwide, translated into a dozen or more languages, and recognised as a modern classic, it failed to comply with what they felt the public wanted.

It was the story of *Genevieve* all over again; the budget for *The Riddle of the Sands*, although many times greater, taking into account costs and inflation, was just as inadequate. If we believed in it enough, we would have to make it in spite of them, as Henry Cornelius did with *Genevieve* all those years ago.

Tony Maylam, with a writer colleague, had produced a script which was as faithful as could be to the book, but immediately there were problems with our friends in Wardour Street about the sex and violence, or 'action' as they put it, which, in their eyes, was entirely lacking. Scenes of a scantily-clad girl clinging to wreckage in storm-tossed waves, a man in the water, his face streaked with blood, fighting for survival, this was the stuff to desecrate the garish posters which would advertise the film, and it was not there in the script. Changes had to be made or there would be no backing forthcoming. With the minimum possible alteration, Tony managed to satisfy them, although I, with my small say in things, tried to fight these changes, to no avail.

In the meantime, *Dulcibella*, crucial to the making of the film, had to be found. As a result of three or more years' search, I had uncovered her complete history. Through a number of extraordinary coincidences I had stumbled upon people who had the information that I wanted.

One day, working up in the gear store of the yard where I kept my boat, I got into conversation with Robert Bowker who, I discovered, was republishing the book. An even greater fanatic than myself, and one who implicitly believed in a lot of it being fact, he had just retraced Childers' voyage in his own yacht, following faithfully every course while using information and charts published in the book. Apart from obvious changes which one might expect with the passage of some 70 years, it was exactly as described, proving beyond doubt in his mind that it all really happened. He planned to include an extensive appendix, setting out all his theories and findings. Over several days of talks we exchanged notes and were able to help each other considerably.

Dick Stower, a naval architect and yacht designer with Laurent Giles, was my next lucky find. I wrote to them asking for help in finding a suitable boat, and he replied, telling me that he was another disciple, having written his own book, not for publication, setting out all his research. It transpired that an uncle of his who lived on the Isle of Wight had once owned Childers' yacht, then in her last years of decay, where she lay on the beach outside his house. The then youthful Dick, a student, had carefully drawn her lines and recorded every detail of what remained.

A conversion from a pulling and sailing lifeboat, we would either have to build from scratch or find something to convert. With his help we found an old motor cruiser in the West Country which he felt would fit the bill. A more unlikely candidate would be hard to imagine, but his skilful eye had detected, beneath the ugly additions of cabin and wheelhouse, the shape of an old lifeboat. It transpired that she was built by the same yard, the Thames Ironworks, just two years after Childers' yacht.

Extensive work was needed to recreate *Dulcibella* and rig her once again as a yacht. Week after week, month after month passed without getting the go-ahead and the money from Rank, so that no start could be made. At last came the OK, with just eight or so weeks before we had to start shooting because of weather and other considerations. Could Dick do it in time? Yes, he could, if they worked round the clock with a massive bill for overtime. We had no option, and she cost twice what she need have done. In my experience, this is a perfect example of too little too late, a disease which seems to infect every film I have worked on.

The hunt for locations proved difficult. We had to shoot at least the key scenes around the Frisian Islands because of the distinctive nature of the terrain and the tides. At low water, miles and miles of sands cut by channels and waterways, marked with saplings still with leaves on, at high water a vast open sea with a necklace of islands, the change taking place with miraculous speed and frightening effect. These tides controlled everything, limiting shooting to a very short period, and of course they changed from day to day. With just eight weeks to shoot the film, we could only take a number of master scenes with the artists, leaving most of the atmospheric shots to a second unit. This was photographed by Arthur Wooster, who with a minuscule unit, but free of the pressures which constrict you when working with artists and a full crew, patiently achieved some beautiful work on my behalf which contributed largely to mood and atmosphere so essential to the picture.

We also needed a small gauge, period railway and water where we could work unrestricted by tide, plus a lot of other ingredients, and they had to be close together with no time in our schedule for travel. Drummond, almost miraculously, found all these in Holland, at a place called Enkhuizen, with a small harbour opening onto the Ijsselmeer, that vast, tideless man-made sea. The little town was unspoilt and could pass easily for Germany, the country was flat and intersected by dykes, just as described in the book, and there was a perfect period railway, now the property of a conservation society. We would all live on a Rhine cruise boat, which sported 60 cabins, with *Dulcibella* tied up snugly alongside. A compromise here and there, but it was all too good to be true.

Tony worked tirelessly on the script, night and day using every moment to plan the very last detail. He came down to Shepperton Studios, where I was working, to have lunch with me, his arms full of schedules, breakdowns, plans and sketches of each scene. I tried to warn him that in the real world, away from the planning stage of things, awful, unseen things go wrong. Advance planning, often entirely lacking in this undisciplined industry, could contribute nothing but good so long as one remained completely flexible. It is all rather like the victim in *Mastermind*, trapped in the sinister black chair, who lets the seconds tick by while he ponders the unknown answer. That way lays certain death and the quicker you say pass, and get on to the next question, the better. Perhaps unkindly, I told Tony the story of Mark Robson and *Nine Hours to Rama*, recounted in an earlier chapter, first to warn him that life would not always be what we hoped, but, rather, depended on what we made out of it on the day.

Our first day's shooting was in the little railway station with the train drawing in. We awoke in our waterborne cells to the sound of a gale and with a foot of snow covering the landscape. Holland being as flat as it is, whichever way you turned there was an awful lot of snow in the shot. The film was set in late summer! What else could we do? An eight-week schedule did not cater for days without shooting. Well, there was a fairly long dialogue scene on the train, but of course we could not see out of the windows. Could it be rewritten for night? We could then try and cover the carriage windows with tarpaulins and sheets of black polythene. For several hours the grips struggled in the gale to lash it all down, while the artists, including Michael York, Jenny Agutter and Alan Badel, waited in the station's only room. In the cramped space available, camera angles were dictated by where we could physically get the equipment and 'art' had to take second place. Almost every lamp was reflected in the windows and the crinkled polythene beyond. At last we were ready for the first shot. In came the artists and the extras, clothes, hair, eyebrows, moustaches and beards covered in frozen snow. When they spoke, clouds of vapour came out of their mouths, the words drowned by the roar of the wind and the flapping canvas and plastic, from time to time torn from its lashings to reveal Antarctica outside. The sound man could not record the words; they would have to be dubbed later. Through a tougher baptism than most, Tony soldiered on and we completed our quota of screen time for the day, which looked good on the report sheets, permeating a sense of well-being back in the offices where, I assume, they are read. Tony survived the day with good humour, and with a wry smile said to me, 'I see what you mean, Chris.' The only sign of stress was a rash which developed on his face and remained persistently until the end of shooting.

Then there was the question of the cover set, something we could have around with us at all times, to be erected in a church hall, barn or any large empty building as a place of refuge we could repair to if weather conditions became impossible. The yacht's cabin was the perfect answer. Small and compact, it was the setting for page upon page of dialogue between Davis and Curruthers. Along with the drawings for the yacht conversion, Dick Stower had produced a lovely set of sketches and drawings of the cabin, perfect in every detail for period. The art department, such as it was, decided to improve on these, adding perhaps a personal though distinctly unnautical touch. It was erected for the first time as a try-out in a small warehouse, and the result filled most of us with total dismay.

Extended in size for some reason, it bore a fairly close resemblance to a 1960s mobile home.

Calling for volunteers from among the sailors on the crew, we set about 'nauticallising' it with saws, hammers and 101 bits and pieces picked up at local chandlers, until it was transformed into a very passable version of what Dick had designed. The next question was where to put it. We finally settled on an old barn on the outskirts of the town where, hopefully, it would be quiet enough to record sound. On the first day in there, driven in by continuous rain, we discovered that it had been taken over by a large colony of starlings, whose chorus of chirping drowned all the dialogue and was, anyway, an incongruous background to conversation in the cabin of a small yacht at sea. Experts were called in to exorcise the building and some dummy hawks were perched on the beams, all to no avail. The starlings quickly established a rapport with the stuffed replicas, perching on the beams all round them, the noise level increasing as they obviously became a topic of bird conversation. The news spread, and the numbers multiplied as visitors flocked to see the exhibition. The sound man, bearded and in appearance not unlike Rasputin, armed himself with an old brass foghorn and a 12-bore shotgun. As the camera turned over for a take, he would leap up from the recorder, blasting on the horn like a forlorn steamer lost in fog and firing blanks into the air. This eccentric and slightly alarming performance produced a period of magical silence, but tended to leave the actors speechless and slightly stunned.

For the many shots at sea not involving the sand and the islands in the background, the placid waters of the Ijsselmeer were, so to speak, on our doorstep. The one real problem we had was a storm sequence. We decided to shoot it in a montage of close shots which, hopefully, we could control, with the camera and a skeleton crew on board the yacht, just 35–feet long. In the bow we perched two local fishermen with a portable pump. They turned up in full survival gear, adding a touch of the incongruous for any bystander watching our antics. The day dawned bright and clear, the sea a mirror. The yacht was artificially heeled over, the sails pulled out with nylon thread to make them look as though they were full of wind, the firemen sprayed water over everything, mostly into the camera lens, and we endeavoured to blot out the sunlight with smoke pots and smoke machines placed on other boats. The light and fickle breeze changed direction constantly so that, just as all looked well, and we were ready to shoot, we emerged into brilliant sunshine, the illusion of our little man-made storm snatched from us by the Deity who controls these matters.

Such are the problems, hidden away in the pages of a script, and beyond the wildest dreams of those who sit in offices and plan budgets. We made it in our eight weeks, and on budget, the result one that I think we can all still feel proud of. In the meantime, the distributors had lost what little interest they may have had and, in my opinion, made no attempt to sell the film. It was released in 1978 and enjoyed a spasmodic showing, considerable critical acclaim but made no profit.

Apart from satisfying an enthusiastic desire to see it made, it was the one occasion in my whole career when I had a percentage in the profits. Alas, my dream of great riches flowing in to comfort my declining years has remained unfulfilled. I still watch the post each day, so far in vain, for the first cheque.

* * *

Here I feel my tale must end. In sifting through my memories extending over nearly 50 years, I realise that I have been very selective. This is not by careful design but rather because of the person I happen to be. Things long-forgotten came to light while many more lay buried forever. Had I kept a conscientious day by day diary, I have the feeling that the result would be much the same. Going back all those years to the question asked me by the lady at Government House in Malta – 'Are they really so awful?' – I would have to reply strongly in the affirmative.

But my answer would be qualified by feelings of great affection and admiration coupled with thanks for many a helping hand along the way from those in all departments of the film industry with whom I had the privilege to work.

Credits

The Drum

GB 1938

Director:	Zoltan Korda
Producer:	Alexanda Korda
Writers:	Lajos Biro, Arthur Wimperis, Patrick Kirwan, Hugh Gray
Photographers:	Georges Périnal, Osmond Borradaile
Trainee Camera Technician:	Christopher Challis
Music:	John Greenwood, Miklos Rosa
Art Director:	Vincent Korda
Editor:	William Hornbeck
Stars:	Sabu, Roger Livesey, Raymond Massey, Valerie Hobson, Desmond Tester, Francis L Sullivan

A Matter of Life and Death

GB 1946

Writers/Directors:	Michael Powell, Emeric Pressburger
Producers:	Michael Powell, Emeric Pressburger
Photographer:	Jack Cardiff
2nd Unit Camera Operator:	Christopher Challis
Music:	Allan Gray
Production Designer:	Hein Heckroth
Stars:	David Niven, Roger Livesey, Kim Hunter, Marius Goring, Raymond Massey

Black Narcissus

GB 1946

Writers/Directors:	Michael Powell, Emeric Pressburger
Producers:	Michael Powell, Emeric Pressburger
Photographer:	Jack Cardiff
Camera Operator:	Christopher Challis
Music:	Brian Easdale
Stars:	Deborah Kerr, David Farrar, Sabu, Jean Simmons, Kathleen Byron, Flora Robson, Esmond Knight

The End of the River

GB 1947

Director:	Derek Twist
Producers:	Michael Powell, Emeric Pressburger
Writer:	Wolfgang Wilhelm
Photographer:	Christopher Challis
Music:	Lambert Williamson
Stars:	Sabu, Esmond Knight, Bibi Ferreira, Robert Douglas, Antoinette Cellier, Raymond Lovell, Torin Thatcher, James Hayter

The Red Shoes

GB 1948

Writers/Directors/ Producers:	Michael Powell, Emeric Pressburger
Photographer:	Jack Cardiff
Camera Operator:	Christopher Challis
Music:	Brian Easdale
Production Designer:	Hein Heckroth
Editor:	Reginald Mills
Stars:	Anton Walbrook, Moira Shearer, Marius Goring, Robert Helpmann, Frederick Ashton, Leonide Massine, Ludmilla Tcherina, Esmond Knight, Albert Basserman

The Small Back Room

GB 1949

Writers/Directors:	Michael Powell, Emeric Pressburger
Producers:	Michael Powell, Emeric Pressburger
Novel:	Nigel Balchin
Photographer	Christopher Challis
Music:	Brian Easdale
Stars:	David Farrar, Kathleen Byron, Jack Hawkins, Leslie Banks, Robert Morley, Cyril Cusack

Gone to Earth

GB 1950

Writers/Directors/ Producers:	Michael Powell, Emeric Pressburger
Photographer:	Christopher Challis
Music:	Brian Easdale
Production Designer:	Hein Heckroth
Stars:	Jennifer Jones, David Farrar, Cyril Cusack, Esmond Knight, Sybil Thorndike, Edward Chapman, George Cole, Hugh Griffith, Beatrice Varley

The Elusive Pimpernel

GB 1950

Writers/Directors/ Producers:	Michael Powell, Emeric Pressburger
Photographer:	Christopher Challis
Production Designer:	Hein Heckroth
Music:	Brian Easdale
Stars:	David Niven, Margaret Leighton, Cyril Cusack, Jack Hawkins, Robert Coote

The Tales of Hoffman

GB 1951

Writers/Directors/ Producers:	Michael Powell, Emeric Pressburger

Photographer:	Christopher Challis
Music:	Jacques Offenbach
Music conducted by:	Sir Thomas Beecham with the Royal Philharmonic Orchestra
Production Designer:	Hein Heckroth
Stars:	Robert Helpmann, Pamela Brown, Moira Shearer, Frederick Ashton, Leonide Massine, Ludmilla Tcherina

Angels One Five

GB 1952

Producer:	John W Gossage
Writer:	Derek Twist
Photographer:	Christopher Challis (Air Scenes: Stanley Grant)
Director:	George More O'Ferrall
Music:	John Wooldridge
Stars:	Jack Hawkins, John Gregson, Michael Denison, Dulcie Grey, Veronica Hurst, Humphrey Lestocq

Twenty-four hours of a Woman's Life

GB 1952

Producer:	Ivan Foxwell
Writer:	Warren Chetham Strode
Director:	Victor Saville
Photographer:	Christopher Challis
Music:	Robert Gill, Philip Green
Stars:	Merle Oberon, Leo Genn, Richard Todd, Stephen Murray, Isabel Dean, Peter Illing

The Story of Gilbert and Sullivan

GB 1953

Producers:	Frank Lauder, Sidney Gilliat
Writers:	Sidney Gilliat, Leslie Bailey
Director:	Sidney Gilliat
Photographer:	Christopher Challis

Musical Director:	Sir Malcolm Sargent
Production Designer:	Hein Heckroth
Stars:	Robert Morley, Maurice Evans, Peter Finch, Eileen Herlie, Dinah Sheridan, Isabel Dean, Wilfred Hyde White

Genevieve

GB 1953

Producer/Director:	Henry Cornelius
Writer:	William Rose
Photographer:	Christopher Challis
Musical Director:	Muir Mathieson
Music:	Larry Adler (who also played it)
Art Director:	Michael Stringer
Stars:	Dinah Sheridan, John Gregson, Kay Kendall, Kenneth More, Geoffrey Keen, Joyce Grenfell

Saadia

US 1953

Producer/Writer/ Director:	Albert Lewin
Photographer:	Christopher Challis
Music:	Bronislau Kaper
Stars:	Cornel Wilde, Mel Ferrer, Rita Gam, Cyril Cusack

The Flame and the Flesh

GB 1954

Producer:	Joe Pasternak
Writer:	Helen Deutsch
Director:	Richard Brooks
Photographer:	Christopher Challis
Music:	Nicholas Brodszky
Stars:	Lana Turner, Carlos Thompson, Bonar Colleano, Pier Angeli

Footsteps in the Fog

GB 1955

Writer:	Dorothy Reid
Director:	Arthur Lubin
Photographer:	Christopher Challis
Music:	Benjamin Frankel
Art Director:	Wilfred Shingleton
Stars:	Stewart Granger, Jean Simmons, Bill Travers, Finlay Currie

Oh . . . Rosalinda (die Fledermaus)

GB 1955

Producers/Directors/ Writers:	Michael Powell, Emeric Pressburger
Photographer:	Christopher Challis
Editor:	Reginald Mills
Production Designer:	Hein Heckroth
Music:	Johann Strauss
Lyrics:	Dennis Arundell
Choreography:	Alfred Rodrigues
Stars:	Michael Redgrave, Mel Ferrer, Anthony Quayle, Anton Walbrook, Ludmilla Tcherina, Dennis Price

Raising a Riot

GB 1955

Producers:	Ian Dalrymple, Hugh Perceval
Production Manager:	John Brabourne
Writers:	Ian Dalrymple, Hugh Perceval
Director:	Wendy Toye
Photographer:	Christopher Challis
Editor:	Austin Dempster
Art Director:	Joseph Bato
Music:	Bruce Montgomery
Musical Director:	Muir Mathieson
Stars:	Kenneth More, Mandy Miller, Shelagh Fraser, Lionel Murton, Michael Bentine

Quentin Durward

GB 1955

Producer:	Pandro S Berman
Writer:	Robert Ardrey
Director:	Richard Thorpe
Photographer:	Christopher Challis
Music:	Bronislau Kaper
Stars:	Robert Taylor, Kay Kendall, Robert Morley, Marius Goring, Alex Clunes, Wilfred Hyde White, Ernest Thesiger, George Cole

Battle of the River Plate

GB 1956

Producers/Writers/ Directors:	Michael Powell, Emeric Pressburger
Photographer:	Christopher Challis
Music:	Brian Easdale
Stars:	John Gregson, Anthony Quayle, Peter Finch, Bernard Lee, Ian Hunter, Lionel Murton

The Spanish Gardener

GB 1956

Producer:	John Bryan
Writers:	Lesley Storm, John Bryan
Director:	Philip Leacock
Photographer:	Christopher Challis
Music:	John Veale
Stars:	Dirk Bogarde, Michael Hordern, Cyril Cusack, Geoffrey Keen, Maureen Swanson, Lyndon Brook, Bernard Lee, Rosalie Crutchley

Ill Met by Moonlight

GB 1956

Producers/Writers/ Directors:	Michael Powell, Emeric Pressburger

Photographer:	Christopher Challis
Music:	Mikis Theodorakis
Stars:	Dirk Bogarde, Marius Goring, Cyril Cusack, Michael Gough

Miracle in Soho

GB 1957

Producer/Writer:	Emeric Pressburger
Director:	Julian Amyes
Photographer:	Christopher Challis
Music:	Brian Easdale
Stars:	John Gregson, Belinda Lee, Cyril Cusack

Windom's Way

GB 1957

Producer:	John Bryan
Writer:	Jill Craigie
Director:	Ronald Neame
Photographer:	Christopher Challis
Music:	James Bernard
Stars:	Peter Finch, Mary Ure, Natasha Parry, Robert Flemyng, Michael Hordern

Rooney

GB 1958

Producer:	George H Brown
Writer:	Patrick Kirwan
Director:	George Pollock
Photographer:	Christopher Challis
Music:	Philip Green
Stars:	John Gregson, Barry Fitzgerald, Muriel Pavlow, June Thorburn, Noel Purcell, Liam Redmond, Eddie Byrne

Floods of Fear

GB 1958

Producer:	Sydney Box

Writer/Director:	Charles Crichton
Photographer:	Christopher Challis
Music:	Alan Rawsthorne
Stars:	Howard Keel, Anne Heywood, Harry H Corbett, Cyril Cusack

The Captain's Table

GB 1958

Producer:	Joseph Janni
Writers:	John Whiting, Bryan Forbes, Nicholas Phipps
Director:	Jack Lee
Photographer:	Christopher Challis
Music:	Frank Cordell
Stars:	John Gregson, Peggy Cummins, Donald Sinden, Reginald Becksmith, Nadia Gray, Richard Wattis, Maurice Denham, Nicholas Phipps, Joan Sims, Miles Malleson

Blind Date

GB 1959

Producers:	Sydney Box, David Deutsch
Writers:	Ben Barzman, Millard Lampell
Director:	Joseph Losey
Photographer:	Christopher Challis
Music:	Richard Rodney Bennett
Stars:	Hardy Kruger, Stanley Baker, Micheline Presle, Robert Flemyng, Gordon Jackson

Sink the Bismarck

GB 1960

Producer:	John Brabourne
Writer:	Edmund H North
Director:	Lewis Gilbert
Photographer:	Christopher Challis
Musical Director:	Muir Mathieson

Music: Clifton Parker
Stars: Kenneth More, Dana Wynter, Geoffrey Keen, Michael Hordern, Maurice Denham, Esmond Knight

Never Let Go

GB 1960

Producers: Julian Wintle, Leslie Parkin
Writer: Alun Falconer
Director: John Guillermin
Photographer: Christopher Challis
Music: John Barry
Stars: Richard Todd, Peter Sellers, Elizabeth Sellars, Adam Faith, Carol White, Mervyn Johns

Surprise Package

GB 1960

Producer/Director: Stanley Donen
Writer: Harry Kurnitz
Photographer: Christopher Challis
Music: Benjamin Frankel
Stars: Yul Brynner, Noel Coward, Mitzi Gaynor, Warren Mitchell

The Grass is Greener

GB 1960

Producer/Director: Stanley Donen
Writers: Hugh and Margaret Williams
Photographer: Christopher Challis
Musical Director: Muir Mathieson
Music/Lyrics: Noel Coward
Stars: Cary Grant, Deborah Kerr, Robert Mitchum, Jean Simmons, Moray Watson

Flame in the Streets

GB 1961

Producer/Director:	Roy Baker
Writer:	Ted Willis
Photographer:	Christopher Challis
Music:	Phil Green
Stars:	John Mills, Brenda de Banzie, Sylvia Syms, Earl Cameron, Johnny Sekka, Ann Lynn, Wilfred Brambell

Five Golden Hours

GB 1960

Producer/Director:	Mario Zampi
Writer:	Hans Wilhelm
Photographer:	Christopher Challis
Music:	Stanley Black
Stars:	Ernie Kovacs, Cyd Charisse, Kay Hammond, George Sanders, Dennis Price

HMS Defiant

GB 1962

Producer:	John Brabourne
Writers:	Nigel Kneale, Edmund H North
Director:	Lewis Gilbert
Photographer:	Christopher Challis
Music:	Clifton Parker
Stars:	Alec Guinness, Dirk Bogarde, Anthony Quayle, Tom Bell, Nigel Stock, Maurice Denham

The Victors

GB 1963

Producer/Writer/ Director:	Carl Foreman
Photographer:	Christopher Challis
Music:	Sol Kaplan

Stars:	George Peppard, George Hamilton, Albert Finney, Melina Mercouri, Eli Wallach

The Long Ships

GB 1963

Producer:	Irving Allen
Writer:	Berkely Mather
Director:	Jack Cardiff
Photographer:	Christopher Challis
Music:	Dusan Radic
Stars:	Richard Widmark, Sidney Poitier, Russ Tamblyn, Rosanna Schiaffino, Oscar Homolka, Colin Blakely

A Shot in the Dark

US 1966

Producer/Writer/ Director:	Blake Edwards
Photographer:	Christopher Challis
Production Designer:	Michael Stringer
Music:	Henry Mancini
Stars:	Peter Sellers, Elke Sommer, George Sanders, Herbert Lom, Tracy Reed, Graham Stark

The Americanization of Emily

US 1964

Producer:	John Calley
Writer:	Paddy Chayevsky
Director:	Arthur Hiller
Photographer:	Christopher Challis
Music:	Johnny Mandel
Stars:	Julie Andrews, James Garner, Melvyn Douglas, James Coburn, Liz Fraser, Joyce Grenfell, Keenan Wynn

Those Magnificent Men in their Flying Machines

GB 1965

Producers:	Stan Marguilies, Jack Davies
Writers:	Jack Davies, Ken Annakin
Director:	Ken Annakin
Photographer:	Christopher Challis
Music:	Ron Goodwin
Production Designer:	Tom Morahan
Stars:	Sarah Miles, Stuart Whitman, Robert Morley, Eric Sykes, Terry-Thomas, James Fox, Alberto Sordi, Gert Frobe, Jean-Pierre Cassel, Karl Michael Vogler, Irma Demich, Benny Hill, Flora Robson, Sam Wanamaker, Red Skelton, Fred Emney, Cicely Courtneidge, Gordon Jackson, John Le Mesurier, Tony Hancock, William Rushton

Return from the Ashes

GB 1965

Producer/Director:	J Lee Thompson
Writer:	Julius J Epstein
Photographer:	Christopher Challis
Music:	Johnny Dankworth
Stars:	Ingrid Thulin, Maximilian Schell, Samantha Eggar, Herbert Lom

Arabesque

US 1966

Producer/Director:	Stanley Donen
Writers:	Julian Mitchell, Stanley Price, Pierre Marton
Photographer:	Christopher Challis
Music:	Henry Mancini
Art Director:	Reece Pemberton
Stars:	Gregory Peck, Sophia Loren, Alan Badel, Kieron Moore, Carl Duering

Kaleidoscope

GB 1966

Producer:	Elliott Kastner
Writers:	Robert and Jane Howard-Carrington
Director:	Jack Smight
Photographer:	Christopher Challis
Music:	Stanley Myers
Art Director:	Maurice Carter
Stars:	Warren Beatty, Susannah Yorke, Clive Revill, Eric Porter, Murray Melvin

Two for the Road

GB 1966

Producer/Director:	Stanley Donen
Writer:	Frederick Raphael
Photographer:	Christopher Challis
Music:	Henry Mancini
Stars:	Albert Finney, Audrey Hepburn, Eleanor Bron, William Daniels, Claude Dauphin

A Dandy in Aspic

GB 1968

Producer/Director:	Anthony Mann
Writer:	Derek Marlow
Photographer:	Christopher Challis
Music:	Quincy Jones
Stars:	Laurence Harvey, Tom Courtenay, Mia Farrow, Harry Andrews, Peter Cook, Per Ascarsson

Chitty Chitty Bang Bang

GB 1968

Producer:	Albert R Broccoli
Writers:	Roald Dahl, Ken Hughes
Director:	Ken Hughes
Photographer:	Christopher Challis

Music:	Irwin Kostal, Ken Adam
Music/Lyrics:	The Sherman Brothers
Stars:	Dick Van Dyke, Sally Ann Howes, Lionel Jeffries, Robert Helpmann, Gert Frobe, Benny Hill, James Robertson Justice

Staircase

US 1969

Producer/Director:	Stanley Donen
Writer:	Charles Dyer
Photographer:	Christopher Challis
Music:	Dudley Moore
Stars:	Richard Burton, Rex Harrison, Cathleen Nesbitt, Beatrix Lehmann

The Private Life of Sherlock Holmes

GB 1970

Producer:	Billy Wilder
Writers:	Billy Wilder, I A L Diamond
Director:	Billy Wilder
Photographer:	Christopher Challis
Music:	Miklos Roza and Alexander Taurner
Stars:	Robert Stephens, Colin Blakely, Genevieve Page, Clive Revill, Christopher Lee, Catherine Lacy, Stanley Holloway

Villain

GB 1971

Producers:	Kastner, Ladd, Kanter
Writers:	Dick Clement, Ian La Frenais
Director:	Michael Tuchner
Photographer:	Christopher Challis
Music:	Jonathan Hodge
Stars:	Richard Burton, Ian McShane, Nigel Davenport, Joss Ackland, Cathleen Nesbitt, Donald Sinden, T P McKenna, Fiona Lewis

Villain

GB 1971

Producers:	Kastner, Ladd, Kanter
Writers:	Dick Clement, Ian La Frenais
Director:	Michael Tuchner
Photographer:	Christopher Challis
Music:	Jonathan Hodge
Stars:	Richard Burton, Ian McShane, Nigel Davenport, Joss Ackland, Cathleen Nesbitt, Donald Sinden, T P McKenna, Fiona Lewis

Catch Me a Spy

GB 1971

Producer:	Steven Pallos
Writers:	Dick Clement, Ian La Frenais
Director:	Dick Clement
Photographer:	Christopher Challis
Music:	Claude Bolling
Stars:	Kirk Douglas, Trevor Howard, Tom Courtenay, Mariene Jobart, Patrick Mower, Bernadette Lafont, Bernard Blier

Mary Queen of Scots

GB 1971

Producer:	Hal B Wallis
Writer:	John Hale
Director:	Charles Jarrott
Photographer:	Christopher Challis
Music:	John Barry
Stars:	Vanessa Redgrave, Glenda Jackson, Trevor Howard, Patrick McGoohan, Nigel Davenport

The Boy Who Turned Yellow

GB 1972

Producers:	Roger Cherrill, Drummond Challis
Writer:	Emeric Pressburger
Director:	Michael Powell
Photographer:	Christopher Challis
Music:	Patrick Gowers, David Vorhaus
Production Designer:	Bernard Sarron
Stars:	Esmond Knight, John Dithtam, Nick Eddison, Helen Weir, Brian Worth, Laurence Carter

The Little Prince

US 1974

Producer/Director:	Stanley Donan
Writer:	Alan Jay Lerner
Photographer:	Christopher Challis
Production Designer:	John Barry
Music/Lyrics:	Frederic Loewe, Alan Jay Lerner,
Stars:	Richard Kiley, Steven Warner, Bob Fosse, Gene Wilder, Joss Ackland, Clive Revill, Victor Spinetti, Graham Crowden

In this House of Brede

US 1975

Director:	George Schaefer
Photographer:	Christopher Challis
Stars:	Diana Rigg, Judi Bowker, Gwen Watford, Pamela Brown

Mister Quilp

GB 1975

Producer:	Helen M Straus
Writers:	Louis Kamp, Irene Kamp
Director:	Michael Tuchnmer
Photographer:	Christopher Challis

Musical Director:	Elmer Bernstein
Music:	Anthony Newley
Production Designer:	Elliott Scott
Choreography:	Gilian Lynn
Stars:	Anthony Newley, Michael Hordern, David Hemmings, Sarah-Jane Varley, David Warner, Paul Rogers, Jill Bennett

The Incredible Sarah

GB 1976

Producer:	Helen M Strauss
Writer:	Ruth Wolff
Director:	Richard Fleischer
Photographer:	Christopher Challis
Music:	Elmer Bernstein
Production Designer:	Elliott Scott
Stars:	Glenda Jackson, Daniel Massey, Yvonne Mitchell, Douglas Wilmer, David Langton, Simon Williams, John Castle, Edward Judd, Peter Sallis

The Deep

US 1977

Producer:	Peter Guber
Writers:	Peter Benchley, Tracy Keenan Wynn
Director:	Peter Yates
Photographers:	Christopher Challis, Al Giddings, Stan Waterman
Music:	John Barry
Production Designer:	Tony Master
Stars:	Jacqueline Bisset, Robert Shaw, Nick Nolte, Lou Gossett, Eli Wallach

The Riddle of the Sands

GB 1978

Producer:	Drummond Challis
Writers:	Tony Maylam, John Bailey
Director:	Tony Maylam

Photographer:	Christopher Challis
Music:	Howard Blake
Stars:	Michael York, Simon MacCorkindale, Jenny Agutter, Alan Badel, Jurgen Andersen

Force Ten from Navarone

GB 1978

Producer/Director:	Guy Hamilton
Writer:	Robin Chapman
Photographer:	Christopher Challis
Music:	Ron Goodwin
Production Designer:	Geoffrey Drake
Stars:	Robert Shaw, Edward Fox, Franco Nero, Harrison Ford, Barbara Bach, Richard Kiel

SOS Titanic

US 1979

Producer:	Lou Morheim
Writer:	James Costigan
Director:	William Hale
Photographer:	Christopher Challis
Editor:	Rusty Coppleman
Production Designer:	Herbert Westbrook
Music:	Howard Blake
Stars:	Harry Andrews, Ed Bishop, Maurice Roëves, Norman Rossington, Helen Mirren, Ian Holm

The Mirror Crack'd

GB 1980

Producers:	John Brabourne, Richard Goodwin
Writers:	Jonathan Hales, Barry Sandler
Director:	Guy Hamilton
Photographer:	Christopher Challis
Music:	John Cameron
Production Designer:	Michael Stringer

Stars:	Angela Lansbury, Geraldine Chaplin, Elizabeth Taylor, Rock Hudson, Tony Curtis, Edward Fox, Kim Novak, Marella Oppenheim, Charles Gray

The Nightingale

GB 1981

Producer:	Richard Goodwin
Directors:	Christine Edzard, Richard Goodwin
Photographer:	Christopher Challis
Animator:	Christine Edzard
Stars:	Richard Goolden, Mandy Carlin, John Dalby

Evil Under the Sun

GB 1982

Producers:	John Brabourne, Richard Goodwin
Writer:	Anthony Shaffer
Director:	Guy Hamilton
Photographer:	Christopher Challis
Music:	Cole Porter
Production Designer:	Elliott Scott
Stars:	Peter Ustinov, James Mason, Diana Rigg, Maggie Smith, Colin Blakely, Jane Birkin, Nicholas Clay, Roddy McDowall, Sylvia Miles, Dennis Quilley

First Love – Secrets

GB 1983

Producer:	Chris Griffin
Writer:	Noella Smith
Director:	Gavin Millar
Photographer:	Christopher Challis
Stars:	Helen Lindsay, Anna Campbell Jones, John Horsley, Daisy Cockburn

Top Secret!

US 1984

Producers:	Jon Davison, Hunt Lowry
Writers:	Jim Abrahams, David Zucker, Jerry Zucker, Martyn Burke
Directors:	Jim Abrahams, David Zucker, Jerry Zucker
Photographer:	Christopher Challis
Music:	Maurice Jarre
Production Designer:	Peter Lamont
Stars:	Val Kilmer, Lucy Gutteridge, Peter Cushing, Jeremy Kemp, Warren Clarke, Michael Gough, Omar Sharif, Christopher Villiers

Steaming

GB 1985

Producer:	Peter Mills
Writer:	Patricia Losey
Director:	Joseph Losey
Stars:	Vanessa Redgrave, Sarah Miles, Diana Dors, Patti Lowe, Brenda Bruce